Campaigning for literacy

Campaigning for literacy

Eight national experiences of the twentieth century, with a memorandum to decision-makers

By H. S. Bhola

Unesco

The designations employed and the presentation of material throughout this publication do not imply the expression of any opinion whatsoever on the part of Unesco concerning the legal status of any country, territory, city or area or of its authorities, or concerning the delimitation of its frontiers or boundaries.

Published in 1984 by the United Nations Educational, Scientific and Cultural Organization
7 place de Fontenoy, 75700 Paris
Typeset by Text Processing, Clonmel, Ireland
Printed by Imprimerie de la Manutention, Mayenne

ISBN 92-3-102167-2

Preface

This study, *Campaigning for Literacy*, is one of a number of Unesco publications devoted to analysis of the worldwide problem of illiteracy and means of overcoming it through improved understanding and more effective action. It advocates the literacy campaign as the most appropriate and adequate means for dealing with large-scale illiteracy and presents eight case-studies of national campaigns as examples and illustrations of this approach. As the selection of case studies suggests, literacy campaigns have often been launched soon after a revolution or the achievement of independence. The author contends, however, that mass literacy campaigns are not the exclusive province of any particular ideology, but are possible within any society that desires them.

The literacy campaign is usually contrasted with the selective and intensive approach used in the functional literacy pilot projects. *The Experimental World Literacy Programme: a Critical Assessment* published by Unesco and UNDP (United Nations Development Programme) in 1976 recounts the experience of such pilot projects in eleven Member States. It may, therefore, be advantageous to read the present study in conjunction with the account of the Experimental World Literacy Programme, in order to contrast two quite different approaches to combating illiteracy. Unesco has not advocated either of these approaches as superior to the other. The approach adopted must depend upon the nature of the illiteracy problem and the means of action available for confronting it. The Organization's *Second Medium-term Plan (1984 – 1989)* observes in this connection: 'The recent history of literacy work has shown that, although selective literacy strategies designed to assist particular groups and focusing on certain specific development objectives may have proved effective, remarkable results have also been achieved by systematic campaigns directed at all sectors of the population and able to generate a truly collective momentum.'[1]

1. Unesco, General Conference, Fourth Extraordinary Session, Paris, 1982, *Second Medium-term Plan (1984–1989)*, p. 72, Paris, 1983 (Unesco doc. 4XC/4 Approved).

While the age-groups at which literacy campaigns are directed vary from country to country, they are normally intended for out-of-school youth and adults. Such campaigns, however, are frequently complemented by, and less frequently co-ordinated with, efforts to extend the coverage of primary schools and, ultimately, to achieve universal primary education. Indeed, one of the important consequences of adult literacy campaigns is the positive community and family attitudes towards schooling of children which they engender. In this connection, the education of mothers appears of particular importance. In recognition of the interrelationship between education of parents and children, Unesco's *Second Medium-term Plan (1984 – 1989)* proposes a global approach to the problem of illiteracy which aims at simultaneously educating children, youth and adults: i.e. at education for all. In many situations, this comprehensive approach appears the most effective manner for rapidly increasing the literacy level of a population and thereby speeding the transition from an illiterate to a literate society. The reader should, therefore, bear in mind that the literacy campaign is normally only one aspect of a broader education and development strategy.

The manner in which the present study was commissioned and prepared is explained in Chapter 2. It draws upon case-studies prepared by authors appointed by governments or institutions as well as upon other published and unpublished sources of information. In presenting the case-studies, Professor Bhola seeks both to evoke the motivating spirit of the campaign and to analyse its organization and operations. The study is addressed to literacy workers, educational administrators, development planners, policy-makers and politicians in countries disadvantaged by high rates of illiteracy as well as in societies where universal adult literacy seems tantalizingly within reach.

The report is divided into four main parts. The first (Chapters 1 and 2) covers the background and context of the study, its nature and objectives, and the methodology used. The second part (Chapter 3) is an analysis of the justifications for literacy promotion which seeks to answer three inter-related questions: Why literacy? Why can't literacy wait? and, Why are mass literacy campaigns necessary? The third and main part (Chapters 4 to 11) presents case-studies of campaigns in the Union of Soviet Socialist Republics, the Socialist Republic of Viet Nam, China, Cuba, Burma, Brazil, the United Republic of Tanzania and Somalia. (More recent campaigns, such as those in Nicaragua and Ethiopia, are not covered because at the time this study was planned and carried out these campaigns were in an early phase and sufficient information was not available for preparation of complete case-studies.) The final part (Chapters 12 and 13) is presented in the form of a memorandum to decision-makers and a set of conclusions deriving from the examination of historical experiences and an analysis of the development process.

This study was prepared for Unesco by the International Council for Adult Education (ICAE) which commissioned Professor H. S. Bhola of Indiana University as its author. Professor Bhola has been deeply involved in carrying out and writing about literacy work for nearly three decades. He has served as Acting Director of Literacy House, Lucknow, India; as Unesco's Senior Technical Adviser to the Work-oriented Functional Literacy Programme in the United Republic of Tanzania; as editor of the series of training monographs titled 'Literacy in Development' published by the International Institute for Adult Literacy Methods (Tehran); and as consultant to the German Foundation for International Development, the United States Agency for International Development and other governmental and non-governmental organizations.

An earlier draft of *Campaigning for Literacy* was discussed at an international seminar convened for this purpose in Udaipur, India from 4 to 11 January 1982 by the ICAE, the German Foundation for International Development and Seva Mandir, a non-governmental organization engaged in literacy work in the Udaipur area. The text was amended by Professor Bhola to take account of the suggestions and comments made during this seminar. Each case-study was also submitted by Unesco to the national authorities of the country concerned for verification and, in certain cases, corrections were introduced. The final manuscript was then revised for publication by Unesco.

Lastly, the reader is cautioned that the assertions made and opinions expressed in this publication should not necessarily be considered as representing the official views of Unesco or those of the numerous governmental and non-governmental bodies which contributed to the preparation and review of this study.

Contents

CHAPTER 1

Background and context

As we enter the 1980s, illiteracy remains a worldwide problem. There are today more than 800 million illiterates in the age-group 15 years and older. Unless drastic measures are taken, there will be many millions more in the future.

The world map of poverty is also the world map of illiteracy. The illiterate are desperately poor, hungry, sick, abused and powerless. Fortunately, development planners are now beginning to see illiteracy as the bottleneck to development. Universal adult literacy is, slowly, becoming a vision full of hope.

The late 1970s saw some important national initiatives to promote literacy in the Third World. Ethiopia, India, Iraq, the United Republic of Tanzania and Kenya, to name only a few, have conducted mass literacy campaigns with some degree of success. Nicaragua has completed a campaign which has attracted considerable international attention. Bangladesh, Nigeria, the Sudan and Venezuela are in the process of launching campaigns. Yet it must be said that the last thirty years do not represent an era of great effort by developing nations for the eradication of illiteracy in the Third World. Third World nations have spent their resources on what they believed to be more deeply felt deprivations and more immediate needs.

Unesco has taken a leading role in the fight against illiteracy. Unesco's interest in literacy goes back to its very inception in 1946; and through its work, the Organization has kept the problem of illiteracy in the public eye, has exhorted Member States to undertake literacy promotion; has assisted them in building institutional capacity for the training of personnel in fundamental education and literacy; and has sought to create a knowledge base for literacy work by undertaking important studies and surveys.[1]

1. W. S. Gray, *The Teaching of Reading and Writing*, Paris, Unesco, 1956. (Second enlarged edition, 1969.)

The World Conference on Adult Education in Montreal, Canada, in 1960, put adult illiteracy on the world educational agenda. Unesco was asked to promote action that would lead to the organization of a vast literacy campaign to improve the desperate conditions then prevailing.

The World Conference of Ministers of Education on the Eradication of Illiteracy was held five years later in Tehran; and the concept of functional literacy was born. This new concept implied

more than the rudimentary knowledge of reading and writing that is often inadequate and sometimes chimerical. Literacy instruction must enable illiterates, left behind by the course of events and producing too little, to become socially and economically integrated in a new world order where scientific and technological progress calls for ever more knowledge and specialization.[1]

This concept of functional literacy, which focused on the economic aspect and on productivity to such an extent that it came to be called work-oriented literacy, was put into practice in the form of the Experimental World Literacy Programme (EWLP) conducted during 1967-73. Eleven experimental projects were carried out under this programme, in Algeria, Ecuador, Ethiopia, Guinea, India, Iran (now the Islamic Republic of), Madagascar, Mali, the Sudan, the Syrian Arab Republic and the United Republic of Tanzania.

A review of the EWLP now available shows that the experimental programme made important qualitative contributions to the field of literacy. It provided systematic and tested experience in regard to the planning, organization, financing and methodology of literacy work; it served as a training ground for a large number of cadres of national and international literacy workers and it kept the problems of illiteracy visible, thereby convincing policy-makers and planners in the Third World that the task had to be undertaken and as rapidly as possible.[2]

Two important developments have since taken place in the field of adult literacy. The exclusive focus on economic skills in the EWLP has been broadened—one might say transformed. Literacy is now seen as a strategy for liberation. The aim is to teach not only how to read the word but also how to read the world. The Declaration of Persepolis affirmed that literacy is

not just the process of learning the skills of reading, writing and arithmetic, but a contribution to the liberation of man and to his full development. Thus

---

1. World Conference of Ministers of Education on the Eradication of Illiteracy, Tehran, 8-19 September 1965, *Final Report*, Paris, Unesco, 1965.
2. Unesco/UNDP, *The Experimental World Literacy Programme: A Critical Assessment*, Paris, Unesco, 1976.

conceived, literacy creates the conditions for the acquisition of a critical consciousness of the contradictions of the society in which man lives and of its aims; it also stimulates initiative and his participation in the creation of projects capable of acting upon the world, of transforming it, and of defining the aims and objectives of an authentic human development.[1]

An understanding has also emerged that the selective and intensive approaches of the EWLP will not by themselves resolve the problems of illiteracy, and that strategies for the eradication of illiteracy must be commensurate with the dimensions of the problem. It is against this background that Unesco is now examining the mass campaign as a promising strategy for the eradication of illiteracy worldwide.

While collaborating with Member States in the development and implementation of an international strategy for the eradication of illiteracy, Unesco continues to examine issues, problems, organization and methods of literacy promotion through a systematic research programme. An important part of the current programme is a comparative study concerning the interrelationship between development and literacy and the results of national campaigns in the twentieth century, a report on which is included in the present work.

BIBLIOGRAPHY

BATAILLE, L. (ed.). *A Turning Point for Literacy; Proceedings of the International Symposium for Literacy, Persepolis, Iran, 1975*. Oxford, Pergamon Press, 1976.

BHOLA, H. S. Development Policy Outcomes of Adult Literacy Research. *Literacy Research in Developing Countries*. Ottawa, International Development Research Center, 1978. (Report of the Bellagio IV Workshop on Educational Research with Special Reference to Research on Literacy.)

GRAY, W. S. *The Teaching of Reading and Writing*. Paris, Unesco, 1956. (Second enlarged edition, 1969.)

INTERNATIONAL COUNCIL FOR ADULT EDUCATION (ICAE). *The World of Literacy: Policy, Research and Action*. Ottawa, International Development Research Center, 1979.

UNESCO. *Estimates and Projections of Illiteracy*. Paris, Unesco, Office of Statistics, 1978. (Unesco doc. CSR-E-29).

UNESCO/UNDP *The Experimental World Literacy Programme: A Critical Assessment*. Paris, Unesco, 1976.

WORLD CONFERENCE OF MINISTERS OF EDUCATION ON THE ERADICATION OF ILLITERACY, TEHRAN, 8-19 SEPTEMBER 1965. *Final Report*. Paris, Unesco, 1965.

1. L. Bataille (ed.), *A Turning Point for Literacy: Proceedings of the International Symposium for Literacy, Persepolis, Iran, 1975*, Oxford, Pergamon Press, 1976.

CHAPTER 2

Nature, objectives and methodology

A definition of the objectives of this study was included in the contract document signed between Unesco and ICAE. According to this document, the study was to involve:

1. Elaboration of a general introduction highlighting the historical, social, economic and cultural background within the framework of which nations have developed their educational systems in general and literacy efforts in particular during the twentieth century, explaining the objectives of the methodological approach of the study.
2. Description—in a chronological order—of the characteristic features of the most important national literacy campaigns in the twentieth century.
3. Comparative evaluation of the various experiences of different countries with a view to drawing up certain generally valid recommendations to be respected in organizing new nationwide campaigns in the countries still suffering from high illiteracy rates.

What was required was clearly a 'policy study', a study especially designed for policy-makers and planners, with a definite theory-into-practice orientation. Such a study had to be 'forensic' in nature, that is, it must build a closely reasoned argument which would (a) convincingly demonstrate the role of literacy in development, within different social and political settings; (b) delineate different policy options available to literacy planners and policy-makers; and (c) argue for the campaign strategy as a preferred alternative among available policy options.

This kind of argument, however, should not be merely politically persuasive. It must be a reasoned discourse that used tested theory and research, and collected, organized and interpreted data according to the accepted canons of social science research.

The study is based on two types of materials: (a) the available theory and research showing the relationship between literacy and development and establishing the conditions under which such relationships may or may not hold; and (b) case histories of various selected literacy campaigns of the twentieth century. While the theoretical and research materials are more and more easily available to literacy researchers, case histories of literacy campaigns are not so easy to find. Most of the methodological problems of this study in fact revolve around the acquisition and use of case materials on literacy campaigns of the twentieth century. The various methodological procedures and issues involved in the study are discussed below.

Selection of campaigns

First, a sample had to be chosen from all the mass literacy campaigns conducted in the twentieth century. In making this selection, the first criterion related to the differentiation of cultural, historical, political and socio-economic settings. The countries chosen were Brazil, Burma, China, Cuba, Somalia, the United Republic of Tanzania, the Union of Soviet Socialist Republics and the Socialist Republic of Viet Nam; thus the sample covers Latin America and the Caribbean, Africa above and below the Sahara, South-East Asia, China and the Soviet Union. The campaigns involved a variety of languages—Burmese, Chinese, Kiswahili, Portuguese, Russian, Somali, Spanish and Vietnamese—and in certain cases included the adoption or modification of alphabets and the use of a multitude of languages.

The campaigns also represent different historical periods: the Soviet campaign was conducted in the 1920s, whereas the Burmese, Somali and others were conducted more recently. The study does not cover campaigns which have been initiated within the last few years, since some time must pass before results can be evaluated in terms of developmental gains. Another criterion used in selection concerned the perceived success of the campaign and the consequent interest it held for professional literacy workers.

All the cases selected turned out to be examples of the mobilization of a people, although each campaign used a strategy.

Preparing case-studies

A survey of published materials on selected literacy campaigns had shown that those available were sketchy, scattered and often journalistic. Moreover, most of the available materials had been written during or immediately after the campaigns and often did not deal with developmental consequences, which were of paramount importance to this study. In almost all cases it was necessary to look back on the campaigns and re-evaluate their impact.

It was, therefore, decided to contact the governments of each of the countries concerned and request them to suggest authors able and willing to contribute case-studies of their respective national campaigns to the overall Unesco/ICAE study. This was considered desirable since Unesco (and to some extent ICAE) prefers to work through official channels in Unesco Member States. The pragmatic reasons were that authors identified by governments would often be government officials or people with access to government libraries, archives and related data. There were also economic reasons. Given the fees which could be paid to authors, it would not have been possible to attract independent scholars to undertake the research and write the case-studies. Once a government agreed to contribute a case-study and proposed an author or authors, it would make the important additional contributions of staff time and secretarial services for the study's completion.

Guidelines for writing case-studies

The case-studies had to include descriptions and analyses of the cultural, historical, and socio-economic settings in which literacy campaigns were conducted. They had to include all possible details about organization and mobilization; planning and administration; choice of language and pedagogic considerations; recruitment and training of teachers; and production and distribution of reading and follow-up materials. Finally, they had to include analyses of the results of the campaigns. The overall objective of each case-study was to articulate the relationships between social context, policy, planning, strategy and results; and to show what relationships could be revived in other settings.

To assist the authors in this task, a set of guidelines was prepared to serve as a check-list of questions to be answered and issues to be faced. These guidelines required a more or less standardized format which would make possible comparisons between campaigns and an accumulation of experience.

Comparative analysis of cases

Data analysis must precede comparative analysis; hence, the case-studies contributed by authors or teams of authors from the different countries were first analysed in terms of what they had to teach us. One special characteristic of this data which must be kept in mind is that these studies were contributed by government officials or establishment scholars. In government documents, typically, we hear a lot about declarations and manifestos and very little about manifestations; a lot about officially stated objectives, but nothing much about latent unstated objectives which suit the governing élite. Governmental studies often omit any mention of breakdowns in planning and strategy, of insufficient public motivation and of distrust, and of corruption among public officials. It was possible that case-studies contributed by government officials would exaggerate results and make no mention of unanticipated and unwanted consequences.

Bias is not, of course, the sole province of bureaucrats, but bureaucrats and establishment scholars do have additional constraints that must be kept in mind in an analysis of case materials commissioned from government sources. In developing the shorter analytical versions included in this report, additional sources were also used in order to present a balanced picture. Special efforts were made to obtain descriptions and analyses of the literacy campaigns from non-government sources and, in some cases, from sources outside the countries concerned. Typical criteria of historical construction and historical criticism, involved in the re-enactments of case-studies, were used.[1]

The comparative perspective

The comparing and contrasting of experiences within different national literacy campaigns was essentially for the purpose of cumulation of experience for use across societies. The comparative approach consisted of the following: on the one hand, various features of a national campaign were shown to be correlated in special ways which differed from society to society; on the other hand, specific features of a campaign were shown to be correlated with specific characteristics of the society in which the campaign took place and to be valid across societies. Thus we were able to separate the unique features of campaigns which may not survive in other cultures from general features which could be transferred and revived in other cultural settings. Comparative analysis had to involve a multiplicity of perspectives based on a variety of questions: What particular socio-political configurations lead to the initiation of mass literacy campaigns or to the use of a particular set of mobilizational and pedagogical strategies? What particular social and psychological syndromes determine successful mobilization and public motivation to make contributions to the campaigns? What set of planning and political decisions lead to the actual use of literacy by the newly literate? And so on.

1. See R. G. Collingwood, *The Idea of History*, New York, Oxford University Press, 1956.

Planning implications

One objective of the study was to draw from the comparative analysis 'certain generally valid recommendations to be respected in organizing new nationwide campaigns in the countries still suffering from high illiteracy rates.'

Yet while we can use phrases like 'trend analysis' and 'strong inference', the fact of the matter is that we know little about the methodology of 'practical reasoning' and of a 'science of human affairs'. Proceeding from the case materials and their comparative analysis to recommendations addressed to planners and policy-makers necessarily involved a creative effort. That effort has been made, and it is hoped that the material now included in Chapter 12 of this report will be of practical use to decision-makers.

BIBLIOGRAPHY

BHOLA, H. S. A Policy Analysis of Adult Literacy Versus Universal Primary Education: Child is the Father of Man—and Man of the Child. *Viewpoints in Teaching and Learning*, Vol. 55, No. 4, 1979, pp. 22-35.

COLLINGWOOD, R.G. *The Idea of History*. New York, Oxford University Press, 1956.

DUNN, W. N. *Reforms as Arguments*. Paper prepared for the international conference on the political realization of social science knowledge and research, 'Towards New Scenarios', in memoriam Paul F. Lazarsfeld, Institute for Advanced Studies, Vienna, June 18-20, 1980.

GAUTHIER, D. P. *Practical Reasoning*. Oxford, Clarendon Press, 1963.

REIN, M.; WHITE, R. Policy Research: Belief and Doubt. *Policy Analysis*, Vol. 4, No. 2, 1978, pp. 239-71.

RIVLIN, A. M. *Systematic Thinking for Social Action*. Washington, D.C., Brookings Institute, 1971.

———. Forensic Social Science. In: P. W. Jackson, et al., *Perspectives on Inequality*. Cambridge, Mass., Harvard University Press, 1973. (Harvard University Reprint Series, No. 8.)

CHAPTER 3

Why literacy? Why can't literacy wait? Why are mass literacy campaigns necessary? Issues for the 1980s[1]

The battle for non-formal education seems to have been won not by reason but by circumstance. That education had something to do with development had been realized for some time, but the education considered was formal education. Then a crisis and a challenge arising simultaneously forced a change in thinking.

The crisis was in formal education (Coombs, 1968). Educational planners were overwhelmed by the scarcity of resources, the burgeoning school-age populations, the endemic wastage and stagnation within the formal education system, the abysmally low quality of the system's products, and the socio-economic vacuum which 'graduates' of the formal education system entered as school-leavers. The challenge was national development. Peasants, workers, housewives needed to be informed, influenced, taught new skills and resocialized to enable them to participate in the processes of development. Educational planners were faced with the reality that non-formal education not only was necessary but was immediately necessary.

Yet the victory for non-formal education has not been a victory for adult literacy. Notwithstanding some recent successes with literacy and literacy campaigns as seen in Brazil, Nicaragua, the United Republic of Tanzania and the Socialist Republic of Viet Nam, educators continue to show ambivalence towards adult literacy (Verner, 1974). Characterizing literacy as 'gradualism' (Postman, 1970), they want to concentrate on non-formal education *without* literacy. The argument is that adult illiterates are not motivated to become literate; that they do not typically have an immediate use for literacy skills in their milieu; and that the information and skills they

1. The material in this chapter was presented to the International Adult Education Section of the Adult Education Association (United States) at its National Conference, St. Louis, November 1980; it was later published in *Convergence*, Vol. 14, No. 1, 1981, pp. 6-23.

urgently need can be communicated to them through non-print media without any need for them to become literate first. It is contended that development must come first, and that this will create needs for literacy which can be met when they arise (Crone, 1979).

Those advocating the cause of adult literacy assert that literacy cannot be postponed: it is needed in the short run, it is needed in the middle run, and it is needed in the long run (Bhola, 1979). Literacy and non-formal education without literacy are not merely two different instrumental approaches to promoting development; they constitute a choice between two different epistemologies (Goody, 1968; McLuhan, 1962), between two different processes of formation of individual identities and structural relationships. Literacy is thus not merely a vehicle for development information, but a potent partner in development. For that reason, it cannot simply be replaced by non-print media performing equivalent educational tasks so as to fulfil equivalent development objectives.

If illiterate adults are not motivated and if the social milieu does not at present offer functional uses for literacy, the important developmental challenge is to fashion new needs, to teach new motivations, to reconstruct environments. Non-formal education without literacy is by no means secure from problems of motivation and an unresponsive milieu. The task of teaching adult literacy may seem harder but it is perhaps also more significant. Therefore, the proponents of adult literacy assert, non-formal education should always be based upon a programme of adult literacy, with literacy being one of the central objectives.

As we enter the Third Development Decade, the argument is by no means settled and the issue is still very much alive. Policy-makers and planners all over the developing world will be hearing arguments from both sides as they engage in the difficult process of making choices among educational approaches and strategies to serve development objectives. But simple assertions pro and con will not be enough. The argument for adult literacy and the logic of non-formal education without literacy must be laid down clearly and discussed fully if policy-makers and planners are to make the right choices and justify the choices made.

Section 1: Why literacy?

A simple answer to the question Why literacy? would be: Literacy for development. This answer raises further questions: Does literacy promote development? Is literacy the only route to development? Or is it, at any rate, the preferred alternative?

Literacy has been defined in many different ways, from reading the word to reading the world (Bataille, 1976). We need not, however, make objectives and methods part of the definition of literacy as has sometimes been done (Unesco, 1978; Freire, 1970a). Literacy can be defined in instrumental terms as the ability to read and write in the mother tongue or in a national language where this is required by cultural and political realities. Numeracy—the ability to deal with numbers at a primary level—is typically considered part of literacy.

Development is, however, a value enterprise and definitions of development, therefore, have to include values about both means and ends. For instance, development must, almost always, mean more production; but improved production must be accompanied by just distribution. The health of the state must be balanced by a concern for the health of its people. Citizens must be taught critical consciousness so that they can engage in the creation and renewal of social and political structures through genuine participation.

Illiteracy need not, of course, be equated with ignorance. Yet, in theorizing about the possible role of literacy in development, we are implicitly making negative assessments regarding the influence of illiteracy on the developmental processes. We are saying that while illiteracy may not be ignorance, yet it is an unsatisfactory condition. The need for a reorientation in values and norms, and the importance of fostering the political, economic and social skills of citizens have to be accepted as part of the development agenda. The question is: Will literacy create or facilitate the emergence of the desired effects in adult men and women who will then take part in the development processes?

A taxonomy of literacy effects

In the following sections we present a taxonomy of literacy effects which can be used by policy-makers and planners in justifying their plans for literacy promotion in the service of development. A few statements should establish the framework for subsequent discussion:
1. The taxonomy of literacy effects includes those effects which have been known to appear, and also those which, it is claimed, will appear when adults become literate. In other words, the justifications given here are not limited to those based on research, on historical analysis or empirical findings; justifications arising from theory and ideology are also included. Policy-makers and planners must sometimes put into practice what seems theoretically compelling, and must often take action to follow up their ideological commitments. There is no reason why these types of justification should not be included in a taxonomy of real or claimed effects of literacy.
2. Literacy may be acquired within the setting of an adult literacy class, or may have been acquired in school and retained. Some of

Nature of justification / Loci of effects	Cognitive	Developmental			Cultural	Ideological
		Economic	Political	Social		
Individual	1	2	3	4	5	6
Family	7	8	9	10	11	12
Community	13	14	15	16	17	18
Nation	19	20	21	22	23	24
World Community	25	26	27	28	29	30

FIG. 1. A taxonomy of justifications for literacy promotion.

the research on literacy effects is in reality a discussion of schooling effects. Inkeles and Smith (1974) have suggested that the effects of schooling on individuals includes socialization in modern values. Thus, literacy acquired in school may have effects in regard to the 'technology of intellect' (Goody, 1968) as well as to the 'contexture of attitudes'. In the taxonomy presented above we have included effects of literacy irrespective of whether it was acquired in a school setting or within the setting of an adult literacy class.

3. In evaluating the evidence concerning literacy effects, it may be useful to think in terms of three different types: the cognitive effects of pure literacy (Type P), the social effects of literacy (Type S), and the instrumental effects (Type I).

Type P effects result purely from the cultivation of the ability to encode and decode a language, irrespective of what language is used, of what is read during and after the acquisition of literacy, or of the uses to which the newly acquired literacy skill is put.

Type S effects relate to the new definition given to the newly literate person by himself and by others in his environment. These effects may relate to the realignment of status, economic and power relationships, and to the development of mutual expectations that follow once the new literate has been initiated into the magic circle of the literate and can 'make the stones speak'.

Type *I* effects are those which result from the uses to which literacy is put by those who teach literacy and by those who learn to read. These instrumental effects may come from the content of the message that is taught; from the predispositions and the possibilities that literacy creates in regard to seeking and handling information; and from the participation and decision-making skills that have been learned by adult participants.

Literacy planners and policy-makers will have to learn to distinguish between these various types of effects in order to be aware of which effects are amenable to planning and control for instrumental uses and which ones are not.

Figure 1 represents, horizontally, the kinds of effect which can be used to justify literacy promotion in a society; and, vertically, the loci of such effects. Examples for some of the thirty cells of the taxonomic matrix suggest themselves more easily than for others. Change in the technology of intellect will be an example for cell 1; human rights for cell 6; scholarization of children for cell 10; abolition of class structures for cell 21; better prospects for a new international economic order for cell 26, etc. For other cells, possible and plausible effects will require research.

Effects of literacy on the individual

The cognitive effects of literacy (especially writing) on individuals— the effects of Type *P*—have received considerable attention from students of culture and cognition. The new literates' modes of perceiving and thinking about the world are thought to change so radically as to constitute a new 'technology of intellect' (Goody, 1968). McLuhan has talked of the new epistemology of print that changes the way in which the literate individual acquires and organizes knowledge of the surrounding reality (Rosenthal, 1968). In-depth interviews with new Tanzanian literates suggest that new literates do feel they have become new persons; and part of these new definitions use cognitive categories (Kassam, 1979). The list of characteristics that accrue from literacy include individualism, objectivity, the holding of individual opinions, a capacity for logical analysis and context-independent abstract thinking, a sense of history and universalism.

Development theorists as well as development planners have asserted that literacy does often mean higher income for the new literate both in urban and rural settings. In the rural setting, the new literate is able to make use of such economic institutions as extension activities, rural banks and marketing co-operatives. In the urban setting, literacy contributes to higher income, to safety on the job, and to the possibility of unionization to protect economic interests.

If literacy does not result in increased participation in political institutions, it certainly equips the individual for possible participation. While it is not out of the question for illiterates to participate in political institutions within the community, leadership in such institutions as the Panchayats in India and the Tanzanian party cells is becoming more and more difficult for illiterates. Participation in political institutions above the local level has now become almost impossible for them. As Lenin asserted half a century ago and others have rediscovered since (Mulira, 1975), the illiterate stands outside politics.

The new literate acquires the most significant status gains in the shift from illiteracy to literacy. Literacy is truly an initiation into the magical circle of the literate (Bhola, 1979). Literacy is a categorical skill: first the individual is illiterate, then the individual is literate. It is also a demonstrable skill, and thus has built-in social certification. Other forms of non-formal education, regardless of the amount or significance of the information that may be communicated through them, do not have the same aura. Literacy releases the individual from a sense of personal inferiority, from the relationship of dependency and subservience, and allocates a new status and potential.

Some studies have been comprehensive in their approach, analysing the effects of literacy and illiteracy on both the technology of intellect and the contexture of attitudes of individuals, and how these, in turn, affect the economic, social and political development processes. Speaking at the International Seminar organized by ILO, Unesco and FAO in Turin (1968), Magderez and Henkes pointed out the following constants that seemed to accompany illiteracy: 'difficulty in perceiving images; atechnicality; absence of scientific mentality; inability to reason and consequent dependence on intuition; difficulty in rationalization and calculation'. The personality of the illiterate, they went on to say, demonstrated an affective and intuitive existence in which the irrational and the fantastic are developed to the utmost (Fakouri, 1973).

On the other hand, literacy acquired through schooling contributes to the resocialization of the individual and the acquisition of overall individual modernity with these characteristics: keeping informed about the world and taking an active role as a citizen; valuing education and technical skill; aspiring to advance oneself economically; stressing individual responsibility and seeing the virtues of planning, including family planning; approving social change and being open to new experience of urban living and industrial employment; manifesting a sense of personal efficacy; freedom from absolute submission to received authority in family, tribe, and sect, and the development of newer non-parochial loyalties; and the concomitant granting of more autonomy and rights to those of lesser status and power, such as minority groups and women. (Inkeles and Smith, 1974.)

The cultural effects of literacy at the individual level may lie in the development of the individual as a maker of culture. Reading involves decoding the meanings carried within the linguistic code; and writing involves stating one's meaning in the same linguistic code. This experience of codification and decodification is transferred to the existential world in which the individual lives. The individual learns to decodify the social and political realities as codified (or structured) by others. At the same time, this literate individual is able to codify realities as personally experienced. This might mean conscientization and a possible emergence from a culture of silence (Bhola, 1979.)

Literacy also opens up new options for the enjoyment of culture. The literate can use the print mode to enjoy the cultural forms and creations of peoples and lands far and wide, instead of being limited to the merely oral and local.

Finally, literacy has been justified on purely ideological grounds. The Universal Declaration of Human Rights (United Nations, 1967) recognizes ignorance as an obstacle to the self-fulfilment of the individual. As literacy exemplifies one of humankind's paramount achievements—the invention and use of symbolic systems—illiteracy is the denial of an essential element of the human heritage and the imposition of an intellectual bondage.

Literacy and the family

Study of the effects of literacy at the family level has not attracted as much attention from researchers and policy-makers as it deserves. There are, however, some important questions: What would it mean to have the head of the family literate? What would it mean to have both husband and wife literate? What would be the effects if the wife were literate and the husband not? What is the quality of life within a fully literate family? What advantages might accrue to a literate family in the community in contrast with a non-literate family?

Theory would suggest that a literate family might enjoy individuation and diversity of interests, access to greater information and to the functional processing of such information, and, generally, a higher level of discourse. This might mean economic survival or at least a greater economic outreach. There might also be a different pattern of family expenditures in a literate family in contrast with a family that is not literate; and the literate family might generally command better communication and living skills.

One aspect on which we do seem to have some information concerns the scholarization of children within literate families. Unesco's evaluation report on the EWLP did not find much hard data to show that parents' literacy was related to the scholarization of their children, yet a positive relationship was beginning to appear consistently (Unesco, 1976). The implications of this finding in regard to increased returns from primary education should be obvious. The impact on the general socialization of children by literate parents should also be quite clear.

An issue which is receiving increased attention is the high rate of illiteracy among women in developing nations and its implications for the educational attitudes and welfare of the family. This growing awareness reflects both an increased consciousness of sex-related biases and the growing disparity between men and women in respect of literacy. Whereas in 1970, there were 139 million more illiterate women than men in the world, by 1980 this gap had increased to 170 million and was expected to reach 194 million by 1990. This disparity is the direct result of unequal schooling opportunities and, hence, unequal school participation. In 1981, for example, it was estimated that 79.5 per cent of all boys in the 6 to 11 age group were enrolled in school but only 68 per cent of the girls. In many parts of the developing world, the discrepancy is considerably greater than is suggested by the above figures for the world as a whole.

It is, of course, correct to observe that these differences are deeply rooted in the cultures of many developing—as well as developed—societies and correspond to traditional divisions of labour: 'the women in the hut and the men at the hunt'. Yet it is also apparent that development action should be aimed at improving the status of the more disadvantaged and that this implies that special attention needs to be given to education for women. Such action can also be justified by the crucial role that mothers play in setting the tone of family life and in transmitting to future generations the attitudes and values upon which development may ultimately depend. As the Director-General of Unesco emphasized in his 1979 International Literacy Day address:

The family is . . . the setting more than anywhere else where children, especially in their early years, find the affection and security essential for their equilibrium and self-fulfilment and for the harmonious development of their young personality. It is there that they acquire their first notions of life. Hence, the cultural environment of the family generally exercises a decisive influence in shaping children's future.

Literacy and the community

Effects of literacy at the community level have, again, not been much studied by literacy workers and educational planners. What is the critical mass of literate adults and children that makes a community literate? How does this critical mass of literates affect life in the community? Equally important, how does a literate, as compared with an illiterate, community fare in terms of acquisition of economic and educational resources, and how does it resist internal colonialism, exploitation and mere neglect?

Even though hard data are not available, once again it seems reasonable in the light of current theory to expect that literate communities will demand and get educational institutions (schools, libraries, reading rooms), economic institutions (rural credit banks, co-operatives), and political institutions of self-government. Literate communities may also experience significant demographic transformations through changes in fertility and mortality rates and the shift of some age groups to the cities.

Literacy and society

Literature on culture and cognition has sought to establish the effects of literacy on the cognitions of individuals and characteristics of cultures. Literate cultures, it is suggested, undergo detribalization, exchange myth for history, acquire a future and with it a predisposition to plan, adopt hierarchical organization and use objective criteria for recruitment to such organizations (McLuhan, 1962; Havelock, 1976). While critics of this literature have sometimes dismissed these assertions as interesting but not empirically provable, it is clear that a literate society, by definition, will have a greater fund of symbolic skills that literacy itself engenders.

The developmental argument—that there is a positive relationship between the level of literacy in a society and the economic, social, and political development of that society—has been more frequently made and more strongly argued.

The relationship between education and material wealth in a society was pointed out early on by the English economist Alfred Marshall (Marshall, 1930). Later, in the 1950s, Theodore W. Shultz of the University of Chicago renewed economists' interest in the role of education in productivity; in his Nobel Lecture on 10 December 1979, he returned to the theme of the importance of quality human capital in breaking the cycle of poverty.

Studies that have accumulated in the meantime have pointed to the significant effects of literacy on economic development. Bowman and Anderson (1963) found that all countries with per capita incomes of over US $500 a year in 1955 had 90 per cent literacy or better; and all countries with per capita income of less than $200 had literacy rates of 30 per cent or below. Literacy levels of 30 to 70 per cent had no systematic correlations with levels of income. The researchers found it tempting to conclude that a literacy rate of 30 to 40 per cent was a pre-requisite to incomes exceeding $200 in most cases and $300 in all cases. Inflation has, of course, raised these thresholds and wealth from oil or other mineral resources has made the correlations less perfect than those cited by Bowman and Anderson, but the connection between literacy and economic development remains strong and constitutes persuasive evidence of a cause and effect relationship.

In another frequently quoted study, Blaugh (1966) found that literacy contributed to economic development in different ways: (a) raising the productivity of new literates, and also of individuals working in association with literates—the so-called spillover benefit of literacy; (b) expediting the flow of general knowledge to individuals (e.g., instructions about health and nutrition) and thus reducing the cost of transmitting useful information; (c) stimulating the demand for vocational training and technical education; (d) acting as a device for selecting the more able and enhancing their occupational mobility; and, finally, (e) strengthening economic incentives, meaning the tendency for people to respond positively to a rise in the rate of reward for their efforts. Not surprisingly, he found the map of world illiteracy and the map of world poverty to be congruent.

Phillips (1970), Versluys (1977) and Rafe-uz-Zaman (1978) have all provided support for the connection between literacy and economic development in their reviews of studies conducted within different socio-economic settings and different political cultures.

Blaugh's study pointed to the spillover effects of literacy and to its role in expediting extension information and in stimulating demand for vocational training and technical education. These *generative* effects of literacy must, of course, be given the attention they deserve and should enter into our calculations of the returns on literacy.

Even more important are considerations of the national futures that are made possible by literacy. Development need not mean Western-style industrialization and bureaucratic nightmares. But development cannot be conceived of without technology and the rationalization of human organization. Technology should have a human face, but it will have to have 'reading lips' as well. A scientific culture will be impossible without literacy and the print to disseminate it. A rational social organization to serve a welfare state is not possible without literacy.

A variety of assertions have been made in regard to the political effects and consequences of literacy on society. Understandably, the effects of literacy have invariably been governed by the values and priorities of the different political regimes. Indeed, literacy has been used by the power élite as an effective mode of affiliation of the masses to weld a people into a nation-state (Almond and Powell, 1966) or to create particular kinds of political culture (Meyer, 1971). Literacy alone
may not create a just society, but it is important for the establishment and sustenance of egalitarian and participative institutions.

Literacy also has been justified in terms of its positive effects on the new literate's social status and, consequently, on the existing class structures. It is claimed on behalf of the national literacy campaigns of Cuba and Somalia, for example, that their most important social-structural effects include: the elimination of a sense of inferiority from among the newly literate who had previously accepted their disadvantage as deserved and, therefore, natural; the creation of a class consciousness among newly literate, but still poor, groups, who can now analyse their socio-economic conditions in terms of a class struggle and thus work together as a class to defend themselves from the exploitative classes; and the de-élitization of members of the urban élite, who went to live among the rural poor and learned to respect the traditional ways of life and culture, gaining a feeling of solidarity with the rural poor. In a larger historical perspective, sociologists and economists have found that literacy (acquired through schooling within the formal education setting) has created conditions for upward mobility for the individual and led to more equitable class structures.

Literacy may also have significant demographic effects. In Sri Lanka, literacy status was closely linked with improved health practices and infant mortality was lowest in the areas where literacy was highest (Isenman, 1978). An analysis recently undertaken for the World Bank (Hicks, 1979) suggested that levels of literacy explain the differences in life expectancy across countries more fully than variations in such factors as calorie intake and protein consumption, the accessibility of clean water, the number of doctors per capita, or the overall measure of the gross national product.

Some social analysts and students of social change have used the concepts of overall individual modernity and overall modernization of societies. Lerner (1958) asserted that 'literacy is indeed the basic personal skill that underlies the whole modernization process'. Literature in this tradition is extensive. In a study of Fijian society, a relationship was found between literacy and social change that included the decline of traditional customs, changes in social status, agricultural and domestic innovation, population change and disease, travel and knowledge of the world, intemperance and other vices, age and sex ratios in traditional economic occupations and in the evolution of new occupations, games and pastimes, dress, moral attitudes, and cognitive change (Clammer, 1976). Modernization is by no means all good!

Finally, Third World Nations have offered ideological justifications for promoting literacy at the national levels. They have called illiteracy the shame of nations which must be eradicated. Illiterates have been presented by the national élites as dumb cattle serving the needs of the élite classes, and making hardly any contributions to their own history and heritage.

Illiteracy is seen as a danger to the principle of the equality of man. It not only violates the individual's right to education; it is one of the major obstacles to the effective enjoyment of other human rights. As René Maheu, a former Director-General of Unesco, declared in Tehran, on the occasion of the United Nations International

Conference on Human Rights on 23 April 1968: 'To try to understand, in order to try to choose and to determine what one wants, one must first be able to read. In times when men are more and more dependent on the intermediacy of signs, to be unable to read means isolation in the world and this is true despite the proliferation and propaganda of images.'

What is true at the national level is also true at the international level. Literacy—universal literacy—must be considered an indispensable tool for the new international order that is being sought by the world community. The new international order cannot be built upon a humanity that is divided into two species, one literate and the other illiterate. Nor can the task of bringing about a new international economic, social, political and information order be left to small cliques in different societies. The masses must be enabled to understand the global economy and the global polity. Who has the resources? Who has the instruments of production? What does one get for what one gives? Who consumes too little and who consumes too much? Who has the power to enforce a world order that seems patently unjust? The masses must understand the distribution of power among nations and the uses to which that power is put, learn who interprets the world for them, who determines what we see, hear and emulate. This cannot be achieved while there are more than 800 million illiterates in the world.

Negative effects and abuses of literacy

In discussing the effects of literacy on the individual, the family, the community and society, we have so far dealt solely with the positive aspects, listing arguments in favour of literacy and citing research in support of the promotion of literacy. The discussion would be incomplete, however, if we neglected the argument on the other side.

With a shift in our framework of values, many of the effects of literacy may indeed appear in a bad light. According to McLuhan, literacy has brought 'linear thinking in science and mathematics, linear development in music, self-centredness in man, fragmentation in human society, and chauvinism everywhere . . . ; also detachment, hierarchical organization, and bureaucratization' (Rosenthal, 1968). From the humanistic perspective, these characteristics are clearly not desirable.

Verne (1975) has talked of literacy as bringing about a 'dispossession of speech' by giving the illiterate the impression that books are the only possible source of culture and teaching him to devalue the importance of his own discourse in his own eyes. We know from historical experience that literacy has not always been used exclusively for conscientization but also for mystification and for creating and reinforcing dependencies. Finally, it is alleged that literacy is part of the 'gradualist plot' (Postman, 1970) to deny to the people what is their due simply because they are not yet literate.

According to a Tantric saying: By what one rises, one may also fall. Some of the consequences of literacy may be unavoidably negative but, when not deliberately abused, literacy is positive and potent. Literacy cannot wait.

Section 2: Why can't literacy wait?

In considering the first question, Why Literacy? we have presented a whole range of justifications for literacy promotion at the individual, family, community, national and international levels. Some students of communication and social change suggest, however, that the question should not be 'Why literacy?' but rather 'Why can't literacy wait?' Within the present developmental context in most developing countries, why not provide the necessary communication systems right now, using non-print media?

Verner (1974) makes a case for non-formal education without literacy when he says

The content of the programmes must be geared to the functional need for learning as perceived by the participant. In most cases this will eliminate literacy as a necessary prerequisite because the underprivileged adult has survived without it. In time, after other more urgent needs have been met, literacy may then itself become a need. Underprivileged adults have a greater need to learn marketable skills than to become literate. With advances made in instruction, it is possible for illiterates to acquire vocational skills.

On the other hand, Jeffries (1967) makes the case for literacy both as an end and as a means:

I suggest that it is fundamentally wrong, in the practical situation in which the world is placed, to hold back the teaching of literacy while education and social programmes are being developed. It is only by a complete reversal of traditional attitudes and by regarding the eradication of illiteracy not only as an end in itself, but as an end which must be attained at once and at all costs that the world has any realistic hope of achieving it.

In evaluating the argument for non-formal education through different media now and non-formal education with literacy later, various tasks must be undertaken:

1. The dialectical relationship in the process of change between needs as perceived by the participant and needs as projected by the development élite must be examined;

2. Assumptions made about the motivational and informational capacities of the non-print media must be analysed; and
3. The meaning of the 'now – later' part of the argument must be properly understood within a programmatic framework.

First, we must face the fact that planning social change is not merely a matter of meeting the perceived or felt needs of participants within educational and developmental programmes. It is more significant to change current perceptions, to fashion new needs and to make participants aware of new needs envisaged by the leadership. This is not to suggest that change means the imposition of central visions or the creation of artificial needs. What we do suggest is that change is based on a dialectic between the needs perceived by participants and those projected by the leadership. Thus, literacy does not have to be bypassed in the developmental process simply because participants do not perceive the need for it and have survived without it. The challenge is to make literacy a felt need.

Secondly, the argument in support of non-formal education conducted through non-print media rests upon uncertain assumptions regarding the capacity of non-formal education to motivate participants and the effectiveness of these media in transmitting development messages. It should not be assumed that non-formal education programmes without literacy are by nature more motivational and in greater demand or, indeed, even better tolerated than formal literacy classes. Programmes of family planning, nutrition, health and agriculture have been rejected by potential participants, who go on living with poor health and malnutrition just as they go on living without literacy.

The assumptions about the informational capabilities of the non-print media are even more untenable. As we have indicated earlier, the print and non-print media are not simply two equivalent alternatives with the same goal. In choosing between literacy and these media, we are choosing between two epistemologies, two different chemistries of cognitions and two different patterns of social effects. Reading is a thinking process; hearing and seeing involve quite different mental processes. In developed societies, in spite of the proliferation of broadcast media, most information is communicated in print. The media cannot operate alone and often require the assistance of print to make their point.

There are inherent problems in receiving information through broadcast media. We retain only 20 per cent of what we hear and only 50 per cent of what we see and hear (*Media Asia*, 1974). Illiteracy in fact supports the spread of misinformation since messages have been distorted anywhere from 29 to 57 per cent, depending upon the complexity of the message, when handled by illiterates (Singh, 1973). This means that extension workers have to go back to participants again and again to make minor adjustments in the initial message or to remove distortions. Written information, however, can be verified by returning to the text from which it originates.

Broadcast media do not help people to become independent consumers of information. On the contrary, listeners and viewers become increasingly dependent upon the outside sources of information. Finally, the listener and the viewer have no control over such media. Print media are much more amenable to user control than are radio and television. A community-based rural newspaper is much easier to create than community radio or television.

Finally, we must ask what planners mean by 'now' or 'later' when they discuss the implementation of literacy programmes. Do those who propose that literacy should wait mean waiting a few decades, if necessary, for the economic and political forces in a society to generate the social demand for literacy? Do they mean to withhold allocation of funds from plans for literacy promotion until a particular level of radio and television facilities has been achieved and put to use? Or do they use the word 'later' in terms of the life of a particular programme of non-formal education meaning that we should wait for the participant in a programme to ask for literacy and offer non-formal education without literacy for the time being? On the other hand, what do those who propose literacy programmes now want? Do they mean teaching literacy to participants on the first day, on the very first encounter; and literacy simple and direct, without motivational frills?

The problem has to be taken out of the temporal framework of 'now and later' and put within a programmatic framework. Development planning makes history; we simply cannot wait for history to come to our rescue by creating a social demand for literacy some time in the future. The urge to seek development via the non-print media as we try to respond to immediate communication needs may be an empty hope and a false economy. To wait for individual participants within our programmes to demand literacy once they have understood and internalized the need for it is to misunderstand the dynamics of planned change and to stultify the role of leadership in development processes. At the same time, we do not have to hit participants on the head with a blackboard in the very first encounter.

What we do need is an approach to programme development in which literacy is central but in which the disabilities of the illiterate are not accentuated in the process of teaching literacy. While we are engaged in making part of the population literate and serving their information and development needs, we must not exclude the illiterate part of the population from developmental concerns or increase the relative burden of illiteracy by withholding services and inputs from the illiterate. This implies a design orientation on the part of the programme planner that involves a 'systematic' integration of literacy with the economic, political and social sectors of society, a central role for literacy both as an end in itself and as a means for development, and functional utilization of the media both for motivation and for amelioration.

Section 3: Why are mass literacy campaigns necessary?

Within a policy-making framework, three programme options for literacy promotion within societies may be conceptualized: (a) the diffusion approach, (b) the selective–intensive approach, and (c) the mass approach.

In this section, we will very briefly analyse the logic underlying each programme strategy and evaluate experiences involving these three different approaches. We will try to show that, in comparison with other approaches, the mass approach seems to be the most promising for the eradication of illiteracy.

The diffusion approach assumes that literacy will come through universal elementary education. As the graduates of the elementary schools enter adulthood and join the economy and as the older generations pass away, literacy will have been diffused throughout the society. This, the 'long siege' approach, seeks to eradicate illiteracy through attrition.

Those who promote this approach believe that childhood and adolescence are the best periods of life for learning; and that, on the other hand, adults are not competent learners. Even when adults do have the mental capacity for learning, they are supposedly overwhelmed by obligations to the family and to the community. If adults have survived without literacy thus far, why not, it is asked, let them muddle through life, instead of taking already scarce educational resources away from the children?

We have already shown some of these assertions to be untenable. Adults are excellent learners since as they learn they also increase their learning ability. And no adult should be too busy to learn because of family and community obligations. Indeed, learning to read and write should be seen as an unfulfilled obligation to the family and the community which must no longer be neglected. Moreover, the resources for adult literacy are seldom diverted directly from elementary education. Quite often a programme for adult literacy would mean greater overall allocations to education. We must also remember that expenditures on adult literacy are likely to improve the rate of returns on formal elementary education (Bhola, 1979).

Quite apart from the logic of the arguments for and against, the experience of developing countries in the post-colonial period indicates that, in most countries, our hopes of eradicating illiteracy through attrition will not be fulfilled for decades, in the context of existing demographic trends.

The selective and intensive approach seeks to promote literacy among those select economic regions, select occupational groups and select age cohorts which offer the highest promise of economic returns, and to work with them intensively for maximum effect. This approach accepts the central role of literacy in the process of development, but it makes segmented commitments. The hope is that after the economic take-off within the selected sectors, there will be spillover to other economic sectors and these will then become eligible for intensive material and literacy inputs. In the meantime, the unstated assumption is that mass literacy will be a waste.

The literacy campaign approach is a mass approach that seeks to make all adult men and women in a nation literate within a particular time frame. Literacy is seen as a means to a comprehensive set of ends, economic, social-structural, and also political. I have suggested elsewhere that a national literacy campaign can serve as a moral equivalent of the 'Long March' (Bhola, 1979). In too many countries of the Third World, the struggle for independence has been outside the direct experience of the masses. Independence has been good news, but most people have been spectators rather than participants in their independence movement. The mobilization necessary for a successful literacy campaign can provide the people with a deeply felt political experience resulting in a sense of nationhood.

The launching of a mass campaign is a declaration of 'business *not* as usual'. This can allow for a mobilization of commitment and resources impossible to achieve under other conditions. By giving the campaign a mass orientation, a large part of the population are able to participate in it as learners or instructors or in one of the many other roles that a campaign requires and creates.

Concluding remarks

Policy choices cannot be made by a systematic and deterministic process of deduction. Assertions about what *is* and what *will* most likely follow are not unequivocal. Research is inadequate, theories are untested. Politics and ideologies confound us further.

In the arguments presented above, research may not always be persuasive, but theory is compelling. Theory gives us an idea of what literacy has done to individual identities and to collective consciousness in literate societies and compels us to think what it might do in the Third World. Where theory also falters, ideology takes over. Literacy is a human right. How dare we question? How dare we not campaign?

REFERENCES

ALMOND, G. A.; POWELL, G. B. JR. 1966. *Comparative Politics: A Developmental Approach*. Boston, Mass., Little, Brown.

BATAILLE, L. (ed.). 1976. *A Turning Point for Literacy: Proceedings of the International Symposium for Literacy, Persepolis, Iran, 1975*. Oxford, Pergamon Press.

BHOLA, H. S. 1979. A Policy Analysis of Adult Literacy Versus Universal Primary Education: Child is the Father of Man and Man of the Child. *Viewpoints in Teaching and Learning*, Vol. 55, No. 4, pp. 22-35.

BLAUGH, M. 1966. Literacy and Economic Development. *The School Review*, Vol. 74, No. 4, pp. 393-415.

BOWMAN, M. J.; ANDERSON, A. C. 1963. Concerning the Role of Education in Development. In: Clifford R. Geertz (ed.), *Old Societies and New States*. Glencoe, Ill., Free Press.

CLAMMER, J. R. 1976. *Literacy and Social Change*. Leiden, E. J. Brill.

COOMBS, P. H. 1968. *The World Education Crisis: A Systems Analysis*. New York, Oxford University Press.

CRONE, C. D. 1979. What Are We Learning? *World Education Reports*, No. 18, January.

FAKOURI, E. 1973. Some Psychological Aspects of Literacy Programmes. *Literacy Work*, Vol. 2, No. 4, p. 21.

FREIRE, P. 1970. *Cultural Action for Freedom*. Cambridge, Mass., Harvard Educational Review. (Monograph Series, No. 1).

GOODY, J. (ed.). 1968. *Literacy in Traditional Societies*. Cambridge, Cambridge University Press.

HAVELOCK, E. A. 1976. *Origins of Western Literacy*. Toronto, Ontario Institute for Studies in Education.

HICKS, N. L. 1979. *A Note on the Linkage Between Basic Needs and Growth*. Washington, D.C., World Bank. (Mimeo.)

INKELES, A.; SMITH, D. H. 1974. *Becoming Modern: Individual Change in Six Developing Countries*. Cambridge, Mass., Harvard University Press.

ISENMAN, P. 1978. *The Relationship of Basic Needs to Growth, Income Distribution and Employment: The Case of Sri Lanka*. Washington, D. C., World Bank. (Mimeo.)

JEFFRIES, C. 1967. *Literacy—A World Problem*. New York, Praeger.

KASSAM, Y. O. 1979. *Illiterates No More: The Voices of New Literates from Tanzania*. Dar es Salaam, Tanzania Publishing House.

LERNER, D. 1958. *The Passing of Traditional Society*. Glencoe, Ill., Free Press.

MARSHALL, A. 1930. *Principles of Economics*. 8th ed. New York, Macmillan.

McLUHAN, M. 1962. *The Gutenberg Galaxy: The Making of Typographic Man*. New York, New American Library.

Media Asia. 1974. Vol. 1, No. 3, p. 35. (Based on a study made by Socony Vacuum Company, Singapore.)

MEYER, J. W. 1971. Economic and Political Effects of National Educational Enrolment Patterns. *Comparative Education Review*, Vol. 15, February, pp. 28-43.

MULIRA, E. E. K. 1975. *Adult Literacy and Development*. Nairobi, East African Literature Bureau.

PHILLIPS, H. M. 1970. *Literacy and Development*. Paris, Unesco.

POSTMAN, N. 1970. The Politics of Reading. *Harvard Educational Review*, Vol. 40, No. 2, pp. 244-52.

RAFE-UZ-ZAMAN. 1978. Why Literacy? *Literacy Discussion*, Vol. 9, No. 1.

ROSENTHAL, R. (ed.). 1968. *McLuhan: Pro and Con*. Gretna, La., Pelican.

SINGH, K. N. 1973. *Communication Strategy for Rural Change*. Paper read at Regional Conference on Communication and Change in Rural Asia, Bangalore, 27 August-3 September, 1973.

UNESCO. 1976. *The Experimental World Literacy Programme: A Critical Assess-ment*. Paris, Unesco.
——. 1978. *Estimates and Projections of Illiteracy*. Paris, Office of Statistics, Unesco. (Unesco doc. CSR-E-29.)
UNITED NATIONS. 1967. *A Compilation of International Instruments of the United Nations*. New York, United Nations.
VERNE, E. 1975. *Literacy and Industrialization: The Dispossession of Speech*. Paper presented to the International Symposium for Literacy, Persepolis, Iran, 3-8 September 1975.
VERNER, C. 1974. Illiteracy and Poverty. *Literacy Discussion*, Vol. 5, No. 2, pp. 303-14.
VERSLUYS, J. D. N. (ed.). 1977. *Research in Adult Literacy*. Tehran, International Institute for Adult Literacy Methods.

BIBLIOGRAPHY

ARNOVE, R. F.; ARBOLEDA, J. Literacy: Power or Mystification? *Literacy Discussion*, Vol. 4, No. 4, 1973, pp. 389-414. (Special issue, 'Functional Literacy: One Approach to Social Change', ed. by H. S. Bhola.)
BERRY, J. W.; DASEN, P. R. *Culture and Cognition: Readings in Cross-Cultural Psychology*. New York, Harper and Row, 1974.
BHOLA, H. S. Notes Towards a Theory: Cultural Action as Élite Initiatives in Affiliation/Exclusion. *Viewpoints*, Vol. 48, No. 3, 1972, pp. 1-37.
BOWMAN, K. J.; ANDERSON, A. C. *The Participation of Women in Education in the Third World*. Chicago, Ill., University of Chicago Press, 1978.
BRUNER, J.; OLVER, R.; GREENFIELD, P. *Studies in Cognitive Growth*. New York, Wiley, 1966.
CARNOY, M. *Education and Cultural Imperialism*. New York, David McKay, 1974.
CHIAPPETTA, M.; BURKE, R. C. *Characteristics of Illiterates and Program Hypotheses*. 1977. (Final report, AID/TA-C-1203)
COLE, M.; SCRIBNER, S. *Culture and Thought*. New York, Wiley, 1974.
COLE, M., et al. *The Cultural Context of Learning and Thinking*. New York, Basic Books, 1971.
EISENSTEIN, E. L. *The Printing Press as an Agent of Change*. Cambridge, Cambridge University Press, 1979. 2 vols.
FARUQEE, R. *Sources of Fertility Decline: Factor Analysis of Inter-Country Data*. Washington, D.C., World Bank, 1979.
FREIRE, P. *Pedagogy of the Oppressed*. New York, Herder and Herder, 1970.
——. *Education for Critical Consciousness*. New York, The Seabury Press, 1973.
GRAFF, J. J. *The Literacy Myth*. New York, Academic Press, 1979.
HABERMAS, J. *Toward a Rational Society*. Boston, Mass., Beacon Press, 1970.
HARBISON, F. H. *The Education-Income Connection*. Paper prepared for the Princeton-Brookings Income Distribution Study, 1974.
——. *A Human Resource Approach to the Development of African Nations*. Washington, D.C., The Overseas Liaison Committee of the American Council on Education, n. d.
HERZOG, W. A. JR. *The Effects of Literacy Training on Modernization Variables*. Doctoral dissertation, Michigan State University, 1967.
ILLICH, I. 1970. *Deschooling Society*. New York, Harper & Row.
ILLICH, I.; VERNE, E. 1976. *Imprisoned in the Global Classroom*. London, Writers and Readers Publishing Cooperative.
INTERNATIONAL COUNCIL OF ADULT EDUCATION (ICAE). *The World of Literacy: Policy, Research, Action*. Ottawa, International Development Research Center (IDRC), 1979.

IRWIN, M.; ENGLE, P. O.; KLEIN, R. E.; YARBROUGH, C. *The Relationship of Prior Ability and Family Characteristics to School Attendance and School Achievement in Rural Guatemala.* Unpublished manuscript, 1977. Available from M. Irwin, Michigan State University, East Lansing, Mich.

M'BOW, AMADOU-MAHTAR. Literacy: A Vital Component of the New Economic Order. *Unesco Features*, Nos. 709/710, 1976.

ROGERS, E. M.; HERZOG, W. Functional Literacy among Colombian Peasants. *Economic Development and Cultural Change*, Vol. 14, No. 2, 1966.

ROGERS, E. M.; HERZOG, W.; with SVENNING, L. *Modernization among Peasants: The Impact of Communication.* New York, Holt, Rinehart & Winston, 1969.

ROY, P.; JESUDASON, V. Research Combines with Action in Indian Villages. *World Education Reports*, No. 18, January, 1979.

SARAF, S. N. *Role of Functional Literacy in Co-operative Development in Afghanistan.* Kabul, 1974. (Unesco Literacy Project.)

SCHUMAN, H.; INKELES, A.; SMITH, D. H. Some Social Psychological Effects and Non-effects of Literacy in a New Nation. *Economic Development and Cultural Change*, Vol. 16, No. 1, 1967.

STICHT, T. G. *Literacy and Vocational Competence.* Columbus, Ohio, National Center for Research in Vocational Education, Ohio State University, 1978.

STRUMILIN, S. G. *Problemi Ekonomiki Truda.* Moscow, 1975.

SUNKEL, O.; FUENZALIDA E. The Transnationalization of Capitalism and National Development. Falmer, Sussex, Institute of Development Studies, University of Sussex, 1977.

UNESCO. *Illiteracy and Human Rights.* Paris, Unesco, 1968.

——.*Literacy: 1965-67.* Paris, Unesco, 1968.

——.*Illiteracy, a Major Obstacle to the Effective Enjoyment of Human Rights.* Paris, Unesco, 1968.

——.REGIONAL OFFICE FOR EDUCATION IN ASIA. *Disparities in Levels of Illiteracy and Educational Attainment in Countries of the Asian Region.* Bangkok, 1977.

VALENZUELA, J. S.; VALENZUELA, A. Modernization and Dependency. *Comparative Politics*, Vol. 10, No. 4, 1978, pp. 535-57.

CHAPTER 4

The literacy campaign in the Union of Soviet Socialist Republics, 1919-39

The national adult literacy campaign of the USSR came officially into being with the signature by V. I. Lenin of the Decree of the Council of National Commissars on the Liquidation of Illiteracy among the Populations of the Russian Soviet Federal Socialist Republic (RSFSR) on 26 December, 1919.

At the time the Decree was signed, Lenin hoped that illiteracy would be wiped out in the USSR by the tenth anniversary of the October Revolution, that is, in about eight years. To his contemporaries, this calendar might have seemed quite credible. But the problem of illiteracy, which affected 70 per cent at the time, proved to be more intractable than initially imagined. It was in 1939 that the literacy campaign was officially closed; and even in that year, literacy was less than universal among the Soviet population aged 9 to 49: 87.4 per cent for both sexes—93.5 per cent for men and 81.6 per cent for women.

It was not, however, for lack of will, faulty direction or insufficient effort that the goal was not achieved sooner. The task was colossal and the conditions under which the literacy campaign of the USSR was first declared and then implemented were far from perfect.

Looking back on the mass literacy campaign of the USSR, it is difficult not to be impressed. It was, after all, the first attempt by a state to make all its people literate—men and women, rural and urban, workers and peasants, speaking more than a hundred tongues, spread over half a continent constituting the largest country in the world. While official accounts may sometimes seem to paint too glowing a picture, the vision, the commitment, the innovativeness can never be questioned. The literacy campaign in the USSR remains the ancestor of all modern mass-literacy campaigns.

Historical background and setting

The Bolshevik Revolution of October 1917 did not mean the end of uncertainty. The war was still going on. The economy was in dire straits. People were dying of hunger as the result of a terrible famine. Scarcities were endemic. The Decree on the liquidation of illiteracy which Lenin signed and which is now preserved in the Lenin State Library was itself written on rough grey wrapping paper.

The Bolsheviks inherited a country as large as a continent, peopled by many nationalities speaking some 122 languages. It was not only linguistic differences that they had to contend with. There were differences in the levels of economic development and of education in social structures, religious affiliations, political and cultural traditions, values and norms of public behaviour and in patterns of life in the family and basic psychological constitutions.

The literacy campaign had little to build upon in terms of education or communication infrastructures. Education had been grossly neglected during the Tsarist regime. Communication infrastructures to reach and teach the peoples of the USSR were completely inadequate. There were 100 million people in the RSFSR when the campaign was launched, with an illiteracy rate of 70 per cent. Under the Tsarist regime, literacy was increasing at a snail's pace: 10.5 per cent per year. At this rate the elimination of illiteracy would take between 150 and 300 years. It was in this historical and educational context that Lenin decreed:

All the population of the Republic between the ages of 8 and 50 who are unable to read or write must learn to do so in their own language or in Russian, as they wish. This instruction will be given in state schools, both those already existing and those being set up for the illiterate population under the plans of the People's Commissariat for Education.

For the elimination of illiteracy, the subsidiary bodies of the People's Commissariat for Education may use People's Centres, churches, clubs, private houses, suitable premises in factories, works, Soviet establishments and so on.

Those who avoid the obligations laid down by this decree and those who prevent illiterates from attending classes are liable to criminal charges.[1]

The Decree and the campaign that followed were acts of both courage and commitment. This is especially evident when we realize the multinational and multilingual character of the Soviet Union and the commitment of the government to pursue a multilingual policy in all significant areas of education and administration.

1. Summarized from the article, 'Ot likvidacii negramotnosti k vseobščemu polnomu srednemu obrazovaniju' [From the Elimination of Illiteracy to Universal Full Secondary Education] by G. Lobancev, published in the Soviet *Učitel'skaja gazeta* [Teachers' Journal] on the sixtieth anniversary of the signature by Lenin of the Decree of the Council of National Commissars on the Liquidation of Illiteracy among the Population of RSFSR.

The purpose of the campaign and the driving forces behind it

The driving force behind the literacy campaign was the Revolution; the political revolution had to be complemented by a cultural revolution.

The literacy campaign of the USSR is always associated with Lenin and it was indeed Lenin's campaign. But it was also a Marxist-Leninist campaign and a utilitarian one. Lenin legitimized the campaign by associating himself personally with it. He twice addressed the 1919 Russian Congress of Extra-School Education, pointing out the crucial importance of adult education and of literacy for reconstruction of the nation. It was at this congress that a special section for extra-school education was created. Lenin signed the famous Decree for the eradication of illiteracy and Nadezhda Konstantinovna Krupskaya was appointed to head the special department for extra-school or extra-mural education.

The campaign was deeply rooted in Marxist-Leninist ideology. The masses had to be given a new consciousness and an opportunity to participate in the political process. This called for political education. As Lenin had said, addressing the Second All-Russian Congress of Soviets on 8 November 1917: 'In our opinion, the strength of the state lies in the awareness of the masses; a state is strong only when the masses are well informed, can pass judgements on any issue, and can make their own decisions.' (Nozhko, 1968, p. 26). It is obvious why education is such an important unifying theme of Marxian social analysis.

The campaign also had many concrete utilitarian purposes. The many nationalities, each speaking a language of its own, had to be formed into one nation and political culture. Lenin understood and asserted the direct relationship between literacy and politics. 'An illiterate person,' said Lenin, 'is outside politics and he has to be taught his ABC. Without this there can be no politics.' (Lenin, 1950).

Finally, the mass literacy campaign had to become the instrument of Soviet modernization, a tool for constructing a scientific, technical and secular future for the country. The authorities seemed to understand even as early as the 1920s that the task of changing a traditional social and economic system into a modern industrial culture could not be achieved without the aid of literacy.

Preparation for the campaign

The campaign went through a fairly long gestation period. The idea was embedded in almost all the declarations and addresses made by senior Party and government representatives during 1917-19. The first movement towards literacy began after the February Revolution of 1917. The First All-Russian Congress of Soviets met on 2 June of that year and published the Declaration of the Rights of the Peoples. The right of every citizen to an education and the right to choose the form and language of instruction was part of the Declaration. In September 1917, a conference was held on adult education; this meant that the Declaration was not intended only for the school-going or school-age population but also for adults beyond the school age. In other words, the generations then at work in factories and fields were not to be written off.

After the October 1917 Revolution, a Second All-Russian Congress of Soviets reaffirmed the Declaration of Rights. The focus on the adult was not abandoned. On 11 November 1917, the newly appointed People's Commissar of Education, A. V. Lunacharsky gave an address to citizens: 'Adults too will want to be rescued from the humiliation of being unable to read and write. Schools must occupy a prominent place in the general plan of education.' (Nozhko, 1968, p. 26).

In March of 1919, the Eighth Communist Party Congress called for government support for 'self-education and self-development for workers and peasants through the creation of a network of extra-scholastic institutions.' (Nozhko, 1968, p. 26). Then in May 1919, the First All-Russian Congress of Extra-Scholastic Education was held, giving birth to the famous Decree of December 26, 1919.

There was, however, no formal preparatory phase in the campaign or any pilot study in the contemporary sense of these terms. There was no elaborate research apart from a fact-finding survey. This survey involved the registration of all illiterates in towns and villages. Its purpose was not only to determine the number of illiterates in the communities, but also to obtain information on age, occupation, place of employment, engagement in social work, the number of children in the family and the times most suitable for studies.

Mobilization of the people

This, the first national adult literacy campaign in the world, remains even today a model of mobilization and innovation. As we have stated earlier, Lenin himself consecrated the campaign when he signed the Decree. All the instruments of information and propaganda were then orchestrated to take the message to the masses in the fashion of a modern 'high pressure' advertising campaign (Medlin et al., 1971, p. 61).

Hundreds of thousands of copies of the literacy decree were published and distributed among the masses. Appeals from leaders were circulated. Slogans were coined: 'Let the literate teach the illiterate'; 'Teach people at all costs and under all conditions'. All possible media were pressed into service—newspapers, posters, billboards, radio, cinema and the theatre. As late as 1926-27, a play 'How Ugly to Be Illiterate' was published and distributed.

There was mobilization of the people by the people. 'Activist' workers and peasants recruited illiterate workers and peasants for literacy classes. Former illiterates spoke to small groups at special meetings, explaining how they had studied, under what conditions and what benefits had accrued to them now that they could read and write.

Marshalling governmental and private resources

As the potential learners were being motivated and mobilized to participate and become literate, structural and technical resources, both public and private, were also mobilized. First and foremost, the campaign was supported by a new organization of public education. A new Commissariat of Education had been established with Lunacharsky as its head. Krupskaya headed the special department of extra-scholastic education. Admittedly, the new Commissariat had its share of problems. In the early years, for instance, education had to compete with programmes in the arts, ballet and the theatre and was relatively disadvantaged. The Commissariat was unable to provide good management and had become a place of employment for poets, artists and others, who were often without any previous experience in such work (Fitzpatrick, 1970). In an effort to improve the situation, the Commissariat underwent successive reorganizations. In 1918, forty-two different departments had separately submitted their budgets to the central collegium of the Commissariat, among them the subdepartment of adult schools, the subdepartment of social education and the committee on literacy. In 1920, the Commissariat was divided into five sectors and in 1921 it was reduced to three main departments to streamline decision-making.

Radiating from the central system, newly organized regional, district and local departments of public education were asked to meet with representatives of the local population to draft local plans for the eradication of illiteracy, to make local censuses, to identify teachers, to fix the length of courses and determine days and times when groups should meet to study. Allocations of state budgets were made and authorizations given for the use of school buildings when unoccupied, of churches, clubs, homes, offices, firms and factories.

Mobilization of technical resources

Technical resources also were mobilized. All those who were literate were asked to teach the illiterate. Volunteers were drawn from trade unionists, school students and members of the Komsomol, the communist youth organization. Well-known authors were enlisted to write primers for adults and to write follow-up books for new readers. To discover and mobilize technical talent among the general population, primer competitions were organized. All this effort was supported by a really impressive governmental programme of language research in almost all of the languages used in the USSR.

The people's response

The Soviet literacy campaign had cast its seeds on fertile ground. Writing about the people's response to the Commissariat's out-of-school programmes in general, Krupskaya noted in 1919: 'Every day we are told by visiting comrades how the masses are longing for knowledge.' (Ivanova, 1959, p. 134.) It cannot have been too difficult to translate this hunger for knowledge into hunger for 'knowledge through literacy'.

It need not be assumed, however, that all was plain sailing in terms of people's motivations and responses. There was reluctance, hesitation and even active resistance. Nozhko (1968, p. 27) reports that 'many elderly people refused to learn to read and write because of their age or the fact that their parents and grandparents were illiterate and had managed without book knowledge.' Organized active resistance, according to official accounts, came from the bourgeoisie and the kulaks who had a stake in the status quo and were uncertain of the future being built by the Bolsheviks. In addition, many Muslim and Jewish religious leaders and leaders of traditional cultures in the outlying areas showed a certain resistance because they saw in the campaign a threat to their religious beliefs. But overall no serious resistance developed and by the late 1920s, overt criticism would have been unthinkable.

The conduct of the campaign

The implementation of the campaign was supervised by the Commissariat of Education under the direction of the Party. The organization of the Soviet campaign may be characterized as comprehensive, experimental, multi-level, collaborative and combining centralization and decentralization, at least in the first eight or ten years of the twenty-year campaign.

In 1920, the Extraordinary Commission for the Struggle Against Illiteracy was created. This was an organizational mechanism to handle co-ordination and collaboration with all other organs of the government and the Party, as well as public organizations and voluntary associations. The Commission included representatives of various state and public organizations and had extensive powers and functions; these included motivational work among the masses, registration of illiterates, elaboration of methods of instruction and production of primers and other textbooks, and recruitment of teachers and supervisors to implement the programme. (Ivanova, 1959). In the late 1930s it was abolished and replaced by local commissions. What should be noted here is the fact that the Extraordinary Commission was created and that it lasted almost throughout the whole life of the campaign.

The Extraordinary Commission of 1920 was supplemented in 1922 by the First All-Russian Society for the Liquidation of Illiteracy. This Society can be seen as an organizational mechanism complementary to the Extraordinary Commission. It is mentioned most often in connection with its work with the *likbez* schools.[1] The *likbez* schools were held in all kinds of locations: school buildings, factories, farms and even tents of nomads. Teachers were literate citizens who had been drafted for work in *likbez* schools or who worked during their free time in their own communities. These schools were both vital and innovative since they took the school to the learners rather than asking the learners to come to the school.

In the meantime, efforts were directed towards providing universal general education at primary level. Thus universal primary education and universal adult literacy were conceptualized and implemented in integration with each other.

The Red Army was asked to play its part in the eradication of illiteracy. Literacy education was made compulsory for soldiers.

The organization of voluntary effort

The governmental machinery for conducting the campaign was supplemented by extra-governmental voluntary activities. The 'Down with Illiteracy Society' (*Doloi negramotnost*) was established in 1923—three years after the Extraordinary Commission and one year after the First All-Russian Society—under the chairmanship of Mikhail I. Kalinin, President of the Republic. Lenin joined as a member. This was a voluntary society and anyone above the age of 18 years could acquire membership. Adolescents between the ages of 14 and 18 who were already working could also become members. Children below 14 years old could become Friends of the Society in any of its local branches which numbered 50,000 in 1932. This society did not simply mobilize and motivate. It had its own publishing house which produced adult literacy primers, study aids and manuals, posters and instructional leaflets. It also published a journal for new readers which carried excerpts from fiction, short articles, and definitions and illustrations of difficult words. Hence it functioned as a national technical-professional association of literacy workers. It was dissolved

1. The name is an abbreviated form of *likvadatsiia bezgramotnosti* or 'liquidation of illiteracy'

why? in 1936, after more than twelve years of solid and useful work and only three years before the campaign was officially closed.

In 1928, mid-way into the campaign, the Komsomol (the All Union Leninist Communist League of Youth) joined the struggle against illiteracy and declared a cultural campaign. It directed its attention both inwards to encourage the efforts of its own illiterate members and outwards to remove illiteracy among the masses and to raise their cultural standards.

The Komsomol's cultural campaign lasted three years, during which time some 21 million people learned to read and write, thanks to more than 1,200,000 'soldiers of culture' (Ivanova, 1959). In each district, the local Komsomol selected groups of between five and thirty persons, which were called 'shock brigades'. The functions of these brigades were:

To ensure fulfilment of the programme for eliminating illiteracy in their particular area;

To keep track of class attendance in the area's schools for adults and to recruit educated people to coach the students;

X To draw illiterates and semi-literates into political and educational activities by means of conversations, excursions, newspaper readings and readers' conferences;

To collect public contributions;

To arrange talks and lectures about the cultural revolution and the activities of the Down with Illiteracy Society, to organize anti-illiteracy meetings, to publish newspapers dealing with problems of the literacy campaign, and to organize nursery play centres for the children of mothers attending school. (Ivanova, 1959, p. 138).

The role played by trade unions in the implementation of the literacy campaigns should not be overlooked. Apart from motivating workers and organizing literacy classes, trade unions supplied learning materials to learners and paid teachers (Ivanova, 1959). We must also note the special emphasis on eradicating illiteracy among women. Women's needs and problems received special attention. The government established nurseries, kindergartens and play centres so that women with young children could attend school.

The organization of the campaign in later years

The organization of the campaign changed somewhat in structure, and considerably in spirit, during its final years. In the early 1930s, a new All-Russian Society for the Liquidation of Illiteracy was formed. The Extraordinary Commission of 1920 was abolished and its functions taken over by local committees. These committees were attached to Soviets in the towns, town-districts and villages, and their members included deputies of the local Soviets, teachers and librarians, club managers, outstanding pupils of adult schools, and exemplary workers and farmers. The functions of these committees were far-reaching:

To promote publicity work for the purpose of increasing awareness of the importance of literacy.

To keep track of the progress of schoolwork, and establish the reasons for non-attendance of pupils.

To conduct individual training for those persons desiring to learn but unable to attend school for legitimate reasons, e.g. children to take care of, school hours coinciding with work hours, remoteness from school.

To see that the departments of public education were prompt in supplying the schools for adults with syllabuses and handbooks on teaching methods and in instructing the teachers thoroughly.

To see that the directors of factories and state farms, the managing boards of collective farms and the trade unions organization provided the necessary premises, light and equipment (tables, desks, blackboards, etc.) for adult schools; and that they ensured favourable conditions for regular school attendance. It should be noted that it was the responsibility of trade unions fo fulfil these requirements: to provide classroom spaces, to keep these spaces heated and lighted, to register illiterates and semi-literates, to motivate them to attend school, to keep records of attendance, and to see that workers were given full opportunity by the management to attend schools.

To exercise control over the proper use of funds allocated for the eradication of illiteracy, and to see that none of the money was used for other purposes. These committees were also required to give an account of their activities at presidium meetings of the Soviet and at public meetings.

To contribute to the establishment of what in modern terms would be described as the creation of a literate environment. The committees, with the co-operation of Party leaders and young Communist organizations, also arranged oral recitations and readings of fiction for adult pupils, lectures and talks on politics, labour, hygiene and sanitation. They arranged excursions to museums and exhibitions, established libraries and ensured that bookshops always had an adequate supply of instructional materials and books.

The direction and control that these committees could provide for literacy work at local level can easily be imagined. Organizational control was matched by curriculum control. The early experimentalism and romanticism of the Krupskaya days was gone. There was a stricter definition of literacy and a unity of approach to teaching it.

The coverage of the campaign

The range of the literacy campaign was truly impressive. It encompassed all fifteen republics and the whole population between 8 and 50 years old. One and a half years after the Decree, 200,000 teachers had been mobilized and 5 million participants had been made literate; by the end of the third year, 7 million. The statistics in Table 1 should put the literacy efforts in perspective.

TABLE 1. Percentages of literates among the population (aged 9–49)

Year	Both sexes	Men	Women
Urban and rural population			
1897	28.4	40.3	16.6
1920	44.0	57.4	32.2
1926	56.6	71.5	42.7
1939	87.4	93.5	81.6
1959	98.5	99.3	97.8
1970	99.7	99.8	99.7
Urban population			
1897	57.0	66.1	45.7
1920	73.4	80.6	66.6
1926	80.9	88.0	73.9
1939	93.8	97.1	90.7
1959	98.7	99.5	98.1
1970	99.8	99.9	99.8
Rural population			
1897	23.8	35.5	12.5
1920	37.7	52.5	25.2
1926	50.6	67.3	35.4
1939	84.0	91.6	76.8
1959	98.2	99.1	97.5
1970	99.5	99.6	99.4

Source: TSSU SSSR, *Narodnoe obrazovanie, nauka i kultura v SSSR* [Public Education, Science and Culture in the USSR], p. 21, Moscow, Statistika, 1971.

The pedagogical aspects of the campaign

The learner was free to choose either Russian or his own mother tongue as his language of literacy. Such a choice was by no means a meaningless gesture. Considerable research was undertaken to support the use of local languages in literacy, education and administration. Indeed, linguistic analysis has been most intensely pursued in the Soviet Union since the early days of the regime, and has covered all the various levels of language research—lexical, phonological and grammatical. As early as 1919, a special section of the Department of National Minorities of the Commissariat of Education worked on the development of languages and adaptation of scripts, assisted by local teachers in creating textbooks and literature. By 1926, work had been initiated on dictionaries and lexicons of new political and scientific development (Dimanshtain, 1933, p. 134.)

It should be noted here that after 1927 important changes occurred in the language policy. In one sense, these changes were inevitable. Russian was already the language of the majority, the instrument of international communication, and above all the medium of Marxist ideology and of Soviet politics. It had to become the *lingua franca*. By 1938, Russian had become obligatory in schools, and may have become popular in literacy classes as well. By 1940, the Cyrillic script was used for most languages, replacing the Latin and Turkic scripts. This both facilitated the language-learning and made printing in the various languages more economical.

Three Rs not exclusive but central

Right from the beginning, the Russian campaign had objectives larger than the teaching of the Three Rs. The basic objective of teaching reading and writing, while not exclusive, was always central to the task of accomplishing the larger objectives of creating a new Soviet man, of promoting a cultural revolution, and preparing citizens for active participation in the social, political and industrial life of the country.

Curriculum organization and setting

Learners were recruited into schools for illiterates and semi-literates. Illiterates were classified as those who could neither read nor write or who could read but not write; semi-literates were those whose reading and writing skills were very poor, who were unfamiliar with basic arithmetic and who had finished the school for illiterates.

In the early years, 1919-22, literacy classes lasted only three months. Experience showed that this was too short a period to teach functional literacy. In rural areas, classes were extended to seven months with four hours a day, twelve days a month, making a total of 336 class hours. In urban areas, classes were extended to ten months with three hours a day, eleven days a month, a total of 330 hours. The programme for illiterates covered the first two years of primary school; for semi-literates, the third and fourth years of formal school. Later these two schools were combined into a programme to cover three years of basic education (Deinko, 1957).

Integration between the Three Rs and functional content (social, political and industrial) was mostly obtained through diversified materials taught together within the school setting and by establishing collaborative and supportive relationships with different media and institutions of instruction and information—newspapers, libraries and radio—and with economic and productive institutions. One example of the economic-educational collaboration was the establishment of the FZU (factory-plant schools) in 1920. These schools required minimal previous schooling and were designed to train young people between 14 and 15 years old in mass-production techniques.

Methods of instruction

The aims of the teaching methods were very clear and direct: to teach reading and writing in the shortest possible time, making teaching matter as concrete as possible and using exercises of practical significance such as reading business letters and figuring out one's own pay cheques.

The methods of teaching were a combination of convention and innovation. The primers used global methods and chose emotional themes which remind us of Paulo Freire's choice of words half a century later. One primer, for example, stated (Deinko, 1957):

> We are not slaves
> Slaves, we are not
> Not we are slaves

Primers featured portraits of Marx, Engels and Lenin. Basic social and economic policies of the Party and government were included.

Recruitment of teachers

All schoolteachers were expected to take part in the literacy campaign. They were to teach when required and to act as supervisors and as methods experts for the training of literacy teachers. While all literate citizens were supposed to serve as teachers, the Komsomol 'soldiers of culture' played a special role. They received several months of training during which both instructional methods and Party doctrine were taught.

To improve the effectiveness of literacy teachers, a training system was established. Centres for instruction in adult education methods were opened in various localities under the regional and territorial departments of education and under the Commissariat of Education. These centres had suitably equipped libraries.

Teachers were expected to prepare their lessons carefully, to define the theme of their instruction, to prepare articles for reading and to develop lists of questions for discussion. They were advised to help learners to establish links with resources of education and information outside the classroom. Krupskaya told them: 'The task is to learn to use books as tools for acquiring further knowledge—adult students must be taught to use dictionaries, reference books, and catalogues—the teacher should use newspapers and pamphlets for them, not children's stories' (Moos, 1950, p. 4). The idea of bringing the newspaper into the classroom for a discussion of day-to-day issues was an innovation of great significance. Later, attention was given to preparing differentiated materials to meet the interests of heterogeneous groups.

Instructional materials

In the early years, there were acute scarcities of all material goods and there are stories of students writing with crayons on old newspapers. By 1920, however, 6.5 million copies of a reader had appeared, including 1.8 million for national minorities. Reading materials were distributed free to students, and each learner received five exercise books, two pencils and one pen holder. Ink and kerosene were supplied to all groups.

Later campaigns in world history may have used programmed instructional materials, games and simulations and perhaps slide sets and hand-held videos—all fruits of more recent electronic and instructional technology—but the literacy campaign of the USSR showed tremendous innovation in the use of instructional materials and left little for others to discover. The campaign used primers, study aids and manuals of various kinds. Its most impressive innovation lay in the use of the newspaper and the follow-up reading materials.

Special newspapers and journals were published, among them, the *Down with Illiteracy* journal and the *Peasant's Newspaper for Beginners in Reading*. The *Byednota* (the title may be translated as 'Impoverished Peasant') published a special column for new literates. Pamphlets were published to encourage learners to help themselves: *How to Learn to Write Without a Teacher*, *How to Learn to Count by Oneself*, *The Peasant Scholar*, and *Learn by Yourself*. There were follow-up books both to inspire and to inform the new literate: *About Lenin*, *Helping the Peasant*, and *Contagious Diseases*.

Incentive management

Both teachers and learners were offered suitable incentives. Workers were given two hours off from work for learning activity, without prejudice to their daily earnings or their holiday pay. They were offered higher wages when their schooling was completed and extra privileges such as holiday excursions, tickets for entertainments, book vouchers and bonuses. Arrangements were made for childcare to enable women to attend classes and some were given individual instruction at home. Competitions were held between programmes and 'Challenge Red Banners' awards were given to literates in the Red Army. As for the teachers, the Commissariat was authorized to pay all educated citizens at the salary rate of schoolteachers for literacy teaching, though it is not clear whether it was ever possible to do so.

Examinations for the literacy certificate

The role of examinations must be mentioned in the analysis of the pedagogy of the Soviet literacy campaign. Students were examined by special, legally appointed committees. In order to receive the certificate, a student had to read aloud a short passage, explain its content, answer questions about it, understand common terms, use elementary spelling rules and write short sentences without help, add and subtract six-digit figures, multiply and divide whole numbers, have an idea of fractions and percentages and have mastered metric measures and time. These examinations were conducted in the presence of a representative from the department of education or Komsomol.

Monitoring the progress of the campaign

Evaluation, monitoring, management information systems, are words and phrases that have only recently entered our vocabulary. Yet the question of monitoring—the development of feedback on the campaign's processes and results, the elimination of bottlenecks, the correction of errors, anticipation problems—can be usefully raised in regard to the literacy campaign of the USSR.

The administration system itself was used as a system of monitoring. The Commissariat of Education, with its various commissions and committees, was the nerve centre of this monitoring effort. The role of the local committees in the process was crucial. At their meetings, these committees heard the reports of the public education departments, of trade unions and co-operative organizations and of local enterprises on the progress of the literacy campaign. In turn, the committees gave an account of their activities at presidium or plenary meetings of the Soviets and at public meetings' (Ivanova, 1959). The data sent back to the centre were analysed and used to produce new materials and to train and retrain teachers.

After 1930, monitoring took on a different aspect. The Party watched the work of the campaign closely: successes were noted, praised and rewarded; failures were often criticized.

The literacy campaign

The effects of the literacy campaign may be evaluated in terms of a variety of objectives: Did the campaign succeed in consolidating the political revolution by a cultural revolution? Did it succeed in politicizing the masses in the early post-revolutionary years? Did it create a new socialist man? Did it produce better farmers and better workers and did it enable them to participate in building the new industrial society?

Official accounts and sympathetic commentators from abroad will answer a resounding 'Yes' to all four questions. The Soviet Union was indeed able to create and consolidate a new political culture and part of the credit must go to the literacy campaign. The Soviet Union was able to create a new Soviet man and to fit this new man into a powerful technological and industrial society. Again, the literacy campaign must take part of the credit. A Soviet commentator describes the meanings of the campaign, in concrete and personal terms, as follows:

Graduates of the literacy schools became good workers on the job and active participants in civic life. Learning to read and write helped them to understand their work better and made it easier for them to solve a great number of daily problems of living.

Collective farms likewise put the knowledge acquired in schools to practical use. Here is what a member of the Krestyanka Collective Farm said about her studies: 'I was illiterate before. I took care of the calves [but could not] check their growth against a tabulated scale. I couldn't do it because I was illiterate. Then I entered a school for illiterates. Now I have graduated and feel altogether different on the job. I have none of the difficulties I used to have.'

One of the campaign's most important achievements, impossible to overlook, was to equalize opportunity through equalizing the literacy levels among social classes, among ethnic groups and between the sexes. Table 2 indicates how the peoples of all the fifteen nationalities of the USSR, both men and women, have built for themselves a status of mutual equality on the basis first provided by the campaign.

Another highly significant effect of the campaign was to give the masses the capacity to enjoy education and culture. All the mass media—newspapers, magazines, radio, television, books, libraries, cultural houses and cultural palaces—would have been useless for the common people if literacy had not become universal.

Some lessons of the literacy campaign in the USSR

As we prepare to draw lessons from the Soviet experience, it must be fully understood that a country's initiatives, solutions, choices and

TABLE 2. Literacy of the population in the Union Republics, 1968 (percentages of literates in the 9-49 age group)

	Both sexes				Men				Women			
	1897	1926	1939	1959	1897	1926	1939	1959	1897	1926	1939	1959
USSR	28.4	56.6	87.4	98.5	40.3	71.5	93.5	99.3	16.6	42.7	81.6	97.8
RSFSR	29.6	60.9	89.7	98.5	44.4	77.1	96.0	99.3	15.4	46.4	83.9	97.7
Ukrainian SSR	27.9	63.6	88.2	99.1	41.7	81.1	93.9	99.6	14.0	47.2	82.9	98.8
Byelorussian SSR	32.0	59.7	80.8	99.0	43.5	79.1	90.7	99.5	20.7	41.3	71.4	98.6
Uzbek SSR	3.6	11.6	78.7	98.1	5.6	15.3	83.6	99.0	1.2	7.3	73.3	97.3
Kazakh SSR	8.1	25.2	83.6	96.9	12.0	35.4	90.3	98.8	3.6	14.5	75.8	95.1
Georgian SSR	23.6	53.0	89.3	99.0	29.1	61.2	93.4	99.4	17.1	44.6	85.2	98.6
Azerbaijan SSR	9.2	28.2	82.8	97.3	13.1	36.1	88.8	99.4	4.2	19.2	76.1	96.0
Lithuanian SSR	54.2	–	76.7	98.5	57.1	–	78.7	98.9	51.4	–	75.0	98.1
Moldavian SSR	22.2	–	45.9	97.8	31.2	–	59.0	99.1	12.7	–	33.1	96.6
Latvian SSR	79.7	–	92.7	99.0	80.5	–	94.6	99.4	78.9	–	91.0	98.8
Kirghiz SSR	3.1	16.5	79.8	98.0	5.0	23.9	84.9	99.0	0.8	8.4	74.4	97.0
Tadjik SSR	2.3	3.8	82.8	96.2	3.9	6.4	87.4	98.0	0.3	0.9	77.5	94.6
Armenian SSR	9.2	38.7	83.9	98.4	14.5	53.7	92.7	99.2	2.9	22.7	74.7	97.6
Turkmen SSR	7.8	14.0	77.7	95.4	11.5	18.3	83.0	97.7	2.7	8.8	71.9	93.4
Estonian SSR	96.2	–	98.6	99.6	96.0	–	98.9	99.7	96.3	–	98.3	99.5

Source: Strana Sovetsov za 50 let., 1969, 278.

practices are bounded by economic and political realities. What is or was possible in the USSR may not be transferable without alteration to another political system. With this caveat, the following lessons may be drawn for the consideration of literacy planners and policy-makers.

1. The political will of the leadership, enforced by the institutional power of the state, can work wonders—it can resocialize members of society, transform the social fabric and invent a new future. Cultural revolutions can be brought about; literacy campaigns can be launched and assured of success.

2. This political will must be clearly articulated and must be oriented towards the people. A campaign that will change an entire country into a classroom must be rooted in an ideology that inspires the whole population.

3. The justification for a successful literacy campaign must not be expressed solely in bread-and-butter economic terms. It may be better to justify a literacy campaign in such transcendental categories as a cultural revolution and a new social hope, while at the same time describing its intermediate objectives in terms of political participation and industrial, technological and economic development.

4. There are no substitutes for the twin processes of organization and mobilization. On the one hand, the government must undertake both the administrative and the technical organization of planning and subsequent implementation. On the other hand, people must be mobilized; learners must be motivated to learn; those who can teach and contribute in other ways must be enabled to do so.

5. Universal literacy is possible even in a multinational, multilingual, multigraphic society. The goal of universal literacy in the mother tongue should not be abandoned for pseudo-solutions—information by mass media; non-formal education without literacy, etc.—since literacy is a prerequisite to political participation and modernization. By contrast, the so-called selective and intensive approaches seem severely limited unless subsumed under a mass approach. Equalization through universal literacy should be the ideal; women and the weaker sections of society must not be neglected in the attempt to cover the so-called productive groups.

6. The will to act and to succeed can of itself generate innovation that helps those concerned to rise above absence of infrastructures, lack of technical capacities and scarcities of material resources. The Soviet willingness to launch educational programmes with minimal resources in the conviction that something inadequate is better than nothing at all deserves to be borne in mind.

7. A literacy campaign must be linked with larger educational, economic, political, developmental and cultural policies. After the first step of literacy, the road ahead to further education and development should be clearly in view.

REFERENCES

DEINKO, M. 1957. *Forty Years of Public Education in the USSR*. Moscow, Foreign Languages Publishing House.

DIMANSHTAIN, S. 1933. *Printsipy sozdaniya natsionalnoi terminologii. Yazyk i pismennost narodov SSSR* [Principles for the Establishment of a National Terminology. Language and Literature of the Peoples of the USSR], p. 134, Moscow.

FITZPATRICK, SHEILA. 1970. *The Commissariat of Enlightenment*. Cambridge, Cambridge University Press.

IVANOVA, I. M. 1959. Abolition of Adult Illiteracy in the USSR (1917-1940). *Fundamental and Adult Education*, Vol. 11, No. 3. (Entire issue.)

LENIN, V. I. 1950. *Sochineniya*, 4th ed., Vol. XXXIII, p. 55.

MEDLIN, W. K.; CAVE, W. M.; CARPENTER, F. 1971. *Education and Development in Central Asia*. Leiden, E. J. Brill.

MOOS, E. 1950. *The Educational System of the Soviet Union*. New York, National Council of American-Soviet Friendship.

NOZHKO, K., et al. 1968. *Educational Planning in the USSR*. Paris, Unesco.

BIBLIOGRAPHY

ANWEILLER, O. The Mutual Impact of Soviet and World Education. *School and Society*, Vol. 100, No. 2338, 1972, pp. 45-58.

APANASEWICZ, N. Education in the USSR. In: *An Annotated Bibliography of English-Language Materials, 1965-1973*. Washington, D. C., United States Government Printing Office, 1974. (Doc. ref. OE74-19111.)

BRICKMAN, W. W. A Bibliographic Introduction to Soviet Education. *School and Society*, Vol. 100, No. 2341, 1972, pp. 251-3.

——. Chronological Outline of Soviet Education. *School and Society*, Vol. 100, No. 2341, 1972, pp. 250-1.

——. The Educational Development of the Soviet Union: Introduction. *School and Society*, Vol. 100, No. 2338, 1972, pp. 30-1.

Education and Social Mobility in the USSR. *Soviet Studies*, Vol. 18, 1966-67, pp. 57-65.

The Great October Socialist Revolution and Problems of Rearing the New Man. *Soviet Education*, Vol. 11, No. 2, 1968, pp. 20-57.

HANS, N. *The History of Russian Educational Policy, 1701-1917*. London, P. S. King and Son, 1931.

INTERNATIONAL UNION OF STUDENTS. *Fifty Years of Education in the USSR: 1917-1967*. International Union of Students, 1968.

LEWIS, E. GLYN. The Development of Literacy in the Soviet Union. In: Thomas P. Gorman (ed.), *Language and Literacy: Current Issues and Research*. Tehran, International Institute for Adult Literacy Methods, 1977.

Literacy Discussion, Vol. 7, No. 1, 1976. (Special issue, 'The Development of Adult Education in the USSR', ed. by A. V. Darinsky.)

MEDLIN, W. K.; LINDQUIST, C. B.; SCHMITT, M. L. *Soviet Education Programs*. Washington, D.C., United States Government Printing Office, (Doc. ref. OE14037, Bulletin 1960, No. 17.)

ONUSHKIN, V. G.; SUHOBSKAYA, G. S.; TONKONOGAYA, E. P. *The Eradication of Illiteracy in the USSR*. Paris, Unesco, 1982. (Surveys and Studies.) (Doc. ED/WS/31.)

ROSEN, S. *Part-time Education in the USSR*. Washington, D.C., United States Government Printing Office, 1965. (Doc. ref. OE-14113, Bulletin 1960, No. 17).

The Russian Soviet Federated Socialist Republic. *Great Soviet Encyclopedia*. Vol. 22. New York, Macmillan, 1975.

SHIMONIAK, WASYL. *Communist Education: Its History, Philosophy, and Politics*. Chicago, Ill., Rand McNally, 1970.

STRUMILIN, S. G. The Economic Significance of National Education. In: Mary Jean Bowman, et al. (eds.), *Readings in the Economics of Education*, pp. 413-50. Paris, Unesco/IIEP, 1968.

UNESCO. *Literacy Education: A Selected Bibliography*. Paris, Unesco, 1950. (Occasional Papers in Education, No. 5.)

——. *Literacy Teaching: A Selected Bibliography*. Paris, Unesco, 1956. (Educational Studies and Documents, No. 18.)

——. *History of Adult, Correspondence and Evening Education in the USSR*. Paris, Unesco, n.d.

USSR Education. Moscow, Novosti Press Agency Publishing House, 1975.

WARD, B. A. *Literacy and Basic Elementary Education for Adults: A Selected Annotated Bibliography*. Washington, D.C., United States Government Printing Office, 1961. (Doc. ref. OE-13017, Bulletin 1961, No. 19.)

WORLD BANK. *Educational Reform in the Soviet Union: Implications for Developing Countries*. 1978. (World Bank Staff Working Paper, No. 288.)

ZEPPER, J. T. Recent and Contemporary Soviet Educational Thought. *School and Society*, Vol. 100, No. 2338, 1972, pp. 31-45.

CHAPTER 5

The mass literacy campaign in the Socialist Republic of Viet Nam, 1945-77

The Vietnamese mass literacy campaign was in fact a series of four campaigns, three conducted in the North and one in the South. The first campaign was launched within two months of the August 1945 revolution. During October 1945 and December 1946, it is known to have reached some 3,020,000 people. The second campaign lasted from June 1948 to June 1950 and covered an impressive 8,109,600 people. The third campaign was conducted during 1956-58 and reached 2,161,300, including some 231,700 people belonging to ethnic minorities living in the mountains. By the year 1958, illiteracy had been eradicated from the North, except for a few far-off regions in the mountains. The unification of the country meant that literacy became a nationwide concern. A fourth campaign came into being which, during 1976-1977, reached 1,321,600 people.

What has been called the August 1945 revolution broke out on 19 August of that year, as Japanese occupation collapsed. On 2 September 1945, the revolution triumphed and Ho Chi Minh read the Declaration of Independence. A month later, in October 1945, Ho Chi Minh asked for popular education of the masses and for the eradication of illiteracy throughout the country within one year:

In order to safeguard our independence and to make our country strong and prosperous, each Vietnamese citizen should know his rights and his duties, and he should be capable of contributing to the work of national construction. Above all, everyone should be able to read and write *Quoc Ngu* [the national language].

Those who already know how to read and write should pass their knowledge on to the others. The illiterate should make every effort to learn. Husbands should teach their wives; older brothers and sisters should teach their younger brothers and sisters; children should teach their parents; the master of the house should teach those living beneath his roof.

As for women, they should study all the more assiduously in order to make up for the countless obstacles that have prevented them from obtaining instruction up till now. The hour has struck for them to catch up with men and to make themselves worthy to be full-fledged citizens.

The objectives were clear: politically, the aim was to ensure that people learnt their rights and duties so as to safeguard the revolution; from the socio-economic viewpoint, the aim was to ensure that people worked so as to bring about economic prosperity for all; and national integration required a common language, *Quoc Ngu*, to be learned by all the people. The communal spirit was apparent in the insistence that people had to teach each other and special consideration was given to women and other disadvantaged groups.

While Ho Chi Minh urged that everyone should learn to read and write *Quoc Ngu*, literacy was taught in the languages actually spoken by the people. This meant meeting the linguistic and cultural aspirations of all the various minorities living in the mountains. With a general level of illiteracy of around 80–90 per cent in the year 1945, this was clearly no easy task.

The Vietnamese literacy campaign is a special case in that it was conducted under wartime conditions. This was converted into an advantage by the revolutionaries, who made the literacy campaign an aspect of resistance:

> The vanguard smashes the aggressor, the rear fights ignorance!

> By going to school one shows one's love for the fatherland!

> Each classroom is a propaganda centre for the resistance!

These were some of the slogans. It is important to note that literacy teaching literally merged into political education and military training. Why resist? Why must resistance be long and stubborn? Why is ultimate triumph inevitable? How should we stand up to enemy searches? How can we ensure that the enemy hears nothing and sees nothing? These were part of the curriculum of the literacy classes. In 1953, literacy was linked with agrarian reform and class struggle as well. Reading the word was always linked with reading the world. Literacy was integrated sometimes with economic and political concerns, and sometimes directly with national survival.

The literacy work was followed up with complementary education, a fully-fledged plan of further education for the masses.

The historical background of the campaign

The Socialist Republic of Viet Nam came into being on 2 July 1976. It had had a long and turbulent history, having at one time or another experienced French colonialism, Japanese and Chinese occupation and the American presence. French colonialism had been consolidated in that part of Indochina by 1883. Under colonial rule, little respect was shown for the culture and language of the Vietnamese people and investment in education was meagre.

Typically, there was one incomplete primary school, holding a few elementary classes, for a cluster of five to seven villages. A whole district would have one full primary school, which enrolled about fifty pupils, most of them from well-to-do families. In the whole country there were a dozen secondary and three high schools with limited enrolments, and once again most of those enrolled were the children of the rich, the mandarins and the high-ranking functionaries. It is not surprising that there was 95 per cent illiteracy among a population of some 20 million. By way of providing a perspective, it should be noted that in 1939, there were 500,000 students in all of Indochina, most of whom were in the first and second grades.

There was, of course, a profound desire for freedom among the colonized Vietnamese people. In 1930, the Indochinese Communist Party was founded, and, led by Ho Chi Minh, it took the initiative of declaring independence in August 1945 with the collapse of Japanese rule. The French, however, refused to relinquish their colonial empire and returned in force. A nine-year struggle followed until the French were defeated at Dien Bien Phu in 1954. The Geneva Agreements of 1954 divided the country temporarily into two parts. The promised general elections of 1956 never came about and war broke out between the North and South, with the United States helping the South.. In April 1975, hostilities ceased.

The Socialist Republic of Viet Nam is a country of 329,566 square kilometres. In 1978, it had a population of approximately 49.3 million and a per capita income of US$140. While much had to be done to build a united nation out of one that had been divided by a brutal civil war, many projects vital for national construction had been under way since the mid-1940s. Mass education was one.

The driving force behind the literacy campaign

Clearly, the August 1945 socialist revolution was the driving force behind the Vietnamese literacy campaign. In 1943, as part of the anticolonial struggle, the Communist Party of Indochina had published its *Theses on Vietnamese Culture*. These identified the three fronts on which the Party had to fight and advance: political, economic and cultural.

The cultural front, in turn, was to have three essential characteristics: (a) national, against all enslaving, retrograde, feudal or obscurantist influences; (b) popular, against everything tending to oppose culture and the masses or to separate culture from the masses; and (c) scientific, against everything opposed to science and to progress. Education was to be the instrument of creating the new culture. Hence, the renewal of *Quoc Ngu* and the eradication of illiteracy were among the urgent tasks that were to be attained on the cultural front. The relationship between imperialism, ignorance and underdevelopment was stressed by the Party.

The *Theses* of 1943 guided the revolution of August 1945. A day after the proclamation of the republic on 3 September 1945, Ho Chi Minh assigned three tasks to the nation: to conquer famine, to conquer ignorance, and to conquer foreign aggression. On 8 September, he signed a decree to establish the Department of Popular Education and in October declared the campaign for the eradication of illiteracy within one year.

The timetable may have been somewhat optimistic, but there was no lack of commitment to literacy as an objective that was at the same time ideological, political, cultural and economic.

Preparation for the campaign

Mobilization of the masses and institutionalization of the government effort went hand in hand from the very beginning. The basic principle of organization was the *mass line*. This meant making the masses conscious of the fact that the eradication of illiteracy was their struggle; that they must eventually assume full responsibility for conducting that struggle; and that they must seek their own ways of overcoming the obstacles existing in their communities. However, the mass line was not based on any illusions of revolutionary spontaneity; the role of the Party and the government was crucial in promoting it. They had to conduct the process of awakening, explanation, mobilization and organization among the population. The Party had to be in control and use youth organizations, women's organizations, trade unions, and peasants' associations as the transmission belts for the process of mobilization.

The organization involved four levels of administration: central, provincial, district and village. Each level had literacy committees which were used as a mechanism for the horizontal integration of various interests and the co-ordination of efforts by various departments and agencies. The central literacy committee, for instance, brought together people from the education, health and agriculture sectors as well as representatives of the various mass organizations. There was also a direct liaison with the Central Bureau of the Vietnamese Front. Highly capable cadres were assigned to take charge of literacy work at all the various levels of organization.

The administrative structure came to be termed the 'two-tailed' style of administration for its ability to allow give-and-take between localities and within the various administrative levels. The delegates of the central literacy committee visited the various regions and localities that were reported to have problems. In consultation with the local population, they devised solutions and allocated the necessary resources. Mutual education and communication was also fostered through occasional conferences.

This type of administration required few full-time workers, a greater number of part-time workers and, above all, volunteers. The government had very few full-time employees at the various levels. Development of 'model' courses for cadres and teachers was a government responsibility as was the production of the main didactic materials. Apart from this, the campaign was financed entirely through public contributions.

To provide technical leadership in training and materials production, the Department of Popular Education at the centre was organized into four bureaus: for pedagogical organization, for production of manuals, for logistics and distribution of instructional materials, and for propaganda.

The approaches used in propaganda and mass mobilization can best be described in the words of a leader of the revolution who outlined the mobilization process at the different stages of the literacy campaign:[1]

Books, the press, radio, leaflets and directives are all extremely important. But they are inadequate for penetrating into the heart of the countryside and for persuading people unless they are backed up by living and attractive 'mass' measures such as:
Slogans and tracts for general distribution;
Processions, spectacular forms of propaganda with tambourines, unicorn dances, giant model penholders and exercise books, music . . .;
Groups of artists which, by means of songs, dances, plays and sketches, can inculcate hatred of colonialism and of its wretched legacy, namely illiteracy, and which can exhort people to advance towards the light, represented by the new regime;
The sale of spelling-books to the illiterates; invitation to literates to pass beneath the 'gateway of honour';
The composition of a large number of lively popular songs to deride young people who still hesitate to learn to read and write, along the lines of:

> Being married to an educated man
> can be a great asset.

1. Ngo Van Cat, 'La liquidation de l'analphabétisme et l'enseignement complémentaire pour adultes', *L'éducation en RDVN*, pp. 37-42, Hanoi, 1955. (Études Vietnamiennes, No. 5.) Quoted in Lê Thành Khôi, 'Literacy Training and Revolution: The Vietnamese Experience', in Léon Bataille (ed.), *A Turning Point for Literacy; Proceedings of the International Symposium for Literacy, Persepolis, Iran, 1975*, Oxford, Pergamon Press, 1976.

> But being married to an uneducated one
> is like being married to an ass.

Towards the end of the last stage [of a literacy course], people who encounter a great deal of difficulty or who lack determination are dealt with individually. We try to make them realize the disadvantages of remaining illiterate and the benefits of being able to read and write (such as being able to write to a husband at the front, being able to take notes in a notebook or a register, being able to do simple arithmetic . . .), as well as the misdeeds of the former regime and the glorious perspectives opened up by the new one. Once a person is convinced, he or she becomes a propagandist. The fact that propagandists speak from the heart, and the evidence of the concrete results they have achieved make their powers of persuasion frequently irresistible.

At the end of each literacy course, a solemn prize-giving and certificate distribution ceremony is organized in honour of people who have conquered their own illiteracy, after which onlookers are called upon to register for the following literacy course. Better still, the best pupils are awarded an honourable mention, and ceremonies are organized on the occasion of the presentation of honours to families, villages, districts and provinces that have successfully eradicated illiteracy. Patriotic competitions are organized in order to stimulate people to outdo each other.

But it is also necessary to foil attempts at sabotage, as for example when reactionary elements seek to prevent their wives, children, relatives from learning to read and write. Some of these even go so far as to use violence against pupils, or to commit theft while others are attending class. Reactionary priests preach that by learning the people will lose their religion.

Here, mention should be made of the considerable impact of congratulatory letters sent by President Ho Chi Minh to literacy instructors, to pupils and to regions that achieve successes in the campaign to eradicate illiteracy. Similarly, the Government offers a series of rewards, including the Order of the Resistance and the Order of Labour, to villages, districts or provinces that complete the eradication of illiteracy by fulfilling or even exceeding the norms laid down in the plan.

While a certain number of cadres and teachers wanted to organize regular classes—a tendency that was liable to create difficulties for the masses and to hamper their everyday activities—there were also certain moments, in certain regions, where cadres and teachers strayed from the mass line and used constraint:

They set up road blocks, making all passers-by undergo a spot test designed to detect illiterates;

They barred illiterates from markets, or else forced them to enter markets through a small lateral door so as to humilate them;

They marked the homes of illiterates with a black circle so as to deride them;

They refused to deliver travel permits to illiterates;

They forced illiterates to come to district centres and to bring food with them so they could attend classes.

These last-mentioned measures did not meet with the approval of the leadership since they were coercive and ran counter to the mass line.

Conduct of the literacy campaign

The Vietnamese campaign began in 1945 with three interrelated tasks: registering students; mobilizing personnel and material resources; and designing administrative structures. The registration was carried out by workers of the Department of Popular Education and covered precincts, communes, factories and service organizations. Data were collected on age, sex and profession. All illiterates were accounted for including children, adults and the elderly. In the space of a year, 1945-46, 2.5 million became literate.

Literacy work continued throughout the period of resistance against French colonialism. People who worked and fought during the day learned to read and write during the night. The slogan was: To study is to fight! More than 10 million people became literate during the nine years of resistance, but more than 3 million people between the ages of 12 and 50 remained illiterate and a fresh drive was therefore launched in 1956. By 1958, the North had eradicated illiteracy except in a few far-off regions in the mountains.

Eradication of illiteracy from the mountain regions was difficult. It was not merely a matter of logistics. While most of the population are Viets who live in the plains and speak Vietnamese, there are close on seventy other ethnic groups living in the remote mountain regions. Many of these ethnic groups, representing about 12 per cent of the total population, had no written language. The government, therefore, conducted a campaign which involved the parallel development of a script for the unwritten languages and despatch of 'shock brigades for the fight against ignorance' to the mountains. These brigades were sent to

live amid the local populations, to share their way of life and to take part in production. At the same time as holding literacy classes, they also played an active part in other social activities, notably in prophylactic movements, in the fight against superstition and in the construction of a new life-style. Their example spread rapidly, forming small groups of volunteer instructors among the local populations, and these last greatly enhanced the effectiveness of their activities. Among certain semi-nomad peoples living at altitudes of between 1,000 to 2,000 metres, these groups initiated adult literacy classes for five or six families along with one or more general education classes for children.[1]

By 1961, illiteracy was practically eradicated in the highlands.

In April 1975, 4 million people were still illiterate in the southern half of the country, a million of them adults. A new literacy campaign

1. Nhât Hung, 'L'enseignement au service des minorités nationales', *Regions montagneuses et minorités nationales en RDVN*, p. 119, Hanoi, 1967. (Études Vietnamiennes, No. 15.) Quoted in Lê Thành Khôi, op. cit.

was launched in 1976 and, by December 1977, illiteracy had been eliminated among working people below 50 years old (below 45 for women). In the mountains, the age limit was 40 for both men and women.

The campaign ended officially in March 1978 when a grand festival was held in Ho Chi Minh City to hail the elimination of illiteracy from all over the Socialist Republic of Viet Nam.

Pedagogical aspects of the campaign

In terms of 'curricular integration', the Vietnamese campaign was integrated with the needs of the revolution, of the resistance, and of the war effort.

There were few young literates in villages and hamlets who could serve as teachers. Teachers and students had to be mobilized from general education schools. Progressives and militants from outside the school system also volunteered. They received no remuneration but did receive important symbolic rewards. Ho Chi Minh himself was present at the inauguration and at the end of the first stage of national-level training to express gratitude to the volunteers and to wish them well in their work with the masses.

Rapid teacher training

Ngo Van Cat describes teacher-training strategies and approaches as follows:[1]

There are hundreds of thousands of literacy instructors. How does one go about teaching them all a teaching method capable of producing maximum results in the least possible time?

We have organized accelerated training courses, these being implemented by the regions and the mass organizations. In most cases, these courses are no longer than five or six days in length. In this period, the bulk of the course consists of political and ideological classes, designed to make these trainee-instructors conscious of their responsibility and to make them love the task that is about to be entrusted to them. Only a full understanding of the revolutionary significance of the work they are about to undertake can give them the necessary ardour, making them capable of overcoming all difficulties that may stand in their way.

Problems of the organization of education are also included in the training programme, though this mainly takes the form of discussions concerning the personal experiences of those involved. Accounts of concrete successes already obtained help guide trainee-instructors while strengthening their determination to accomplish the task assigned them by the people and the revolution.

1. Quoted in Lê Thành Khôi, op. cit.

A good many teachers have been granted the accolade Combattant de l'Émulation Patriotique (Hero of Labour), or have received congratulatory diplomas or medals. They have borne aloft their sense of responsibility; they have served the people unconditionally; they have never ceased to improve their teaching methods, overcoming every obstacle in order to lead their fellow countrymen rapidly out of the gloom of ignorance. They have come up with countless innovations in their efforts to teach people to read and write. For example, popular songs have been written so as to help pupils memorize more easily or to distinguish more readily between certain letters that are similar in appearance.

> *i* and *t* have an appendix,
> *i* is short with a dot, *t* is long and is crossed,
> *o* is as round as an egg,
> *ô* wears a hat, while *o'* wears a moustache.

Vietnamese writing is not hard to learn. An ordinary man, studying one hour a day, can learn to read and write within three or four months. At the height of the movement, we organized competitions in which pupils tried to outdo each other, bringing the average learning period down to seventy-two days. Thus organized, this spirit of emulation helped stimulate a certain number of pupils, while inciting others to make still greater efforts to bring down the time required for learning.

The teaching method

As the foregoing indicates, the traditional synthetic method of teaching reading was used. First, letters and sounds were taught; these were combined into syllables; syllables were combined into words and words into phrases and sentences. *Quoc Ngu* was taught in the Latin script. A new method of teaching the alphabet had been pioneered and practised. By this method it took only a couple of months to teach what had previously required five to six months.

The basic literacy text comprised seventy lessons. It dealt first with the eleven vowels and the diacritical markings used for the six tones in Vietnamese. A group of twenty-three consonants were taught next and then the rest of the consonants. The remainder of the lessons were devoted to dictation and reading of texts of five to sixty words. These texts were, of course, frequently revised during the campaign to suit changing circumstances.

A second book, following the basic text, included thirty lessons of 60 to 100 words each. Addition and subtraction were also introduced in this book.

Literacy was completed in three to four months, or 150 to 200 learning hours, with classes meeting one to two hours, six days a week. The definition of a literate changed during the life of the campaign. In 1945, a person was declared literate if he or she was able to write correctly from dictation forty or fifty words, read a short printed text and read numbers up to three digits. In 1956, a more stringent definition was introduced. To be declared literate, a person had to be able to read both print and written script; read and write (from dictation) numbers up to four digits; write from dictation a text eighty words long within forty-five minutes with no more than six mistakes.

Ngo Van Cat has recorded:[1]

Organization of courses

Courses are organized in a wide variety of ways so as to ensure that:
Studies can be undertaken outside working hours;
Studies are organized as a function of working conditions in each region and according to each season;
The organization of studies is appropriate to each category of pupil. In towns, for example, a good many classes are held in the evenings, whereas in the countryside, most classes are held at midday; classes may be suspended at the height of the monsoon season, but these are made up for by extra classes in the mornings, when the peasants are not at work in the fields.
Most classes have relatively few pupils, since they are organized for each hamlet, sometimes even for each family.
Sometimes, for shy young men, 'clandestine' classes have to be organized until they have acquired a little knowledge, and the courage to speak up in a mixed class with girls.
For managers obliged to travel for their work, special classes are laid on so that they can catch up on lessons missed.
The greatest difficulty lies in the organization of classes for fishermen and, generally speaking, for all those people who are obliged to travel constantly for their work; in these cases, it is necessary either to see that they are accompanied by a literacy instructor or to ensure that at least one of their number is capable of teaching the others.
In the countryside, even at the height of the monsoon, when classes have to be suspended, instructors try, by all means imaginable, to get their pupils to revise the lessons they have already learnt: the letters of the alphabet are written up on boards, or on the backs of buffaloes, or on the hats of the labourers themselves; blackboards are set up in the shade of a tree, in the yard where normally they thresh the rice, so that the workers can revise what they have learnt, without wasting time, even while working.
We had to fight energetically the tendency to want to organize regular classes along the lines of school; this type of approach is utterly unsuited to the conditions in which the pupils concerned live and work. We had to fight hardest against this in the latter years of the war on illiteracy.

The necessary means for studying

As the movement spread, so the problem of means became correspondingly

1. Quoted in Lê Thành Khôi, op. cit.

greater and more difficult to resolve, especially during the resistance, for there was a great shortage of books, exercise books, ink, metal pens, etc.

Classrooms. Where ordinary school accommodation proved inadequate, classes were started in private homes. If there was no table available, pupils would place their exercise books on beds to write, or else on upturned baskets. In areas close to forests, masters and pupils could go into the forest to collect wood and bamboo in order to make their own tables and benches, and even to build classrooms.

Spelling-books. During the war, there were not enough of these even for the teachers. Even the most rudimentary methods of printing were brought into use, and pupils undergoing general schooling willingly copied out lessons for illiterates as dictated by their teachers during spelling lessons.

School supplies. Paper was scarce during the resistance, and a good many pupils made use of banana leaves for writing on. Some kinds of leaves and fruits gathered in the forest provide a liquid that can serve as a replacement for ink. If needs be, a wooden stick or a half-baked brick could serve for writing on the floor or the ground.

Where conditions permit, we do our utmost to ease the work of teachers and pupils alike. But once the masses become aware of the importance of study, they are perfectly capable of finding a way round the most daunting obstacles in order to make up for the lack of means.

Individual motivations

The motivation of learners was built upon five arguments.
1. The adult literate should realize that his or her newly independent country needed a body of citizens with a higher level of education than was then prevalent, in order to meet new agricultural, industrial and political responsibilities.
2. The adult literate should realize that the fact that he or she was illiterate was the fault of the former colonial government and that the inability to read and write limits an individual's choices and possibilities in life. The door to education was now open and so there was no longer any reason for the illiterate to remain at a disadvantage.
3. The adult illiterate should realize that education had now become the right of each citizen, and furthermore, a necessity in the new society. Citizens should not lightly renounce one of their rights or ignore a duty to the country.
4. The adult illiterate should be convinced that it was possible to succeed in becoming literate.
5. The adult illiterate should realize that improving the literacy rate and raising the level of education generally in the country was a national concern.

These were not the only elements of the motivational strategy (we have already referred to the social and emotive aspects), nor should it be assumed that the motivational approaches outlined above worked every time and in all cases.

The follow-up programmes: complementary education

The problems of follow-up to the Vietnamese literacy campaign were conceptualized as more than merely providing supplementary reading materials for new literates. The need to broaden the range of useful knowledge of the people was well understood. As early as 1946, Ho Chi Minh had written to those who had joined the battle against illiteracy:

Where illiteracy has already been eliminated, you should take part in the process of patriotic emulation and take a further step forward by teaching our fellow countrymen:
Basic elements of hygiene, so as to prevent sickness;
Notions of science, so as to fight superstition;
The 'four operations,' in order to accustom people to putting order into their
    lives;
The history and geography of our country [a summary of history and
    geography in the form of poems and popular songs] in order to develop
    patriotic consciousness;
The rights and duties of citizens, so that our fellow countrymen can become
    good citizens.

The years of resistance, however, made it impossible to conduct follow-up activities and indeed many of those made literate relapsed into illiteracy. At the end of the resistance in 1954, the need for follow-up came into sharp focus.

It was declared that literacy was merely the first step in raising the cultural standards of the people. Ever higher cultural standards were needed in order to create modern-minded people who could be more productive and could make socialist reconstruction possible. The new goal was universal first-level general education for all working people throughout the country, with higher levels of education for specialized roles.

A system of complementary education for adults was conceptualized. It was to have three levels, paralleling the three stages of school education: a first level of four years for children 7–10 years old; a second level of three years for children 11–13 years old; and a third level of three years for children 14–16 years old. Both the duration at various levels and the curriculum content differed. The adult complementary education system was to take less time to complete, was to be concise and more practical, and was to emphasize productive and life skills.

Two basic types of schools were planned: schools organized 'on the job', where study was combined with productive labour, and boarding schools, which catered primarily to the needs of youth from ethnic minorities in the provinces.

Three categories of people received complementary education: cadres, youth and workers. Priority was given to those cadres and young people who showed merit in production and combat, the goal being to ensure that all cadres at the provincial and district levels should have a third-level education and some should have university-level education in their area of specialization. All village-level cadres were to receive second-level general education, while some of the 'core' cadres at village level were to receive third-level general education.

Young people of outstanding merit, who were regarded as the leaders of the future, were to attain a third level of general education and to continue their studies later at the university. The majority of young people were to aim at a second-level general education and, eventually, to attain a third-level general education.

The mass of working people were to receive universal first-level general education with special emphasis on production skills and the new socialist way of life.

With the coming of peace in 1954, considerable attention was paid to complementary education; the cultural, scientific and technical level of the workers had to be raised. The 1960 census showed that 327 out of 1,000 Vietnamese in the North had completed the first level of general education; 33 had completed the second; and 5 had completed the third. This was not a wholly satisfactory situation. The First Five Year Plan, 1961-65, gave tremendous emphasis to complementary education. In 1979, over 1,400,000 adults were attending various types of complementary education schools. Attendance figures have remained around 1 to 1.5 million annually since 1960. In 1979, some 1,500 villages in the North had already declared universal first-level general education. Some 20,000 people now in government and Party posts are the product of these complementary education schools.

Two important points should be made in connection with follow-up work in the Vietnamese literacy campaign. First, even at this level, the mass-line principle was followed: once again, people taught people. Second, the first-level compulsory education of children of school age was being rigorously implemented. The link between the primary education of children and adult literacy was fully understood.

Monitoring progress and effects

The national experience with the mass campaign against illiteracy was continuously evaluated and the lessons learned were fed back into the planning and implementation processes. At the local level, an interesting use was made of the inspection teams. When a particular locality had attained its campaign goals, it notified the national committee, which appointed an inspection team to visit the area. The inspection team prepared an evaluation file on the locality comprising three items: a report prepared by the local administration describing the literacy work done in its area compared with the literacy plan originally approved; a list of newly literate persons and the literacy rate of the area on completion of the campaign; and the written work done by the students in their final examinations.

National conferences were also used to bring together principal participants at various levels of the campaign to engage in self evaluation and in evaluation of the results. One such conference was organized in 1976 to evaluate the results of the campaign in the South.

The effects of the Vietnamese campaign

The effects of the Vietnamese campaign have been both significant and far-reaching. The country succeeded in creating a new political culture, making it possible to mobilize the will of the people to defeat a determined and superior war machine and, within less than a decade, at least in the North, bringing a literate voting public into being.

Literacy also had important consequences in terms of productivity and health as well as increasing the participation of women in the work-force and in public affairs.

Lessons of the Vietnamese literacy campaign

1. The power of commitment born of an ideology is very apparent in the success of the literacy campaign. Additionally, it is noteworthy that the campaign derived its legitimacy and received support from the highest levels of power. The President, Ho Chi Minh, inspired the campaign throughout its duration.
2. The Vietnamese campaign demonstrates that with determination no set of conditions is too formidable for a successful literacy campaign. The literacy campaign did not wait for the resistance to come to an end or the war to be over. Indeed, the conditions of war strengthened the resolve of the people to become literate.
3. The use of the mass line in a literacy campaign is not merely a matter of mobilizing human resources. Mass campaigns cannot be conducted by bureaucrats. What is needed are well-trained, well-disciplined cadres with a deep sense of commitment and the willingness to make sacrifices.
4. The cultural ethos of a nation helps when that culture includes respect for education. Linguistic realities are also of major

importance: success is likelier if most people use one language, and if that language is easy to teach.

5. Another important lesson is of a technical nature: what seems to work at an early stage of literacy does not necessarily work at the post-literacy level. Literacy can be a mass movement built basically on the mobilization of teachers and learners through managing incentives suitable to promote and sustain initiative. At the post-literacy stages, the programme becomes more scientific and formal. Know-how is needed for the development of curricular content; more sophisticated methodology must be employed; and instructional materials and class levels must be more carefully differentiated.

BIBLIOGRAPHY

DE FRANCIS, JOHN. *Colonialism and Language Policy in Viet Nam*. The Hague, Mouton, 1977.

LACOUTURE, JEAN. *Ho Chi Minh*. New York, Random House, 1968.

LÊ THÀNH KHÔI. Literacy Training and Revolution: The Vietnamese Experience. In: Léon Bataille (ed.), *A Turning Point for Literacy; Proceedings of the International Symposium for Literacy, Persepolis, Iran, 1975*. Oxford, Pergamon Press, 1976.

SNYDER, S. C. *The Campaign Against Illiteracy in Viet Nam: A Policy Analysis*. Paper written for Professor H. S. Bhola's seminar on Educational Policy Studies, School of Education, Indiana University, 1980.

CHAPTER 6

The anti-illiteracy campaigns in the People's Republic of China: from the 1950s to the 1980s

When the People's Republic of China was established on 1 October 1949, illiteracy rates in China were reported to be as high as 85 per cent among the total adult population and as high as 95 per cent in the rural areas.

Literacy was viewed as a historical goal, central to the total effort of reconstruction, in post-revolutionary China; and the attack on illiteracy therefore began almost immediately after the establishment of the new government. The first specific plan was announced in 1950. In 1951, the Anti-Illiteracy Commission was set up. The government vowed to make 200 million people between the ages of 18 and 40 literate within five to seven years.

The task was huge, and time too short. While enthusiasm was high, the level of success in the early years of 1950-52 was dismally low. New plans were initiated in 1953, 1954 and 1956. In 1956, the Anti-Illiteracy Association was established. The goal was to eradicate illiteracy throughout China in ten to twelve years and to make 95 per cent of the workers in mines and factories literate within two to three years.

From the vantage point of the early 1980s, anti-illiteracy work in the People's Republic of China is seen to fall in three distinct phases: (a) from 1949 to mid-1966—a period of seventeen years (b) from May 1966 to October 1976 (the period of the Cultural Revolution); and (c) from October 1976 to the present (Bo Yu, 1981).

The years 1950–58, however, are of special interest to development planners and literacy administrators and workers, for it was in the 1950s that the role of literacy in the cultural development of China was clearly defined and elaborated in terms of concrete action; an overall institutional framework was established for the provision of literacy services; and organization, methods and techniques were tried out. A model emerged for the successful implementation of anti-illiteracy work, consisting of six interrelated principles: (1) mobilization of the masses to fight against their own ignorance; (2) organization of a teachers' contingent on the basis of 'people teaching one another'; (3) utilization of a teaching method 'integrating theory with practice and study for the purpose of application'; (4) adoption of flexible multiform organizations for the conduct of anti-illiteracy work; (5) consolidation of achievements in anti-illiteracy by promoting programmes of literacy retention among new literates and ultimately establishing universal elementary education for children; and (6) action by the government to project a total commitment to literacy and give guarantees for the fulfilment of the task of anti-illiteracy (Bo Yu, 1982).

In spite of its ups and downs, anti-illiteracy work in China has been marked by considerable successes. Over 100 million illiterates between the ages of 14 and 45 were made literate before 1966. Another 37.7 million were made literate after 1966, in spite of a decade of disruption wrought by the Cultural Revolution from May 1966 to October 1976. The anti-illiteracy efforts, combined with developments in primary and middle school education, reduced illiteracy among young and middle-aged peasants from 80 per cent in the early post-war era to about 30 per cent today, and among workers and employees from 60–70 per cent in the early 1950s to less than 8 per cent today. China's anti-illiteracy efforts are clearly the greatest experiment in mass education in history: a nation of some 970 million people has become a nearly literate society in the space of just over thirty years.

Historical background and setting

The establishment of the People's Republic of China in 1949 ended a turbulent century of Chinese history, a century which saw the forced 'opening up' of China, the slicing of the 'Chinese melon' among the Western nations and its neighbours, and the reduction of a great empire to the status of a semi-colony. The century saw numerous rebellions and uprisings, foreign invasions and a protracted civil war. It saw the fall of the imperial Qing dynasty and the declaration of the first Chinese Republic in 1911 with Sun Yat-sen as President. It saw the founding of the Nationalist Party, the Guomindang, and of the Chinese Communist Party in 1921. It witnessed the coming to power of Chiang Kai-shek in 1925; the Long March of 1934/35; and finally the Communist takeover of China after a full-scale war between the Guomindang and the Chinese People's Liberation Army.

The Communists inherited a vast country, a land mass of some 9.7 million square kilometres, a population of some 550 million, and an ancient, rich and fairly homogeneous culture. The cultural situation was both a help and a challenge. The Chinese Communists could not simply build upon the old rich traditions of Confucianism; they wanted in fact to overthrow it fully and absolutely and replace it with Marxism-Leninism and Mao Zedong Thought. That was the challenge. Yet the homogeneity of the culture, and the respect for hierarchy and authority which Confucianism had ingrained among the people, helped the Communist leadership in the process of introducing Marxism.

The new government had to contend with differences in nationalities, religions and languages; but while there were fifty-four different nationalities, the major ethnic group, Han, constituted 90 per cent of the population. Linguistically, too, China's situation was unique. While there are eight major dialects in Chinese, not mutually intelligible, all are written in the same way. It is only when spoken they differ. Most importantly for the Republic, there was no hostility towards the idea of a common language in any class or age group—a rare circumstance in most developing countries. Religious groups included Buddhists, Muslims, Christians, Confucians and Taoists; yet no resistance seems to have appeared against the government or against its policies.

With the end of the war between the Guomindang forces and the Chinese People's Liberation Army, the Communists were in firm control of the mainland, with the Nationalists confined to Taiwan. The economy was in a shambles and agriculture in complete disarray. Landlords, only 10 per cent of the population, controlled 70 per cent of the land. The government embarked upon a land-reform movement that distributed 46 million hectares of land among 300 million peasants.

The social programme of the administration was as courageous as it was formidable. A new nation had to be built with people imbued with Marxist ideology, trained in new modes and methods of production, participating in a new culture.

The driving forces behind the campaign and its objectives

The sole driving force behind the literacy efforts of the 1950s in China was the revolution that culminated in the declaration of the Chinese People's Republic in October 1949. This declaration had to be made meaningful in terms of peoples' lives. The political revolution had to be consolidated by a cultural revolution.

The cultural revolution in the Marxist sense is basically an educational revolution. Through education the masses have to be taught to rid themselves of their false consciousness, to be imbued with Marxism-Leninism, and to become activists to overthrow oppression and to abolish class structures. And education is not merely ideological, but also technological. New scientific knowledge must be learned and applied in the mines and factories and on the farms and collectives. Education must become the instrument for creating the 'intellectual worker' and the 'worker intellectual'.

As one of the early declarations of the government put it:

The main task of the People's Government in cultural and education work shall be the raising of the cultural level of the people, the training of the personnel for national construction work, the eradication of feudal, comprador and fascist ideology, and the development of the ideology of service to the people. (Chen, 1953, p. 554.)

The cultural revolution embodied in the preceding declaration was to be based on literacy—the essential instrument of the cultural revolution. Mao himself put it unambiguously:

The necessary condition for establishing a new China is to sweep away illiteracy from the 80 per cent portion of China's population . . . . these are not ordinary conditions, nor are they conditions you can or cannot have, but, rather, they are absolutely necessary. (In Hawkins, 1971, p. 90.)

Literacy is thus an absolute condition; for the vanguard of the revolution—the cadres and the activists—but equally for the masses if they are to be brought into the political process, to achieve a new 'socialization' and to work in the new scientifically based economy.

Preparation for the literacy campaigns

If by preparation we mean statistical surveys, feasibility studies or systematic pre-testing of methods and materials, then no preparation was made by the Chinese Government for the literacy campaigns which began in the 1950s. A literacy survey was scheduled for completion as part of the national census, but results did not become available until November 1954. The leaders believed they knew the needs of the masses and how to fulfil those needs. The masses did not have to be studied or asked, especially when the national vision was to be implemented using the 'mass line' and in conformity with 'local conditions'.

However, if preparation is interpreted more broadly to include prior experience with similar work, perhaps on a smaller scale but in somewhat similar settings, then the literacy campaigns that began in the 1950s can be seen as a set of intensified mass campaigns based on earlier pilot projects conducted within areas under communist control.

Respect for the literate was not new to Chinese culture, nor was literacy organization new to the communists who had now proclaimed the People's Republic of China. Literacy and education had been prized in China for thousands of years though only 1 or 2 per cent of the people were literate through most of early Chinese history. Although literacy among women was virtually non-existent, some statistics suggest that during the eighteenth and nineteenth centuries, 30-45 per cent of men and 2-10 per cent of women may have possessed some ability to read and write (Rawski, 1979, p. 23). In the decades immediately preceding the Revolution, however, literacy is known to have declined because of the disruptions wrought by foreign invasions and the civil war.

Marxist revolutions, as observed earlier, are almost always complemented by educational revolutions. The communists had started their educational work as early as the 1920s, concurrently with their military effort. There are numerous descriptions of educational work carried out among the peasants by soldiers of the Red Army during the Long March of 1934-35. In particular, three intensified efforts made during 1937, 1940 and 1944 within the Communist-controlled areas are worthy of consideration.

The 1937 literacy education campaign covered both urban and rural areas. The urban campaign covered miscellaneous employees in cities and used such organizational mechanisms as literacy groups, night schools and half-day schools. These schools tried many innovations, among them books prepared by the students themselves, posters and newspapers and the idea of 'little teachers'—a sort of peer-teaching invented in response to the dire scarcity of trained teachers. The rural areas had their half-day schools, night schools and news-reading groups and—an important innovation—winter-study schools for peasants during the off-season.

The 1940 campaign was a 'mass reading' campaign that sought to popularize revolutionary literature written in the vernacular. The Mass Reading Materials Society, established in 1940, anticipated many of the innovations of the 1960s and 1970s in literacy and the promotion of follow-up literature. Of particular interest was the establishment of a 'mass news reporter' network and 'mass news-reading' groups to enable a two-way flow of information between the masses and the Party. Utilitarian literature for new readers was also produced, including such titles as *Health in Summertime*, *How to Care for Babies*, etc.

For a time, the Winter Study campaign of 1944 became the central task of all Party and governmental work. The approach was pragmatic, flexible, sometimes even contradictory. The curricular emphasis kept shifting from literacy to political education, to war, to production and back. Two important policy-oriented emphases developed during this campaign. To begin with, the education of the cadres, the vanguard of the revolution, was to come first and the education of the masses later:

This is not only because cadres are the vanguard of the masses and as such are in greater need of cultivation and improvement—the objective of their cultivation and improvement is to benefit the masses—but also because there are after all, limits on the nature of the popular education that can be provided in the environment of the peasant villages. (On Regulations and Curriculum in General Education, 1971, p. 197.)

Secondly, adult education was to have priority over the education of children, though children were also to be educated whenever possible. The rationale behind this policy was as follows:

Although educating them is unavoidably difficult, by improving their situation one step through education, we can improve the situation in the war and in production one step, and the results will be immediate. (On Regulations and Curriculum in General Education, 1971, p. 198.)

The government had this valuable experience behind it when it launched its campaigns of literacy promotion in the 1950s, designed to cover the whole of the country. It had envisioned, conceptualized, mobilized, organized, held classes, produced instructional materials, recruited and trained teachers—and experimented with its ideas and its solutions. It was well prepared.

Mobilizing at the national level

Before referring to the informational and mobilizational strategies used by the Chinese in their literacy campaigns, it is important to understand the special meaning and function of mobilization in Chinese society and policy.

In terms of Mao Zedong Thought, mobilization seems to be not merely an instrumental process for disseminating information and organizing public and private initiatives and resources, but a substantive revolutionary experience, collectively shared by the people. Teaching of literacy, improved nutrition, etc., may seem to be objectives for mass mobilization, but in reality these are considered secondary purposes. The primary purpose of mobilization in Mao's view seems to have been to invite the people to participate—if necessary by-passing the Party and the government—in a collective experience of evaluation, analysis and renewal of revolutionary experience, to claim the revolution for themselves and, in the process, to change their deeply held perceptions and values and their images of the future.

This being said, three additional ideas related to mobilization for the national campaigns of the 1950s should be noted: gradual expansion, the mass line and responsiveness to local conditions. These three aspects of planning and implementation affected the total effort of mobilization, and later the conduct of the campaign.

The concept of gradual expansion was itself divisible into three parts: selection of client groups, choice of geographical areas, and priority in terms of curricular emphasis. As already mentioned, the cadres of worker-peasant origin were to be educated first, and then the workers and peasants. In geographical terms, urban-industrial sectors enjoyed priority over rural areas. Within rural areas, choices were made on the principle of 'readiness'. Those areas where land reforms had been completed and the standard of living had somewhat improved were the first to be offered education; others, including national minority areas, disaster areas and areas close to the theatre of war had to wait for the normalization of political and economic conditions. The concept of gradual expansion was also applied to the choice of curricula.

The need to respond to local conditions in the application of educational policies was a key consideration in the mass education effort of communist China. The First National Conference on Workers' and Peasants' Education held on 30 September 1950 stated:

Our worker-peasant education must always respect local conditions and the time factor, advancing soundly step by step. China is a big country . . . [with] political, economic, financial and cultural development unequal in various parts . . . ; there are also different cultural and historical backgrounds. Therefore, top-level policy on worker-peasant education must be adapted to the different conditions prevailing in various areas . . . , employing concrete forms and procedures according to the local conditions at the time [*Peoples' Education*, 1951].

Finally, there was the emphasis on the mass line. This was an ideological view supported by economic exigencies; a combination of virtue and necessity. Mao had laid down the ideological line: 'All work done for the masses must start from their needs and not from the desire of any individual, however well-intentioned.' But the mass line also meant that the masses had to be responsible for their own education; they had to provide the resources and the organization for education in their localities.

The concept of the mass line being central to the mobilization effort, people were to be educated and motivated through contact with cadres. This involved a two-pronged approach. In the organized industrial sector, the operation was conducted through trade unions in factories and enterprises; these provided meeting places and equipment, and literate members of the staff taught the illiterate. In the rural areas, county committees on spare-time education for peasants, composed of representatives of the county government, the new democratic youth corps, and democratic women's associations, were organized for literacy work; these provided the funds, enrolled the teachers—often ordinary people teaching ordinary people—and improvised meeting places.

The conduct of the campaigns

The Chinese literacy campaigns must be placed within an appropriate conceptual and institutional context if their objectives, organization, conduct and contributions are to be fully understood. The Chinese had foreseen, as their ultimate objective, a dual system of education, one for children and another for adults. There was to be a formal education system for children and a parallel formal educational system for adults whereby the latter received an equivalent education in their spare time. This spare-time school system was not limited to any age group and, as Figure 2 shows, took an accelerated form.

The spare-time school system was the formal part of adult education and was complemented by an informal system. The formal system, as can be seen from the chart, was structured along the same lines as the regular school system, although the teaching methods and techniques were flexible. Informal adult education, on the other hand, was organized to meet purely local needs and conditions. It included a variety of topics (physical health, trade union laws and other topics of a practical nature, also art, literature and related cultural topics) and a variety of materials and settings (lectures, illustrative materials, bulletins, broadcasts, choral groups, reading circles, libraries).

Literacy had an essential role to play in this educational scheme for adults. It could be neglected only in the short run and not for long. It was required for entry into the formal adult education system and for a major part of the informal adult education programmes. Literacy was thus viewed as the core of the adult education curriculum and as a basic tool of the cultural revolution in both its political and technological aspects.

Within this context, the literacy campaigns in China can be seen in a new light. The campaigns are revealed as a series of mobilizations within a larger adult education system which itself was in the process of emergence and institutionalization. The mobilizations were helped by specially created temporary organizations such as the Anti-Illiteracy Commission of 1951 and the Anti-Illiteracy Association of 1956.

The actual teaching of literacy was handled by three educational organizations: spare-time schools, short-time schools and literacy schools. Thus, it should be noted that the attack on illiteracy was spearheaded by and through adult primary education.

The administrative superstructure was complex, and the lines of collaboration and control are not always easy to understand. Two

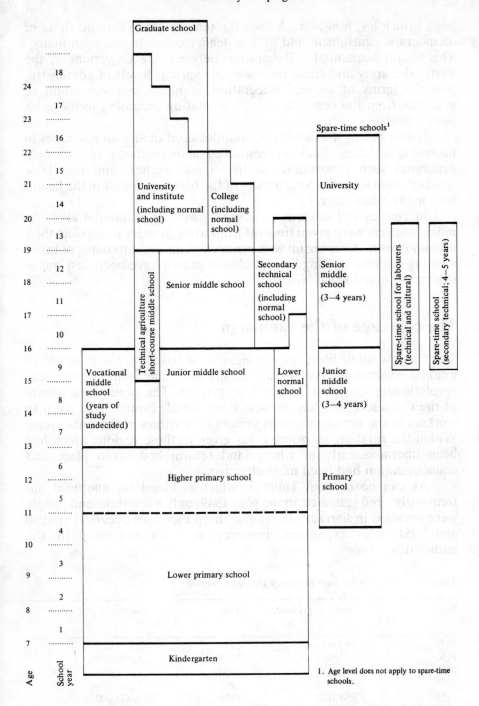

FIG. 2.   School system in the People's Republic of China, 1958. (After Hu Chang-tu (ed.), *Chinese Education Under Communism*, 2nd ed., p. 25, New York, Teachers College Press, 1974.)

basic principles, however, defined the temper of the system: those of 'democratic centralism' and of 'one leader collaborating with many'. This meant horizontal collaboration between the Government, the Party, the army and trade unions at the various levels of administration. In terms of vertical integration, it meant a combination of guidance from the centre and implementation according to the mass line.

It also meant that local communities used their own resources in becoming literate. Lack of resources and emphasis on self-help generated such innovations as the 'mass teacher' and the 'little teacher', who were the forerunners of the barefoot doctor in the health field many years later.

Incentives and rewards were hardly ever of a material kind. At most, teachers were given time off from work in order to conduct their literacy classes. Keeping up with production quotas, attending political meetings and conducting literacy classes cannot have been easy but in the main proved feasible.

The coverage of the campaign

The Chinese adult literacy campaigns were based on the principle of gradual expansion. As already mentioned, the cadres, being the revolutionary vanguard, received top priority. The incremental nature of the Chinese effort has likewise been noted. Priority was given to workers in the urban-industrial sectors rather than in the rural areas. Within the rural areas, priority was given to those regions which had been liberated early or where land reform had taken place and collectivization had been most effective.

As can be seen in Table 3, which is based on unofficial but frequently cited statistics, in the year 1949, only a few thousand people were enrolled in literacy classes but sharp increases occurred in 1950 and 1951. This expansion, however, was not welcomed by the authorities.

TABLE 3. Statistics for anti-illiteracy classes (1949-58)

Year	Number of graduates	Year	Number of graduates
1949	657,000	1954	2,637,000
1950	1,372,000	1955	3,678,000
1951	1,375,000	1956	7,434,000
1952	656,000	1957	7,208,000
1953	2,954,000	1958	40,000,000

Source: Leo A. Orleans, Professional Manpower and Education in Communist China, p. 49, Washington, D.C., National Science Foundation, 1961.

The official report characterized the period as one of reckless expansion and took the cadres to task for 'commandism' and for spreading limited resources too thinly. The change effected in 1952, however, did not please the leadership either, the situation being criticized as over-cautious, conservative and pessimistic.

The marked increase in enrolment in 1953 is explained by the fact that this was the first year of the First Five Year Plan when the people were organized in mutual aid teams and collectives both in industry and in agriculture. The expansions of 1956 and 1957 may have been due to the new anti-illiteracy plan and to the expansion of agricultural co-operatives. The phenomenal increase in 1958 to 40,000,000 enrolments should be seen in the context of the Great Leap Forward and the intense activity surrounding it. Education expanded at a dizzying speed. Communes collectivized almost all of the productive activities of the masses. Hardly anyone was left outside the processes of collectivization or education.

Temporary economic difficulties around 1960 brought anti-illiteracy work to a virtual standstill. After 1962, it was gradually restored but it was only in early 1965 that the economic upturn made the normal development of literacy promotion work possible. By mid-1966, 100 million young and middle-aged adults, in the age group 14-45 years, had been made literate.

The period of the Cultural Revolution (May 1966 to October 1976) is characterized by present-day Chinese analysts as a disastrous one for China's educational activities. Anti-illiteracy work declined as many new literates relapsed into illiteracy and many school age children were unable to attend school.

Literacy promotion resumed in earnest after October 1976 following the end of the Cultural Revolution. In November 1978, the State Council issued the Directive on the Elimination of Illiteracy asking for redoubled efforts aimed at the eradication of illiteracy among the age group 12-45; programmes to assist retention of literacy by those who had become literate; and the institution of five-year universal primary education. Literacy became the core of the four modernizations: modernization of agriculture, modernization of industry, modernization of national defence and modernization of science and technology. As mentioned earlier, 37.7 million young and middle-aged are estimated to have become literate after 1966.

Pedagogical aspects of the literacy campaigns

There was considerable experimentation in the pedagogical aspects of the campaign during the three decades of literacy work in China under review. Only some of the major themes and approaches can be discussed here.

Communist educators make a distinction between method and technique, the first describing the relationships between institutions and learners and the latter describing the relationship between the teachers and learners. Method is thus a way of organizing the study group or unit, while technique is the art of teaching particular subject matter in the classroom situation.

The basic policy concerning the correct teaching method stated that *any* method could be used that would satisfy the peoples' needs, possibilities and customs. This was especially true in the remedial phase of adult education, that is, in the teaching of basic literacy. It was this flexibility that led to so much improvisation and innovation in the organization of classes, groups, schools, teaching roles and curricular combinations.

Vincent Tsing-ching Lin (1963) listed a variety of methods used in literacy promotion during this period, among them: Qi Jianhua's Quick Literacy Method (which sought to teach the illiterates to read and write 1,500 to 2,000 characters in about 150 class hours); the collective teaching method (which brought all learners in the village to a class for distribution of lessons in the morning and then interspersed study throughout the working day); circuit teaching (a teacher assigned to a circuit of villages made his rounds and taught in each village every three to five days, leaving interim teaching to little teachers); little teachers teaching their families what they themselves had learned while assisting the 'big teacher'; location of literacy billboards in every village; the review movement (a sort of follow-up encouraging learners to review their progress and their shortcomings); achievement reports using symbols (the best learner received an airplane, the next best an automobile, others merely received an ox-cart or rice basket); a seat of honour for the top learner; the quiz system (to help in the assimilation of material as well as for diagnostic purposes); the promotion notice board; mutual dictation; question exchange scheme (a type of problem solving calling on those who had already solved such problems); attendance charts; cultural posts (a blackboard placed at the factory gate for workers to revise their lessons); learning contests; reading circles (allowing farmers in paddyfields and women engaged in household chores to learn while they worked); and the method of 'Reading One Hundred Books and Writing One Thousand Words', a follow-up designed to emphasize the need to put literacy to work.

The use of correct technique demanded that the special characteristics of the adult learner be taken into consideration and that teaching be related to the adult's real-life activities. Lectures were downgraded, but there was an emphasis on drill (because of the particular nature of the Chinese characters), study periods, and individual help outside the classroom. The teacher used students to assist his teaching and asked them all to criticize his methods.

While there was a general overall interaction between literacy teaching on the one hand and politics and production on the other, there seems to have been a clear emphasis on literacy teaching in the early stages. The process of teaching students to read, recognize and write characters—that is, to decodify and codify—was not diluted by functional material.

The teaching of literacy was assisted by a clear language policy and a clear-cut definition of what it meant to be literate. As mentioned earlier, eight mutually unintelligible dialects were spoken by the Han, the ethnic group consituting 90 per cent of the Chinese population. The advantage, however, was that all used the same script. Thus, literates could read and understand each others' written messages although they could not understand each other's speech. This was possible because Chinese writing is not phonetic, but ideographic. The language contains some 50,000 characters; not even the well educated, however, know more than 10,000. Newspapers may use no more than 4,000 characters and those who know 1,500 characters are considered literate. Learning these 1,500 characters is by no means a simple task. The President of the Chinese Academy of Sciences calculated that learning to read in Chinese characters took about two years more than was required for the same level of literacy using a phonetic script.

The Chinese did three important things to help the literacy effort. They developed a 'common speech' (basically the Mandarin dialect with Beijing pronunciation), dropping words which were too literary, too élitist, too infrequently used or too parochial. They simplified the characters wherever possible, reducing strokes and using abbreviations. Finally, they developed a phonetic alphabet (*pinyin*), not to replace the Chinese characters but to assist in the teaching of characters by annotating them phonetically. In 1957, on New Year's Day, newspapers and most magazines began to use horizontal as opposed to vertical printing.

Adult illiterates wishing to become literate first became literate in the national language. This policy has received widespread acceptance throughout the country and among groups of all ages. The use of a single language has become an important part of nationalism.

Definitions of the literate, semi-literate and illiterate underwent a process of evolution but the official position has now been definitely set out: those who are letter-blind or who know less than 500 words are considered illiterate; those who know more than 500 words but do not meet the required standard are considered semi-literate; peasants and housewives are considered literate if they know 1,500 commonly used words, are able to read the simplest books and newspapers, and can write informal notes and receipts; cadres and workers to be considered literate must know 2,000 commonly used Chinese characters, read ordinary books and newspapers, and write essays of 200 or 300 words.

Mention has already been made of the problems of teacher shortages which led to such innovations as 'people teaching people' and the use of mass teachers and little teachers. The mass teachers and little teachers were typically guided by full-time professional teachers representing the core of the adult education and literacy movement. Teacher-training institutions at all levels were asked to undertake the training of teachers for work in worker-peasant schools.

Learners were declared literate only after they had finished certain textbooks edited and published by the central administration. Once a person had been declared literate, all-out efforts were made to prevent any relapse into illiteracy.

Monitoring and effects of the campaigns

The processes of mobilization, administration and monitoring seem to have been conducted at the same time in the Chinese campaigns. There is evidence of flexibility, of learning from mistakes and drastic rectifications. In a speech commemorating the tenth anniversary of the People's Republic of China, the Minister of Education provided some noteworthy figures:

Under the leadership of the Chinese Communisty Party and Chairman Mao Zedong, education has made great strides during the past 10 years . . . .

In terms of enrolment, the figures for 1958 compared with those of 1949 are as follows: pre-schools: 31,000,000, or an increase of 237 times; elementary schools: 86,000,000 or an increase of 2.6 times, 85 per cent of all children of school age are now in school; secondary schools: 10,520,000, or an increase of 5.56 times; secondary vocational schools: 1,470,000, or an increase of 2.8 times; higher education institutions: 660,000, or an increase of 3.2 times.

During the past ten years, nearly 2,000,000 specialized personnel of higher and middle levels have been trained and nearly 100,000,000 young workers and farmers have become literate. . . .

1958 was the year of the Big Leap Forward; school enrolment drastically increased at all levels . . . including 60,000,000 attending classes for the eradication of illiteracy and over 30,000,000 in spare-time schools [*Ten Years National Construction*, 1959, Vol. 2, pp. 85-102].

A stocktaking undertaken in 1981 is even more impressive. Fundamental changes have occurred in the educational conditions of peasants and workers. The illiteracy rates for young and middle-aged peasants have dropped from 80 per cent to 30 per cent in the last thirty-two years; for workers and employees from 60-70 per cent to less than 8 per cent; while in the petroleum and chemical sectors of industry, illiteracy is down to 3 per cent. To ensure consolidation of gains, literacy has been linked with spare-time elementary schools; a multiplicity of study groups have been organized; and utilization of literacy skills has been integrated with practical skills and cultural activities. Even more significant gains are indicated by the greater demand for education and culture; heightened production in agriculture as well as in industry; increased political consciousness; and an enhanced moral outlook of society.

Lessons of the campaign

The following lessons may be drawn from the Chinese experience:
1. The Chinese experience is at once impressive and sobering. It shows that, given the right conditions, it is possible, within the space of some thirty years, to plan for and implement a policy aimed at re-socializing a whole nation of almost one billion people and a culture more than 2,000 years old. Nations can be taught to think new thoughts and read and write those new thoughts. Nations can be made literate.
2. The need for an ideological commitment matched by political will on the part of the leadership is again revealed by this case study. The ideology has to be a people's ideology, offering equality and dignity to the masses. Literacy has to be seen as serving those transcendental goals at the ideological level and more concrete political and economic goals at another level. The existence of a strong political leadership is a major factor.
3. The Chinese experience suggests that something more than merely informational goals is essential to mobilization. Mobilization of the masses for national literacy campaigns can provide a collective experience of a revolutionary character.
4. A clear-cut language policy, language reform where necessary, and clarification of the relationship between the national language and minority languages are significant elements.
5. A commitment to act and achieve seems to compensate for the absence of infra-structures, scarcity of material resources, and lack of technical sophistication. Harsh conditions combined with commitment and hope seem to generate innovation in organization, social roles and methodologies.
6. Literacy is assured of success when conducted in a larger context of adult education, political socialization, abolition of class structures and economic development.
7. There is no one correct way to organize for literacy. A nation may declare a literacy campaign independently of the existing institutions of formal and non-formal education or may implement a campaign through such existing institutional structures. It may establish different priorities—vanguard versus the masses, urban versus rural, steel-workers versus miners. It may practise social or

geographical incrementalism. The only things it cannot do are to let the commitment dissipate, to let direction become confused, to let declarations become hollow.

REFERENCES

Bo Yu. 1982. *China's Experiences in Anti-illiteracy Work*. Paris, Unesco. (Surveys and Studies.) (Doc. ED/WS/30.)

Chen, Theodore Hsi'en. 1953. Education in China. *Comparative Education*. New York, Dryden Press.

Hawkins, John. 1971. *Educational Theory in the People's Republic of China: The Report of Ch'ien Chun-jui*. Honolulu, University of Hawaii Press.

Lin, Vincent Tsing-ching. 1963. Adult Education in the People's Republic of China: 1950-58. Berkeley, Calif., University of California. (Unpublished Ph.D thesis.)

On Regulations and Curriculum in General Education. 1971. *Chinese Education*. Vol. 4, No. 3, pp. 195-204.

Orleans, Leo A. 1961. *Professional Manpower and Education in Communist China*. Washington, D.C., United States Government Printing Office.

People's Education. 1951. Vol. 3, No. 1, 1 May.

Rawski, Evelyn S. 1979. *Education and Popular Literacy in Ch'ing China*. Ann Arbor, Mich., University of Michigan Press.

Ten Years National Construction. 1959. Hong Kong, Chi Wen Publishing.

BIBLIOGRAPHY

Abe, Munemitsu. Spare-time Education in Communist China: A General Survey. In: Stewart Fraser (ed.), *Education and Communism in China: An Anthology of Commentary and Documents*, pp. 239-53. London, Pall Mall Press, 1971.

Adult Classes in China: Measures to Fight Illiteracy. *Times Educational Supplement*, 30 December 1960, p. 879.

Barendsen, R. D. Education in Mao's China. *American Education*, No. 2, October, 1966, pp. 14-19.

——. Mao's Educational Revolution. *American Education*, No. 8, May, 1972, pp. 4-13.

Bianco, Lucien. *Origins of the Chinese Revolution: 1915-1949*. Stanford, Calif., Stanford University Press, 1971.

Border Region Government Directive on Winter Study This Year (3 June 1944). *Chinese Education*, Vol. 4, No. 3, 1971, pp. 225-30.

Chai, Winberg. *The Search for a New China*. New York, Capricorn Books, G. P. Putnam's Sons, 1975.

Chen, Theodore Hsi'en. The Maoist Model of Education: Origins and Ideology. *Asian Affairs: An American Review*, July/August 1976, pp. 384-400.

Chronology of the Two-road Struggle on the Educational Front in the Past Seventeen Years. *Chinese Education*, Vol. 1, No. 1, 1968, pp. 3-58.

Directive on the Promotion of Spare-time Education for Peasants: Collection of Laws and Decrees of the Central People's Government, 1949-50. *Chinese Education*, Vol. 2, No. 3, 1969, pp. 58-77.

L'éducation des adultes. *Notes et études documentaires*, No. 3197, 4 June 1965, pp. 23-4.

FANG CHENG. Reform Work in the Chinese Communist Educational System. *Chinese Education*, Vol. 3, No. 4, 1970/71, pp. 228-64.

GAMBERG, RUTH. *Red and Expert: Education in the People's Republic of China*. New York, Schocken Books, 1977.

GIBSON, T. Modern China: Adult Movement. *Times Educational Supplement*, 24 April, 1948, p. 232.

HARDING, HARRY. *Maoist Theories of Policy-Making and Organizations: Lessons from the Cultural Revolution*. Santa Monica, Calif., Rand, 1969.

HARPER, PAUL. Problems of Industrial Spare-Time Schools. In: Stewart Fraser (ed.), *Education and Communism in China*, pp. 255-74. London, Pall Mall Press, 1971.

HO WEI. Successfully Build Half-farming, Half-study Schools and Promote the Village Education Revolution. *Chinese Education*, Vol. 1, No. 3, 1968, pp. 15-37.

HSIAO CHING-JO. *Literacy in the People's Republic of China*. Speech presented at the International Symposium on Literacy, Persepolis, Iran, 4 September 1975.

HU CHANG-TU. *Chinese Education Under Communism*. New York, Teachers College Press, Columbia University, 1974.

I WO-SHENG. Education in Communist China. *Communist China Problem Research Series*, No. 3, 1961, pp. 99-152.

KOBAYASHI FUMIO. *Education in Building Chinese Socialism. Theory and Reality in the Transitional Period*. Tokyo, Institute of Developing Economics, 1976.

Labour Laws and Regulations of the People's Republic of China. Directives on Developing Spare-time Education for Workers and Staff Members, pp. 81-88. Beijing, Foreign Languages Press, 1956.

LI TING-I. *A History of Modern China*. Dartmouth, Oriental Publications, 1970.

LINDSAY, MICHAEL. The Educational System: Early Communism Origins, 1939-1946. In: Stewart Fraser (ed.), *Education and Communism in China*, pp. 27-48. London, Pall Mall Press, 1971.

MAO ZEDONG. Comrade Mao Zedong on Educational Work. *Chinese Education*, Vol. 2, No. 3, 1969, pp. 37-57.

——. Comrade Mao Zedong on Educational Work. *Chinese Education*, Vol. 3, No. 1, 1970, pp. 20-41.

——. On Practice: The Relation between Knowledge and Practice—The Relation between Knowing and Doing. *Chinese Education*, Vol. 3, No. 4, 1970/71, pp. 265-82.

Ministry of Education's Instructions on Strengthening the Teaching of Political Current Events in the Winter of This Year (11 November 1951). *Chinese Education*, Vol. 3, No. 1, 1970, pp. 42-64.

OKSENBERG, MICHEL. Policy Making under Mao, 1949-1968: An Overview. In: John Lindbeck (ed.), *China: Management of a Revolutionary Society*, pp. 79-115. Seattle, University of Washington Press, 1971.

POOL, ITHIEL DE SOLA. Communication in Totalitarian Societies. In: Ithiel de Sola Pool, et al. (eds.), *Handbook of Communication*, pp. 462-511. Chicago, Ill., Rand McNally, 1974.

PRICE, R. F. *Education in Communist China*. New York, Praeger, 1970.

PRIESTLEY, K. E. Education in the People's Republic of China: Beginnings. In: Stewart Fraser (ed.), *Education and Communism in China*, pp. 49-80, London, Pall Mall Press, 1971.

Problem of Transforming General Education in the Base Areas. *Chinese Education*, Vol. 4, No. 3, 1971, pp. 189-94.

PYE, LUCIAN WILMOT. Mass Participation in Communist China: Its Limitations and the Continuity of Culture. In: John Lindbeck (ed.), *China: Management of a Revolutionary Society*. Seattle, University of Washington Press, 1971.

SERRUYS, PAUL L. M. *Survey of the Chinese Language Reform and the Anti-illiteracy Movement in Communist China*. Berkeley, Calif., University of California Press, 1962.

SEYBOLT, PETER. *Yenana Education: The Chinese Revolution, 1937-1945*. Ph.D. dissertation, Harvard University, 1969.

Seybolt, Peter; Chiang, Gregory Kuei-te. *Language Reform in China*. White Plains, N.Y., M. E. Sharpe, 1979.

Yang Hsui-feng. Educational Revolution and Progress: 1949-1959. *School and Society*, No. 89, 4 November 1961, pp. 378-81.

Yu, Frederick T. C. Campaigns, Communications and Development in Communist China. In: Wilbur Schramm and Donald Roberts (eds.), *Process and Effects of Mass Communication*, pp. 836-60. Urbana, Ill., University of Illinois Press, 1971.

CHAPTER 7

The Cuban mass literacy campaign, 1961

One of the most widely known mass literacy campaigns, a campaign that continues to inspire and challenge political leaders and literacy educators in all parts of the world, was announced by Fidel Castro during his address to the General Assembly of the United Nations on 20 September 1960:

In the coming year our people intend to fight the great battle of illiteracy, with the ambitious goal of teaching every single inhabitant of the country to read and write in one year, and with that end in mind, organizations of teachers, students and workers, that is, the entire people, are now preparing themselves for an intensive campaign. Cuba will be the first country in America which, after a few months, will be able to say it does not have one person who remains illiterate.

But the battle against illiteracy in Cuba was one battle in a larger struggle. The larger struggle consisted in the consolidation of the political revolution of 1959 which, in order to survive and to become meaningful, had to be experienced directly by the masses in economic, social and cultural terms. A new political culture had to be created which required mobilization of the masses in the service of the masses; abolition of existing class structures for the creation of a new revolutionary consciousness; and education of the people in new skills of economic production. The mass literacy campaign was to be the decisive battle that would bring victories on all these fronts at the same time.

The Cuban mass literacy campaign of 1961 was noteworthy for its drive and speed. Compared with campaigns in other developing countries, it had the advantage of dealing with a relatively small illiterate population of 979,207 in a nation with an illiteracy rate of no more than 23.6 per cent among the age group of 10 years and over. Moreover, the campaign was carried out in one language only and sought literacy at the first grade level of primary school. Nevertheless, the results were dramatic: in some eight months (April–December 1961) the illiteracy rate had fallen to 3.9 per cent.

The Cuban literacy campaign, of which the mass campaign of 1961 was a first step, covered a span of twenty years. Fidel Castro closed all schools for eight months in order to send everyone of 13 years and older, including teachers, to teach the peasants. This 'army' lodged in the homes of illiterates, teaching small groups of two to three adults—a strategy which not only provided the campaign with the necessary manpower but which had far-reaching educational and social implications. The students acquired a new class consciousness: the girls learned a new identity—an important first step towards the liberation of women in Cuba—and, in due course, girls and boys alike supplied the nation with the essential party cadres, administrators, technicians and teachers.

Background and setting

The Republic of Cuba that came into being with the Revolution of 1 January 1959 is an archipelago comprising hundreds of small keys and islands with a total area of 110,772 km^2. The largest island is Cuba itself which covers 105,007 km^2.

The Spaniards arrived in Cuba and exterminated the indigenous Indian population of between 80,000 to 100,000 people in the late fifteenth and early sixteenth centuries. Later, slave labourers were imported from Africa to work on the sugar and other plantations. Until the early 1930s, sugar determined the demography of Cuba. The population rose from 7,236,000 to 9,738,500 between 1963 and 1978.

Spanish colonialism was overthrown in 1898, but neocolonialism continued, imposed by foreign economic and political power, and bourgeois latifundist oligarchies. When Batista took power in 1952, the situation was already ripe for the revolution that would come six years later. The country was divided into the haves and the have-nots; the urban and rural areas were two different worlds. One half of one per cent of the farm units, owned by the rich, covered 36.1 per cent of the total cultivated land, while three-fourths of the population was living in small huts in the countryside under harsh conditions. Most of the economy was in the hands of foreigners.

Sixty per cent of the population, according to a World Bank report, was undernourished; and 80-90 per cent of the children in rural areas were sick with no medical aid generally available. Only 55.5 per cent of children aged 6-14 were attending elementary schools. In rural areas, this percentage was 40 or less. In the age group 15-19, only 17 per cent attended any institution of secondary education. For rural areas the figure was 11 per cent or less.

The driving force behind the Cuban literacy campaign

The driving force behind the Cuban literacy campaign was the Revolution of January 1959 and the ideology it represented. Fidel Castro, the leader of the revolution, was the dominant figure of the campaign. In 1953 when Castro was on trial, he had made an important statement connecting illiteracy with the underdevelopment of the peasantry. In 1957, a literacy campaign was made part of the ten-point programme set out in the Manifesto of the Sierra Maestro. The rebel army organized schools for children and soldiers in the liberated zones. Within weeks of entering Havana, a literacy campaign for soldiers had been instituted and every police station and camp had become a literacy centre. In March 1959, a National Commission of Literacy and Fundamental Education was established and literacy centres had been started, especially in urban areas. The mass campaign of 1961 was a logical culmination of earlier efforts. If socialism was to be more than a mere idealistic aspiration, if the revolution was to build a socialist reality meeting the needs of the people, the educational level of the people had to be raised so as to improve technology, production and culture. Illiteracy had to be eliminated because it deepened and reinforced class differences produced by economic conditions and gave the exploiting classes a justification for their privileges.

Preparation for the campaign

Literacy work was by no means new to the Cuban leaders as they prepared to launch the mass campaign of April 1961. As already mentioned, literacy had been a part of the revolutionary struggle against the Batista regime. The actions of the new revolutionary government during 1959-60 provided additional groundwork. The establishment of the National Commission for Literacy and Fundamental Education and of the local boards made it possible to test the organization needed for the mass campaign which was due to follow. Useful experience was gained in the training of literacy teachers and in the organization of adult literacy centres in the field. There was an opportunity to work with and evaluate the relative merits of three different primers—by Ana Echegoyen, Maria L. Soler, and Lauback—and to study the approaches followed in each case. Dr Raul Gutierrez had carried out an investigation in 1960 of the active and passive vocabulary among some 3,000 Cuban peasants. This study provided useful information on words used by peasants and on their conversational styles.

Mobilization for the campaign

Fidel Castro's announcement of the mass literacy campaign in his address to the General Assembly of the United Nations on 20 September 1960 legitimized the campaign at home and gave it prominence abroad. A fully literate Cuba was to be achieved within one year, he predicted, and this promise could not be an empty one. Later in the year, on 31 December 1960, Castro made his views clear:

Why have we proposed to eradicate illiteracy in only one year? Because the revolution is developing its work as fast as possible and it is pushing forward very fast. . . . One year will be enough . . . revolutions are capable of doing things like that.

Indeed, the Cuban leadership did not consider the revolutionary programmes to be limited by a lack of human resources but placed trust in the people. The people themselves had to be the resource. Fagen's analysis of this point is instructive:[1]

Viewing almost the entire population as the potential manpower pool for a development effort implies two subsidiary beliefs. The first is that given a bit of initial guidance and a Revolutionary orientation toward work, almost anyone can be helpful in one way or another. Thus all children with a sixth-grade education can teach illiterates (although they cannot teach physics), any housewife who can count and write a simple sentence can be a census-taker, and any peasant who understands why it is a Revolutionary duty to become literate can help in recruiting his *campaneros* for the campaigns. The basic problem is not training the child, the housewife, and the peasant, but locating, recruiting, and motivating them. In the Revolutionary view, people grow to fit the responsibilities thrust upon them.

In the context of the literacy campaign, the foregoing was translated into two principles:
1. If illiterates exist among the people, so too do literacy workers.
2. The one who knows more must teach the one who knows less.

The mobilization of the people and of governmental organizational resources went hand in hand. A National Literacy Commission was established in place of the earlier National Literacy and Fundamental Education Commission. The new National Literacy Commission incorporated all existing mass and revolutionary organizations, among them the Cuban Labour Confederation, the (now) Federation of Cuban Women, the National Federation of Sugar Workers, the Ministry of the Revolutionary Armed Forces, the July 26 movement, the Revolutionary Directory of 13 March, the Popular Socialist Party,

1. R. Fagen, *The Transformation of Political Culture in Cuba*, Stanford, Calif., Stanford University Press, 1969.

the Rebel Youth Association, the Elementary Teachers' Guild, the National Educators' Guild, the National Institute of Agrarian Reform, the National Student Federation, the Federation of Rural Associations and the Confederation of High School Students.

This Commission was complemented by a national co-ordination body for the campaign, located within the Ministry of Education. Similar commissions and boards were installed at municipal level. It was soon found necessary to add an intermediate administrative step at provincial level since the co-ordination of all municipalities from one central office in Havana was found to be impractical. To ensure integration, the upper level commission appointed delegates to the lower level commissions. This administrative and co-ordination system proved to be of great value during the campaign. Meetings of the national co-ordination body were held every fifteen days to check fulfilment of previous agreements, to discuss the progress of the campaign and to decide upon measures for the next period.

By way of achieving technical mobilization of national resources, the National Literacy Commission created four sections: finance, propaganda, technical, and publications. The same structure was repeated at the provincial and municipal levels though the emphasis on the various functions changed from one level to another. For instance, much less publication work was handled at the provincial and municipal levels whereas propaganda work was important at all three levels.

The national co-ordination body brought the work of the four Sections of the campaign into one integrated focus, besides providing a channel for association with outside public and private interests. This was achieved through a membership pattern which included the national co-ordination body, the Section directors of the Commission, some representatives of the mass revolutionary organizations, provincial co-ordinators and delegates of the integrated revolutionary organizations.

These arrangements worked well. By the time the campaign began, the national co-ordination body was ready with 1.5 million copies of the primer *Venceremos* and half a million copies of the teachers' manual, *Alfabeticemos*.

Information and motivation

All the various instruments of information and propaganda—radio, television, posters, billboards, newspapers—were pressed into the service of the campaign. Propaganda posters all over the island exhorted the people:

> If you can teach, teach;
> If you can't teach, learn!

Another appeal was directed especially to the youth of the nation:

> Young men and women,
> Join the army of Young Literacy Workers.
> The home of a family of peasants who
> Cannot read and write is waiting for you now.
> Don't let them down!

Students who went to teach the peasants were organized as the Conrado Benitez brigades (in memory of a murdered teacher) and had a special hymn:

> Cuba! Cuba!
> Study, work and rifle!
> Pencil, primer, manual!
> Teach, teach! We will overcome!

> We are the Conrado Benitez brigade,
> We are the vanguard of the revolution,
> With books raised up
> We will reach our goal,
> To take literacy to all Cuba.

> Through valleys and mountains the *brigadistas* go,
> Performing our duty to the Fatherland, struggling for Peace.
> Down with imperialism, up with liberty!
> We carry with the words the light of truth.

> Cuba! Cuba!
> Study, work and rifle!
> Pencil, primer, manual!
> Teach, teach! We will overcome!

A call upon students and workers

Mobilization, however, did not consist solely of slogans and hymns. With the closing of schools for a period of eight months beginning in April 1961, some 105,664 students of the sixth grade and above became available as teachers. Later in the campaign, the direct participation of schoolteachers in teaching and supervision was made mandatory. The impact of closing the schools was not merely that more than a hundred thousand literacy teachers became available. The psychological impact was even more significant. The decision reverberated thoughout the society. Literacy became the nation's business. Since another 100,000 or more teachers were needed, factory workers were mobilized to teach the peasants. In all, a quarter of a million teachers were mobilized to work in the mass literacy campaign.

War on illiteracy

Another important feature of the mobilization effort in Cuba was the battlefield organization of the mass literacy campaign. The students were organized into the Conrado Benitez brigades and the workers were organized into *Patria o Muerte* (Fatherland or Death) brigades. The *brigadistas* took oaths, wore uniforms, and liberated villages from illiteracy. The campaign was a veritable combat.

The census

Another important action simultaneously comprising information gathering and mobilization of the people was the literacy census that continued well into the campaign. The census was not undertaken by conventional government employees but by thousands of volunteers from all walks of life. The objective was not only to identify and locate illiterates but also to put them in touch with literates who would be their teachers. As a result of this census some 929,297 illiterates were identified. Offices, banks, courts and post offices continued the task of locating illiterates.

The conduct of the mass campaign

The literacy census that began in November 1960 had identified 412,000 illiterates by February 1961, and 546,000 by April 1961. (The census, as already indicated, continued into the campaign period, identifying 648,000 by June 1961 and 985,000 by August 1961.)

On 15 April 1961, the first *brigadistas,* a group of some 1,000 students, arrived at Varadero. Two weeks later 7,500 were undergoing training. In all some 100,000 instructors were trained at Varadero to teach the peasants. A majority of these participants were students—from the sixth grade of primary school, junior high, high school and the university—primary schoolteachers, artists, newspapermen, nurses and others. A brigade of doctors in pedagogy, teacher trainers and researchers was also integrated into the teaching force as specialists.

Table 4 shows the numbers of student *brigadistas* recruited from each province of the country; but these constituted only part of the eventual literacy force. Final figures were as follows: popular instructors, 120,632; workers' brigades (*Patria o Muerte*), 13,016; Conrado Benitez brigades, 100,000; teachers, 34,772; making a total force of 268,420.

The student-teachers were organized into brigades in army style. As each *brigadista* left for the 'battle-front', he or she received a kit containing the following materials: a pair of boots, two pairs of socks, two uniforms, a belt, an olive-green beret, a hammock, a backpack, a

TABLE 4. Contributions to the Conrado Benitez brigades from each province

Province	Female	Male	Total
Pinar del Rio	2,474	2,029	4,503
Havana	19,658	17,015	36,673
Matanzas	2,401	2,670	5,071
Las Villas	8,730	8,064	16,794
Camaguey	4,825	5,040	9,865
Oriente	16,865	15,893	32,758
TOTAL	54,953	50,711	105,664

plastic insignia. The kit also included the following instructional materials: the primer *Venceremos*, the literacy manual *Alfabeticemos*, notebooks, pencils, lists, a lamp. Each *brigadista* was given ten pesos a month for incidental expenses.

Once the location of each student-teacher had been established, the leader of each platoon of *brigadistas* filled in a location card, keeping one copy for himself and forwarding the other to the leader of the company who in turn sent it to the National Commission of Literacy. This was primarily designed to keep parents informed of their children's whereabouts.

It will be noted that the Cuban literacy campaign did not hold conventional literacy classes and that the *brigadistas* met with illiterates in the latter's homes. This prevented absenteeism and resulted in a teacher/learner ratio of 1:3 and sometimes 1:2. More importantly, it gave adult illiterates greater confidence, greater freedom of communication, greater familiarity with the literacy workers; it was helpful to young and inexperienced teachers who were not obliged to stand in front of a large class.

For technical control of the teaching process, twenty-five teachers in each area were organized into a literacy unit, supervised by a unit leader who provided technical advice and counselling to teachers in weekly meetings. The health of the *brigadistas* was the responsibility of doctors, nurses and medical assistants mobilized to care for those in remote areas. Illiterates also were examined and, when necessary, provided with spectacles. Typically, teaching lasted two to three months although in certain situations it could take a little longer.

Table 5 shows the progress of the campaign. The figures for June-August were not encouraging, and to accelerate results, the government took several important measures. First, the Confederation of Cuban Workers was called upon to recruit factory workers as an auxiliary force to the Conrado Benitez brigades; some 20,000 factory workers responded. The workers were organized into *Patria o Muerte* brigades and sent out to teach in the mountains and on the farms. While they were teaching, they received their regular salary from the factory.

TABLE 5. Progress at various stages of the literacy campaign

Category	End of June	End of July	End of August	End of October	End of campaign (21 December)
Illiterates located	684,000	822,000	985,000	988,000	979,000
Persons studying	465,000	594,000	776,000	500,000	n.a.
New literates (cumulative totals)	22,000	62,000	119,000	354,000	707,000

Source: R. Fagen, *The Transformation of Political Culture in Cuba*, p. 50, Stanford, Calif., Stanford University Press, 1969.

Second, at the request of the government, the Federation of Cuban Women and the Committee for the Defence of the Revolution carried out a massive effort aimed at recruiting housewives as learners. The recruiters also served as literacy teachers, bringing many women into the learning process.

Third, the government gave all responsibility for the literacy campaign to Municipal Councils of Education in different areas of the country. These councils were to oversee all aspects of the campaign in their territory including the census of illiterates, deployment and sometimes further training of literacy workers, and the establishment of smaller literacy units and supervision mechanisms.

Finally, in September 1961, four months before the end of the campaign, a National Congress of Literacy was called to evaluate the results and to determine what measures were required to ensure success. The Congress may be seen as a mid-term mobilization of the national effort for the success of the campaign and was attended by 833 delegates from all over the country. It renewed the national commitment to eradicate illiteracy as planned by the end of 1961 and made proposals for the intensification of efforts.

In following up the proposals of the Congress, schoolteachers' direct participation in the campaign was now made mandatory. Every teacher was assigned to some task by his or her local Council: as an instructor, technical assistant or brigade leader. The opening of the new school year was delayed until January of 1962. In the meantime, a 'plan of attendance' was drawn up for young children who were out of school because their teachers had left to teach illiterates. Parents, members of the Association of Young Rebels and other volunteers were asked to organize substitute activities for children out of school.

Acceleration Camps were set up wherever there were large numbers of adult readers who had fallen behind. Adult learners were brought to these camps to spend whole days in learning with

experienced people's teachers and expert educators. Friends, neighbours and community organizers replaced these adults in their places of
work.

When adult learners could not come to the camps, Study Coaches
were sent to them. These specially trained coaches went to the most
isolated areas to recruit and teach adults living and working under
difficult conditions. These coaches numbered no more than a few
hundred but 'their expertise, innovative energy, and intensive training
rendered them dynamic catalysts wherever they went'.[1]

On 22 December 1961, the Year of Education was declared at an
end and Cuban territory free of illiteracy. In 1959, 23.6 per cent of the
population above the age of 10 were illiterate. The campaign contacted
some 979,207 of these and made 707,212 literate during 1961, resulting
in an illiteracy rate of only 3.9 per cent at the end of the one-year
campaign.

Pedagogical aspects of the campaign

Many of the pedagogical aspects of the Cuban mass literacy campaign
have been dealt with indirectly in our earlier discussion of the campaign
in the field: the language of literacy was Spanish and the campaign dealt
only with that language; one single primer was used for the whole
country; the teaching kit, in addition to the primer, included a teachers'
guide; brigadistas were given some training; actual instruction was given
in small groups of two to three adults in their own homes; student
teachers were supported by expert teachers and counsellors; teaching,
typically, lasted two to three months; and the reading level required to
be considered literate was approximately that achieved by children at
the end of the first grade.

The primer, Venceremos (We Will Overcome), was based on three
realities: the reality of the country; the reality of the illiterate reader;
and the reality of the literacy volunteer teacher. It comprised fifteen
lessons, each based on a motivational theme linked with the economic
and social reforms that were taking place at that time. Some of the titles
of the lessons were: The Revolution; Fidel is Our Leader; The Land is
Ours; The Co-operatives; Racial Discrimination; Housing Rights; and
Health and International Unity.

Methodologically, the primer combined the analytical and synthetic approaches and taught recognition and writing of both printed and
cursive letters. Each lesson began with a photo and a sentence
describing the event or subject of the photo. The sentence was divided
into words; words were divided into syllables; and these were, in turn,
combined to make new words and sentences.

1. J. Kozol, 'A New Look at the Literacy Campaign in Cuba', Harvard Educational Review, Vol.
   48, No. 3, 1978, pp. 341-77.

The teachers' manual, *Alfabeticemos* (Let's Learn to Read and Write), comprised three parts: orientation concerning the teachers' jobs and tasks; a clear and simple explanation of the revolutionary process; and a vocabulary including those words which could cause problems of clarity and usage to the teachers themselves.

The section on the revolutionary process was meant to be used for the political education of the student teachers themselves. Only by understanding this material could they conduct discussions of the photo themes in the primer *Venceremos*. Detailed step-by-step instructions on the teaching of each lesson were also provided.

The recruitment and training of teachers

The sources of recruitment of literacy teachers have already been outlined. Most student-teachers underwent one week's training which covered four aspects: physical, social, technical and political. The teachers' manual *Alfabeticemos* was the text on which training was based. In their teaching process, the *brigadistas* were encouraged to be firm and definite but not authoritarian; purposeful, sequential and well organized, but never abusive and never condescending. The following steps were suggested in the teaching of each lesson, as reported by Kozol.[1]

First step: Conversation

Conversation between the *brigadista* and the pupil in regard to the photograph within the primer:
(a) To find out what the pupil knows about the subject of the photo;
(b) To provoke oral expression;
(c) To clarify the concepts.

Second step: Reading

A complete reading of the text (block letters) that appears beside the photo:
(a) First, by the teacher, slowly and clearly;
(b) Second, by the teacher and the pupil at the same time;
(c) Third, by the pupil alone.

Third step: Practice and exercise

(a) Sight recognition of a phrase or sentence that has been selected (Key).
(b) Break-up of a phrase or sentence into syllables.
(c) Examination of each syllable within an exercise.

Technical preparation, as indicated above, was only one part of teacher preparation. Political education was also involved. Each brigadista took

1. Ibid.

an 'Oath of Honour' to honour Cuba; to act with elevated moral and revolutionary principles; to respect the life and customs of the humble peasant; to be disciplined and worthy; never to desert; and to return as better students and more conscientious revolutionaries.

Examinations and certificates

Three simple tests were applied to the illiterates in the process of learning to read: an initial test, an intermediate test, and a final test. The first test was to determine whether the person concerned was illiterate or semi-literate (that is, able to read the first three items of the test but unable to write). The intermediate test was primarily for monitoring progress. The final test was based on the lesson 'The Cuban Fishermen', in the primer. The assumption was that if the person passed the test after reading all fifteen lessons of the primer, he or she was literate. Certificates were awarded to those passing the tests.

The follow-up to the literacy campaign

Immediately after the campaign, some reading material was made available to the new literates so that they could continue reading. *El Placer de Leer* (The Joy of Reading) designed especially for new readers and containing national and international news was published and distributed free. Rural libraries were opened where new readers could go to borrow books.

But the follow-up to the literacy campaign did not merely consist of producing materials and establishing reading rooms. Its significance lies in the fact that it was conceptualized in the larger context of adult education of the masses and the recruitment through education of the erstwhile underprivileged into the service of the revolution. As 100,000 or more *brigadistas* gathered in Revolution Square on 22 December 1961, chanting 'We have overcome', Fidel Castro declared:

Onward, Comrades, onward to new goals, to meet new commitments, to train as technicians, doctors, teachers, engineers and revolutionary intellectuals.

The same day a major scholarship plan for 40,800 young people from localities where there were no junior or senior high schools was announced, with priority to be given to those who came from poor and large families. In this way, follow-up was provided not only for newly literate adults, but also for young people, including many who had left school for almost a year so as to teach on farms, in fishing villages and in the mountains.

A Department of Workers and Peasants Education (later called the Department of Adult Education) was created. Even before the literacy campaign came to an end, the Ministry of Education was making plans for a follow-up course, *Seguimento*. The first course started on 24 February 1962 (two months after the end of the mass literacy campaign) and the first students graduated in December of the same year. The minimum goal for this course was continuously raised: from a follow-up course to the 'technical minimum' and then to the sixth grade. The sixth-grade classes followed three different timetables: the urban timetable (September-June); the sugar-cane timetable (June-December); and the mountain calendar (January-September). In this way it was possible to cover all sectors of the economy—agricultural, metallurgical, fisheries, and military.

In all, some 586,000 people returned to school to strive to achieve the sixth-grade level. By 1966 about 65,500 had graduated and by 1974, over 60 per cent of those who returned to school had achieved sixth-grade competence. The government hoped to win the battle for sixth-grade education nationwide by 1980.

The general fundamental objectives of adult education following on the literacy campaign are worth considering:

1. To facilitate development of the general culture of the unschooled masses, so as to enable them to communicate more effectively and to increase their active participation in the construction of socialism.

2. To guarantee the general basic schooling needed for professional training of a different type at different levels.

3. To contribute to the formation of the multilateral personality of communist workers, peasants and homemakers, by developing the Marxist-Leninist conception of the world and the corresponding moral and ideological convictions.

4. To allow students who for various reasons were unable to complete their studies in the subsystem of general education to complete schooling up to the level of compulsory education.

5. To facilitate the development of students' spiritual needs by extending their cultural horizons and stimulating their cognitive capacities.

6. To stimulate students to undertake self-education, using the diverse organized forms available in the country.

7. To take advantage of the knowledge of foreign languages for the purpose of social communication and as an instrument in work and self-education.

This comprehensive adult education agenda has led to a variety of instructional settings and structures, such as evening and late afternoon schools; schools in work centres and factories; workers' and farmers' faculties; schools for homemakers; family reading circles; language schools; and residual illiteracy classrooms.

Monitoring of literacy actions and their effects

All municipalities kept files on each of the adult learners who joined the campaign. In addition to results on the three tests taken by each learner, the files also contained data on attendance, interests, whether the adult liked reading and writing, level of satisfaction with present job and interest in further education. This material was useful both during the literacy campaign and after the campaign for developing follow-up actions. The files, however, merely provided numerical data on the number of persons declared literate. The more significant effects of the campaign lay elsewhere.

One of the most important results claimed for the campaign was an awakening among the people of a desire for their own culture. There was a definite mass cultural revival. New poets and artists emerged and produced pieces that became part of the consciousness of the people: 'Awakening' (*Despertar*); 'The Hymn of the Conrado Benitez Brigades'; and 'The Story of a Battle' (*Historia de una Batalla*). A trend towards popular literature developed; the people were expressing themselves; a new consciousness was developing.

The campaign engendered a new awareness of the position of workers and peasants in the development of the country, a fuller understanding of socialism. The masses acquired social experience in creating and using mass organizations, and in co-operating with other organizations to find creative solutions to their problems.

The *brigadistas* learned the reality of misery within the countryside. This helped them to identify with the peasants and become interested in solving their problems. The student-teachers saw in themselves the first germination of the new Cuban. On the other hand, the newly literate became active in the conscious construction of socialism. Thus a much-needed integration of social classes took place. Students who had gone to teach later received scholarships to become scientists, teachers, artists and technicians and emerged as the core of the socialist administration in Cuba.

The literacy campaign was not, of course, a panacea for all the problems of a developing nation, but it was more than a first step; it was a great leap forward.

Lessons of the campaign

1. The most obvious lesson is that campaigns are not miracles; successful campaigns result from hard work, technique and organization. And these do not come together without the political will of the leadership.
2. Literacy campaigns cannot be justified in purely economic terms. Ideological justifications are necessary; quite often ideological justifications may even be sufficient.

3. While the availability of resources helps, further resources can be generated through mobilization of the people, if the political will, inspired by an ideology, exists. Closing the schools and sending young people to teach adult learners on farms and in the mountains was a masterly stroke which not only supplied the necessary manpower but also resulted in a campaign for those who taught—they experienced the rural culture, they learned socialism, they became the backbone of the socialist revolution.

4. Finally, literacy campaigns should be evaluated not merely in terms of people made literate but in terms of their effects in cultural, social and developmental terms.

BIBLIOGRAPHY

BOWLES, S. Cuban Education and Revolutionary Ideology. *Harvard Educational Review*, Vol. 40, No. 2, 1971, pp. 472-500.

CARNOY, M.; WERTHEIN, J. Socialist Ideology and the Transformation of Cuban Education. In: Jerome Karabel and A. H. Halsey (eds.), *Power and Ideology in Education*. New York, Oxford University Press, 1977.

FAGEN, R. *The Transformation of Political Culture in Cuba*. Stanford, Calif., Stanford University Press, 1969.

GILETTE, A. Cuba's Educational Revolution. London, 1972. (Fabian Research Series, No. 302.)

KOZOL, J. A New Look at the Literacy Campaign in Cuba. *Harvard Educational Review*, Vol. 48, No. 3, 1978. pp. 341-77.

PRIETO-MORALES, A. *The Literacy Campaign in Cuba*. Report written for the Unesco/ICAE study of literacy campaigns of the twentieth century. 1980.

SEERS, DUDLEY. *Cuba: The Economic and Social Revolution*. Chapel Hill, N.C., University of North Carolina Press, 1964.

CHAPTER 8

The mass literacy movement in Burma: from the 1960s into the 1980s

Slowly but surely and systematically, under the Burma Socialist Programme Party (BSPP), the country is rooting out illiteracy in a unique way.

The Revolutionary Council of the Union of Burma assumed power in March 1962, more than fourteen years after Burma achieved independence. The declaration on the 'Burmese Way to Socialism' was issued on 30 April 1962, asserting that socialism could not be achieved with more than one-third of the nation illiterate.

The first literacy campaign was launched in 1964 as a pilot project in the Meiktila district. After intensive experimentation during 1966-68, a new strategy for literacy promotion was adopted and a long-term plan was approved in 1969.

The Burmese mass literacy movement has certain unique features that are worthy of note. To begin with, it is a mass movement in terms of its ultimate objective, but is selective and geographically incremental in its implementation. The movement focuses on the age group 15 to 59 years; and literacy work is conducted area by area: districts and townships are selected by the Central Literacy Committee on the basis of need, readiness, accessibility and security. Another important feature of the movement is its voluntary nature and the mode of its funding. It is a budgetless campaign, though certainly a most resourceful one. It is a mass movement run by volunteers. None of those involved, from teachers in villages to members of the Central Literacy Committee, draw any salaries or allowances.

In the past fifteen years, more than two million adults have become literate with the help of some 300,000 volunteer teachers, reducing the national illiteracy rate in the early 1980s by some 10 per cent, to 30 per cent of the population. Some 9 million adults, however, are still illiterate and most children in rural areas drop out of elementary school without completing all the grades. The struggle, therefore, goes on.

On each International Literacy Day (8 September) new campaign areas are announced and new beginnings are made, in the hope that one day 8 September will indeed mark the end of illiteracy.

Historical setting

Burma had existed as a unified empire for almost eight centuries before the British annexed it in 1885. Independence was achieved in January 1948. The years of the Second World War had been especially hard on Burma. Twice it became a battlefield: the British had had to withdraw in 1942 under the Japanese onslaught, and in 1945 the Japanese retreated and the Allies returned.

The early post-independence years were a period of conflict and turmoil. In 1962, General Ne Win assumed power and declared the Burmese Way to Socialism. Twelve years later, in 1974, a new constitution was promulgated and the Socialist Republic of the Union of Burma was established.

Burma, a country of 678,528 square kilometres, bordering on Bangladesh, India, China, Laos, Thailand, the Andaman Sea and the Bay of Bengal, has been and remains an object of fascination for many outsiders. Today it is a country of some 32,573,000 people, with an average population growth of 2.22 per cent during the last twenty years. Some 14,433,000 of the total population are between the ages of 15 and 59.

It is basically an agricultural country and 85 per cent of its people live in the rural areas. Rice and hardwoods (including the famous Burma teak) are its two main exports, followed by minerals. There is some oil and gas but only enough for local consumption.

Burma is ethnically rich, comprising descendants of migrants from Tibet and Central Asia; and even today some 126 native languages and dialects are spoken. However, the Buddhist religion has permeated the whole society, creating one culture and unity in diversity. The people share a common sense of history, reinforced by the Burmese language which is widely understood. The Socialist Republic of the Union of Burma is creating a common political culture and welding the many ethnic groups into one nation.

Burma was a highly literate society even before the British arrived in the nineteenth century. This was solely due to the Phongyi-kyaungs, schools attached to Buddhist monasteries. These monastic schools existed in every village and all young boys attended them, some for as long as two or three years, to learn to read and write and to acquire spiritual and secular knowledge. Girls, who could not go to monastic schools, attended common schools inside the village.

Buddhist spiritual values are still important in Burma. This philosophy, combined with the widespread experience of literacy among the masses, has endowed the Burmese literacy campaigns and their implementation with a specific character.

The driving force and objectives of the campaigns

The driving force behind the literacy movement was the Revolution of 1962. Socialism required literacy. The 1965 seminar of BSPP pointed out that if the socialist system is to be set up, every person must have high standards of awareness of their duties and responsibilities. There must be wide knowledge. It is clear that every person must be literate for this situation to become possible. This is why the elimination of illiteracy is to be carried out on a 'mass basis'. The BSPP also justified literacy in more concrete terms. Literacy education was to be integrated with the economy, with earning a livelihood; basic education was to be brought within the reach of all, children and adults. This, of course, meant both universal primary education and universal adult literacy.

The objectives for the literacy movement, as elaborated by the Burma Central Literacy Committee (BCLC) in 1969, were as follows:
(a) first and foremost, to help illiterates to gain literacy;
(b) to develop new ideas and to instil desirable attitudes;
(c) to promote a broader outlook on life;
(d) to encourage more active participation in a more progressive community;
(e) to raise productivity levels and standards of living;
(f) to improve the education level of the whole population; and
(g) to aid in the economic and social progress of the country.
The Burmese also wanted to create a single political culture; and literacy in the Burmese language had to play an important part in bringing this about. One community required one language of communication, so that messages in respect of health and agriculture development could be carried to all the people.

The use of student volunteers each summer was also intended to help resocialize the student community by providing experience of constructive work, knowledge of the rural masses and of rural life, appreciation of the dignity of labour through direct contributions, and thus coming to realize that 'to serve others' interest is to serve one's own'.

'Readiness' and the preparation

The work of the Buddhist monastic schools over the centuries had created a 'readiness' for adult literacy in post-revolutionary socialist Burma. These schools had touched the lives of almost all Burmese youth, and had introduced them not only to religious and moral principles but also to arithmetic, astronomy, medicine, alchemy, art, crafts and architecture. Young girls had studied in the 'house schools', also called the common schools, in the villages.

Under British rule, as under many other colonial regimes, a slow but sure destruction of the indigenous system, and a slow and uneven diffusion of the new Western system of schooling took place: vernacular schools for the rural masses, Anglo-vernacular schools for towns-people, and English schools for a select élite. Yet in 1931, 56 per cent of males and 16.5 per cent of females over the age of 5 were literate—rates approximately four times as high as those reported in India at that time. Among the Burmans alone (excluding all other ethnic groups), the literacy rates were as high as 71.1 per cent for males and 21 per cent for females.

In educational terms, the dark cloud of Japanese occupation from 1942 to 1945 had a silver lining. The occupation years saw the democratization of education through the establishment of a common school for all races and classes, following a common curriculum and taught in a common language of instruction—Burmese. Nothing better could have happened to Burma with regard to the plans of the BSPP some twenty years later.

The years between independence and the socialist revolution, 1948–1962, saw three initiatives that further readied Burma for the mass literacy movement of the mid-1960s. The government of independent Burma passed a Mass Education Act which became effective in March 1949. The Mass Education Council established under the Act undertook to attack illiteracy on two fronts—through traditional schools for children and through new schools for adults. Mass education for adults was conceptualized as something more than the acquisition of the Three Rs. It was meant to be community education for bringing about integrated rural development. Unfortunately, the movement lacked total political commitment; but while its results were less than impressive, it did provide some useful historical lessons in regard to the conditions that must prevail for a mass literacy movement to be successful.

The Burmese Army undertook a more successful action in respect of literacy. A survey of illiteracy in the army in 1954 led to a campaign against illiteracy in 1955 when the Army Education Corps taught its soldiers to 'sharpen the bayonet with alphabets'.

In 1952, the Education Plan for a Welfare State sought, among other things, to ensure universal knowledge of the Three Rs among all citizens of Burma and to prepare them as productive workers and technicians and as good citizens of a democracy. The years 1952-56 also saw the tremendous expansion of primary education. The number of state primary schools rose from 3,335 to 10,146; and enrolment from 468,436 to 1,155,816. By the end of 1956-60 the enrolment ratios for elementary education were 63 per cent (70 per cent if monastic schools are included) of all children of elementary school age. Unfortunately, during these same years adult education was neglected by the government and left to volunteers and voluntary associations. When the revolutionary government took over, enrolment ratios in elementary education were 63-70 per cent, but adult literacy ratios had probably declined from the levels of the 1930s.

The Meiktila pilot project

The 'readiness' described above was complemented with preparation for the literacy movement of the 1960s. In 1964, a pilot project was opened in the Meiktila district, with volunteers from the State Teachers' Training College. This project provided Burmese literacy workers with an opportunity to experiment with various concepts of literacy and literacy objectives, modes of organization, strategies of motivation, curriculum development, preparation of teaching materials, production of teaching aids, recruitment and training of teachers, optimum teaching periods, monitoring and evaluation, and follow-up measures.

Certain concrete conclusions were reached.

(a) It was realized that 'literacy in the summer vacations' would not work. Six weeks of teaching in the months of April and May each year could only make semi-literates who soon relapsed into illiteracy.

(b) The need for much more adequate co-ordination among the various levels of government from national to township to village level was keenly felt. Horizontal co-ordination was also required.

(c) It was appreciated that literacy work could not succeed if it was undertaken merely as an administrative measure. It had to be a mass movement and to be undertaken by the masses on their own behalf.

(d) The reader prepared for illiterate adults needed bigger print and more colourful pictures. The programme also required follow-up materials.

(e) Volunteer student-teachers needed systematic training in the methodology of adult literacy teaching.

(f) Adult illiterates in literacy classes had to be treated as adults and not subjected to the formalized atmosphere of the typical elementary school.

Having absorbed these lessons, Burma was ready for the launching of the wider literacy movement.

Conduct and coverage

A long-term plan was drawn up in 1969 designed to cover twelve years, through three four-year plans, for the country's economic and social development. A strategy for the literacy campaign was developed. It was to be a mass movement; to involve community participation and operate on a voluntary basis; to make use of locally available resources; to concentrate on selected areas, regions or townships; and to be organized with the co-operation of the township and divisional literacy committees, together with the Party and other mass organizations concerned; finally, it was to be conducted all year round.

By 1975, a fully fledged literacy committee had been established, with lines of co-ordination and co-operation with the Party and the government. (Figure 3 illustrates the vertical and horizontal co-ordination built into the administrative structure of the literacy movement.)

The administrative structure reflects the spirit of the New Constitution of 1974 which offered the Burmese people 'centralized decentralism'—local initiative and autonomy under the central leadership and guidance of BSPP. Another important collaborative linkage, which is not shown in the figure, was co-ordination with mass organizations such as the Workers' Association, the Peasants' Association and the Youth Association.

The Central Literacy Committee members (about twenty-five in number) represent all interests: the Party, mass organizations, and government departments, the public, the media, and also trade, transportation and the universities. The Committee works through three sub-committees: one for general organization; another for curriculum development and instructional materials; and a third for the promotion of reading and the establishment of a library movement.

The State/Divisional Literacy Committees are the connecting link between the Central Literacy Committee and the District Literacy Committees. Their main task is to provide supervision and guidance to the leadership in the district committees.

The District Literacy Committees are essentially 'organizing' committees designed:
(a) to form village and factory literacy committees;
(b) to motivate illiterates and literates and to sensitize public opinion in the districts;
(c) to carry out statistical surveys of learners and of volunteers who might teach adult learners;
(d) to allocate duties to volunteer teachers from outside the district;

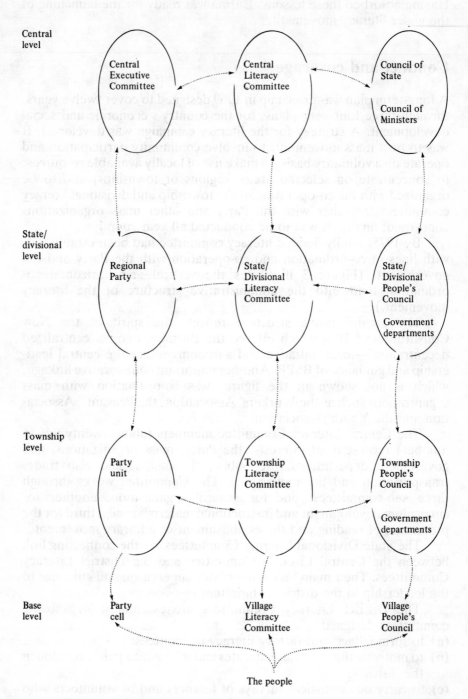

FIG. 3. Lines of co-operation and co-ordination between the government, the
Party and the literacy organization.

(e) to raise funds for the campaign in the district;
(f) to organize reading rooms, reading circles and libraries and to keep these supplied with follow-up materials;
(g) to hold Peoples' Victory ceremonies to celebrate the total eradication of illiteracy from a village; and
(h) to render assistance in problem-solving and evaluation to village committees.

As mentioned earlier, the literacy movement in Burma is incremental in its strategy of coverage, and proceeds area by area and district by district. Districts are selected by the Central Literacy Committee in consultation with the district committees. Work at the village level continues until a whole village becomes literate, taking any time from six months to two years.

Each year a cycle of public mobilization and programme implementation is initiated. BCLC selects campaign areas from a list of suggestions forwarded by the fourteen States and Divisions on the basis of these considerations: How many illiterates are in the area? Are the local people themselves interested? Does BCLC have enough paper to print the necessary number of adult readers, teacher guides and other teaching-learning materials? Are there funds for the purchase of slates, pencils and exercise books? Is there time enough for BCLC to provide guidance and advice to the selected townships? Submissions are made to the Central Literacy Committee during July and August each year, and choices are declared on 8 September, International Literacy Day.

The selected districts have until the end of March (that is, some six months) to prepare for the literacy classes, which are launched in April at the beginning of the school and university summer vacations. These preparations include the following steps: collection of data on illiterate adults in the various communities where classes are to be launched; recruitment of volunteer teachers (emphasis is placed on local recruits—literate villagers, teachers, monks and nuns—who are readily available since there are more literates than illiterates in most wards and villages of Burma. Teachers from state schools and students from colleges and universities also become available during the vacations); training of key literacy workers and of volunteer teachers; sensitizing the public, both literates and illiterates; developing ways and means of funding the movement in the area; choosing locations for literacy centres (flexibility is the rule here so that teachers and learners can decide to meet at a time and place convenient to the group); and collecting materials such as books, chalk, pressure lamps and kerosene lamps.

Figures for the First Four-Year Plan, 1969-72, give an idea of the actual coverage: 75 townships, 15,080 villages, 33,546 Centres, 206,744 volunteer teachers, 840,261 new literates.

The Second Four-Year Plan, 1973-76, was a period more of consolidation and review than of expansion. Follow-up programmes such as village libraries, reading circles and clubs were developed and implemented. Six more districts were added to the earlier area of coverage. Significantly, two of these districts were from the non-Burman areas of Shan State, namely, Ywa-ngan and Kalaw townships. Experience in these districts made the work of the Third Four-Year Plan possible.

In this last plan, 1977-80, the programme was extended to all the seven States and seven Divisions of Burma on the basis of at least one township in each State or Division, thus covering the whole country and all ethnic groups. This meant the addition of sixty townships.

No specific provision is made for the literacy movement in the government budget. Government contributions take the form of unpaid work by government officials. Student volunteers and local literates bear the whole burden of teaching. Peasants house and feed volunteer teachers from outside the community who in turn help by working on the farms of host families. Facilities for holding classes are available rent-free. Materials are printed by the information ministry but the cost of paper, printing and binding is absorbed by the Central Literacy Committee. Learning materials are supplied free to learners. To pay for printing costs and other sundries, funds are collected from the public through donations and by the sale of campaign badges, banners, paper fans, postcards, sling bags, and ash trays.

Pedagogical aspects of the literacy movement

The conceptualization of literacy in Burma was largely traditional, in contrast to the definition of functional literacy within the Experimental World Literacy Programme (EWLP) during 1967-73. No attempt was made to develop a functionally integrated approach or work-oriented materials. In comparison with the more recent radical-humanist view of literacy as constituting not merely the reading of the word but the reading of the world, the Burmese definition could best be described as 'cultural'. The campaign sought to teach reading and writing first and foremost.

The definition of what it meant to be literate was developed specifically in terms of the Burmese programme: 'An illiterate becomes literate when he has covered the whole primer prescribed by BCLC and is able to read a daily newspaper, to write simple messages and to do elementary calculations for daily life. In other words, an illiterate becomes literate when he has passed the literacy test conducted by a group of examiners.'

Literacy meant literacy in the Burmese language, making it possible to teach one language and one script throughout the whole country. The Burmese language belongs to the Tibeto-Burman group of the Sino-Tibetan family of languages. It is not, however, an ideographic language. The Burmese script is a derivative of the Pallava script of South India which is alphabetical. Burmese thus has an alphabet and a script of its own. It is chiefly monosyllabic, and it is a tonal language.

The Burmese language has been the principal literacy medium in the country since the sixteenth century. Burmese is almost the only language spoken in the plains, and it serves as a medium of communication in the hill tracts, where some speak it as a second language. The choice of Burmese as the language of literacy was therefore natural.

The Burmese Mass Literacy Movement uses one curriculum and one primer throughout the country. The view is that Burma has one people, one culture, one common vocation, one religion, one value system, one written language and one set of needs and interests.

The approach used to teach literacy avoids the traditional alphabetical method and equally the new methods of teaching literacy integrated with an economic or political function. It is a mixture of the 'linguistic approach' and the 'look-and-say method'—in other words, a symbol-to-sound transference method. The names of characters are not taught, merely the sounds that they represent. No attempt is made to teach all thirty-three characters of the Burmese language before proceeding to read and write words and sentences. Five to six of the simplest and most frequent characters are taught first and immediately put to work in combination with the three tones of each vowel sound. This gives the adult a sense of achievement on the very first day. It is claimed that this is a very quick way to teach literacy and that adults learn to read and write within 60-100 hours.

The first phase of the literacy class is devoted solely to learning to read. Even numeracy is omitted. Functional content is added during a second phase. In the primer itself the coverage of the content is as follows (percentages): social studies, 25; production knowledge, 20; health education, 16.7; moral practices, 16.7; nature study, 13.3; and religion, 8.3.

Some simple but effective teaching aids have been developed within the programme, among them a 'teaching wheel' to instruct in the sounding of consonants and vowel combination. Alphabet posters and lessons are displayed in public places.

Learner motivation and volunteer participation are stimulated through what the Burmese call 'organization power'. The public is kept informed of the need for literacy through the media and by means of posters and billboards. Even more effective is the use of the so-called 'mass measures', such as: opening ceremonies attended by Government Ministers and other prominent officials; visits by poets, singers, and well-known film personalities; song and dance festivals; send-off ceremonies for village leaders preparing to attend the supervisory course in the capital; mass receptions to welcome volunteers; sale of literacy badges, banners, sling bags, paper fans, postcards, posters, etc.; competitions with prizes for the best performers.

Socialist emulation is encouraged: districts compete with other districts, villages against villages, groups against groups. The first village in the township to achieve literacy is awarded library materials by BSPP. Others earn the right to a 'Victory Celebration'. Teachers and volunteers receive badges in organized ceremonies. It should be noted here that social recognition is the only reward that volunteers receive; there are no monetary rewards. Indeed some volunteers pay their own expenses to travel to their places of assignment. Teachers in schools and universities may get leave-credit.

The basic strategy used in the training of teachers is the 'multiplier method'. During the pre-campaign period of September to March, cadres in all townships selected for literacy work are given basic training at the Centre, covering the importance of the campaign, its aims and objectives; how to collect necessary data and motivational information on learners and volunteers; methods of motivation and organization; the basic method of teaching reading and writing; teaching numeracy; and fund raising. Instructors in these courses include those who are in the midst of ongoing programmes in neighbouring areas and can contribute from their grass-roots experience. After training, these key personnel return to their districts and townships and train second-line personnel who may then train field-level workers and volunteers.

The training of university students seems to be handled at the institutions where they are studying. In a two-week training period they study such issues and themes as: why students in universities should participate in the literacy campaign; aims and objectives of the campaign; attitudes to be observed when living with rural people in the field; how to check supplies such as medicines, instructional materials, gifts for learners; how to co-ordinate with literacy committees at various levels; how to work with and relate to farmers and how to contribute to their work; how to study the cultural and socio-economic environment of the communities and establish the work of the campaign there; how to prepare group reports; how to survey changes in the community; how to solve problems and make suggestions for implementation and action.

Follow-up work

The Burmese literacy movement has paid considerable attention to follow-up work, though the lack of resources has not permitted important gains to be made in this area. After adults have become literate they are normally organized in reading circles which meet twice weekly. Thirteen follow-up books have been produced on such subjects as nutrition, health care, child rearing, sanitation, water conservation, family planning, domestic science, agriculture, veterinary science, stock and poultry farming, and co-operatives. Some 2 million copies of these follow-up books have been distributed. Technical literature has also been produced, such as the *Handbook for Volunteer Teachers* and *Instructions for University Volunteer Teachers*. However, the lack of material resources and scarcity of paper have prevented the extension of the follow-up programme.

Evaluation and monitoring

Monitoring, in the sense of determining flaws and providing correctives at the various stages of the programme and at various levels of action, is part of the general administrative and supervision system. The communication system is well articulated both vertically and horizontally, giving the programme significant organizational power.

Some evaluation is especially concerned with curriculum development and production of materials. Two different sources supply evaluation information: the technicians of BCLC sub-committees and non-technicians participating in the system at various levels. Both sources provide data on organizational experience and on the usefulness of materials, based on observation and experience or on formal interviews and discussions. Several extensive revisions of curricular materials have resulted from such evaluations.

Statistical data are collected from village level and upwards and are reviewed and consolidated at each level before reaching the Central Literacy Committee.

The basis of such data is, of course, the number of people made literate. The achievement tests given to adults provide both a monitoring mechanism and evaluative information on the effects of the programme. The Burmese programme does not use any standardized tests. Tests are conducted by committee members according to rules and regulations laid down by BCLC. Adult learners are tested individually both on passages from the primer and on unseen passages. Those displaying the ability to read and copy, without outside help, the selected texts are temporarily recorded as newly literate members of the locality. This, however, must be confirmed by the Achievement Testing Committee from another village or by the Township Literacy Committee. Reciprocal testing of villages is prohibited so as to guard against reciprocal leniency.

Results of the campaign

Unfortunately, no analyses are available of the political, social or economic effects of literacy on the lives of the Burmese people. The number of volunteer teachers who took part in the mass movement from 1965 to 1980, and the number of those adults who were declared literate give some idea of the dimensions of the programme (see Table 6).

TABLE 6. Progress of the literacy programme, 1965-80

Years	Number of literates	Number of teachers
1965-68	183,510	61,617
1969-72	840,261	206,744
1973-76	66,619	11,279
1977-80	214,067	78,284
	1,304,457	357,924

Lessons from the Burmese experience

1. Once again the significance of the ideological and political commitment of the leadership emerges from the Burmese case-study. There is a definite link between literacy and socialist reconstruction, between literacy and reform, and between literacy and nation-building.
2. The Burmese case-study also indicates that mass literacy campaigns must be mass movements; they cannot be conceptualized as programmes to be designed and implemented by administrators. Literacy campaigns need committed cadres of workers, not cautious, career-oriented civil servants.
3. This does not mean, however, that these campaigns do not need to be well administered. Indeed, ideological commitment must be supported by extensive organization. The mass literacy campaigns must create and use organizational power to succeed.
4. The Burmese Way to Literacy embodies relativism. Burmese socialism would seem to be culturally adapted. It has apparently been found compatible with Buddhism and is spiritual and moralistic in tone. The use of the cultural values of charity and service and of indigenous institutions such as the monastic schools and of monks and nuns in teaching literacy is worthy of note. In terms of organization, while the overall framework was standardized, considerable flexibility was built into the system and considerable attention was paid to local conditions. Finally, as regards the technical aspect, the Burmese chose to use teaching methods appropriate to the realities rather than to follow any methodological orthodoxy of whatever kind.
5. There is perhaps a need to justify literacy at various levels and in different terms. The Burmese justified literacy in transcendental terms of socialism and progress as well as in terms of the Three R's, changed attitudes, and agricultural productivity.

6. By making the literacy campaign a wholly volunteer effort, and by allocating whatever funds were available to programme elements of the campaign rather than to administration, the Burmese prevented any group from using those funds for new employment or for increasing their existing incomes. This can be a very important lesson for countries that face similar situations.

7. Finally, the Burmese campaign is an excellent example of how a country can achieve international visibility and support by linking its work with the work of an international organization. By announcing its literacy plans and targets for the forthcoming year on 8 September, International Literacy Day, Burma gave an international dimension to its national efforts.

BIBLIOGRAPHY

ANDRUS, J. R. Burmese Economic Life. Stanford, Calif., Stanford University Press, 1947.

BURMA SOCIALIST PROGRAMME PARTY. Party Seminar, 1965. Rangoon, 1966.

——. The System of Correlation of Man and His Environment. Rangoon, 1963.

KYI, DAW AHMAR. A Historical Survey of the Literacy Movement in Burma. Rangoon, 1978. (Thesis for M.Ed. degree, Institute of Education.)

LOWE, J. The Education of Adults—A World Perspective. Paris, Unesco, 1975.

MEAD, MARGARET. Cultural Patterns and Technological Change. New York, Mentor Books, 1958.

OO, U. THAN; SOE, U. AYE. Literacy Campaign in the Union of Burma. The Guardian Supplement, 6 September, 1970.

TINKER, HUGH. The Union of Burma. London, Oxford University Press, 1961.

TUT, U. THAUNG; MYINT, U. LAY. Burmese Way to Literacy. Rangoon, Burma Central Literacy Committee, 1980. (Report written for the Unesco/ICAE study of literacy campaigns of the twentieth century.)

CHAPTER 9

The Brazilian literacy movement from 1967 to 1980

The Brazilian Literacy Movement (MOBRAL) was proclaimed on 8 September 1967 to coincide with International Literacy Day. Today MOBRAL is a familiar name to literacy workers throughout the world. Its renown is a result of both its impressive scale and its record of innovation in organization and pedagogy.

MOBRAL is another example of a literacy campaign brought into being under the aegis of public authorities. Law 5379 establishing MOBRAL and defining its mandate was signed by the President of the Republic, Artur de Costa e Silva, on 15 December 1967. MOBRAL's stated purpose is to promote literacy among illiterate adolescents and adults within the overall frame-work of continuing education. Its success in meeting this objective cannot be doubted. In an operation of continental scope, MOBRAL has succeeded in reaching almost all the adolescents and adults in its target population and in teaching many of them to read and write. For the first time in Brazil's history, there has been a considerable reduction in both the absolute number of illiterates and the overall literacy rates.

Contrary to so many other cases, MOBRAL was sustained and supported by material resources commensurate with the task involved. For example, in 1979, MOBRAL spent a total of US$66 million on its various programmes. MOBRAL has been directed by specialists who have put both pedagogy and technology to work in solving the various problems that have arisen.

Background and setting

With an area of 8.5 million square kilometres, Brazil is the fifth largest country in the world in area and the seventh most populous. Its ethnically diverse population was estimated to be 120 million in 1980 and was increasing at a rate of about 3 per cent per annum.

Like many other countries not directly involved, Brazil was greatly affected by the Second World War. Traditional economic patterns broke down or were severely strained. The need to reduce imports led to an industrialization effort that created demands for more and more skilled, and literate, labour.

While the 1950s were prosperous years for Brazil, a sharp decline in the early 1960s was followed by high inflation, widespread social tension and the Revolution of 1964. The new government, in which the military played a prominent role, promised an end to populism and to social and economic difficulties and offered security to foreign investors. The task of social and economic reconstruction was by no means easy. The new government had to deal with a country of great distances and inadequate infrastructures; and with sharp economic disparities between the prosperous south and east, and the poorer north and north-east.

The social divisions were reflected in, and reinforced by the educational system. During the period 1940-70, the literacy rate had risen from 46 to 67 per cent in the population aged 15 and over. The rate in 1970, however, was slightly lower than the average for twenty-six other countries in the same per capita income class. In absolute terms, 2.5 million more illiterates joined the population during the decade 1960 – 70. Literacy varied widely from region to region and between urban and rural areas in 1970. In the rural areas of the north-east region, literacy rates were extremely low, ranging from 19 to 27 per cent from one state to another. Literacy was highest in the urban areas of the south-eastern states, varying from 73 to 82 per cent.

The driving force

The driving force behind MOBRAL was clearly the revolution of 1964 that brought the army to power. The government's plan for prosperity involved building up the formal sector of the economy, for which professionalized labour was a basic necessity. The political task was to establish law and order, to protect the country from subversive forces and to channel the energies of the masses in the service of the country by appealing to patriotism, religious and moral duty, and obligations to the community. Both economic and political considerations indicated the need for a mass instrument of education and socialization. MOBRAL was to be that instrument.

Purposes and objectives

In explaining the birth of the Brazilian Literacy Movement, official commentaries note that the appropriate historical moment had arrived for the nation to rid itself of illiteracy, which in 1970 was calculated at 18.1 million illiterates, or 33.6 per cent of the population of 15 years and older. The time had come to improve the quality of life of most Brazilians, to invite them to participate in the task of national construction, to devote themselves to their own development.

A few preliminary remarks may help to put the purposes and objectives of MOBRAL into perspective. First, its objectives have changed during the last ten years of operation. Different aspects of social and economic realities at home and abroad caught the imagination of Brazil's leaders, giving rise to extensions of programmes and to various new emphases within programmes. Second, changes occurred in the language of justification and in the terms of the campaign's objectives. Finally, as regards programme implementation, MOBRAL has always been more comprehensive than any formal statement of its objectives might have suggested. In focusing on literacy, it did not abandon the leitmotif of lifelong education for adults; in focusing on the professionalization of labour, it did not neglect the wider social and cultural objectives.

At its inception in 1967, MOBRAL's objectives were stated in concrete terms of functional literacy training and, in particular, the lifelong education of adolescents and adults. By the early 1970s, when the economist Mario Henrique Simonsen was President of MOBRAL, the vocabulary of objectives had become strongly economic, and objectives were stated in terms of the professionalization of labour in the formal sector of the economy to improve productivity in the industrial sector.

Over the years, and especially since the mid-1970s, a variety of objectives have been added. The list now includes the personal development of learners; improved opportunities in the job market; the education of children; social mobility and social justice; development of the community through dialogue and critical awareness; political participation through voting; enjoyment of good health, of sports and leisure; consumer education; and valorization, fostering and preservation of the popular culture.

Mobilizing and organizing for action

Brazil's experience with literacy work did not start with MOBRAL. The tradition of voluntary literacy work dates from 1915 when the Brazilian Anti-illiteracy League was established. Sporadic interest continued through the National Crusade for Education (1932); the Campaign for the Education of Adolescents and Adults (1947); the National Rural Education Campaign (1952); the National Campaign for the Eradication of Illiteracy (1958); the Basic Education Movement (1961); the National Education Plan (1963); the Crusade for Basic Christian Education (1966); and various other movements dedicated to the promotion of popular culture.

MOBRAL was proclaimed on 8 September 1967. Three years later, on 8 September 1970, MOBRAL was reorganized and given a new mandate, and initiated its operational phase. Today it is the only national agency for mass education and literacy in the country.

Preparation for the campaign

While the organizational approaches, methodologies and materials of earlier literacy action were informally reviewed and analysed, there was no formal preparation for the launching of MOBRAL's 1970 operational phase. There were no new assessments. The leadership found the socio-political conditions in 1970 sufficient to justify such action. Not even technical vocabulary research was conducted since, it was claimed, the population spoke one language (Portuguese), one dialect, with only minor regional variations which, moreover, were being progressively reduced under the influence of the mass media.

Thus, MOBRAL has not used a 'research into action' model, but rather an 'action and correction' model. Action has not waited on research, but has used whatever research and experience was already available. This pragmatic approach should not, however, be construed as anti-research. Indeed, MOBRAL has built up a formidable feedback system to help in its management. In 1980 its Survey Research Section had a budget of US$86,000, not including salaries, to conduct anthropological, linguistic, pedagogical and statistical surveys, especially in the northern and north-eastern regions.

MOBRAL organization

MOBRAL has three basic organizational levels: Central MOBRAL, State/Territorial[1] MOBRAL and Municipal MOBRAL. Central MOBRAL is a foundation within the government and is supervised by its own Board of Trustees and Board of Administration. This is an innovative organizational arrangement which makes it possible for MOBRAL to use the institutional resources of the government, and of other private and public enterprises, without being inhibited in its policies, plans and actions. Central MOBRAL has recruited a highly qualified team of social scientists and other specialists who constitute the movement's 'brain-trust'. They are organized into fifteen or more 'managements', 'centres', and 'advisory groups'. The next level of MOBRAL organization consists of state and territorial co-ordination,

---

1. A territory does not have the full status of a principal division, since it has no political or administrative autonomy.

where different specialized 'agents' represent the various 'management', 'centres' and 'advisory groups' located in Central MOBRAL. The third level of organization, Municipal MOBRAL, is located in the office of the mayor of each municipality.

The first two levels are part of a management system that develops policy initiatives and programme plans and exerts overall control and supervision. Implementation is, however, handled at the third level by Municipal MOBRAL. The municipalities undertake to do literacy work and to conduct other related programmes under formal agreements with Central MOBRAL. Municipalities are able to practise some limited autonomy in adapting programmes to local conditions and have come to be the mainstay of the operations.

Implicit in the above administrative arrangement is the principle of dualistic administration, that is, centralized supervision and control and decentralized implementation—also used, with considerable effect, in the People's Republic of China.

In the initial stages, Central MOBRAL undertook mobilization along two lines: general mobilization of the masses and administrative and technical mobilization within MOBRAL's institutional system. In general mobilization, MOBRAL used the typical strategies of information dissemination to inform the people and arouse their enthusiasm, using posters, newspapers, press conferences, press releases, radio and television. Effective slogans were devised: *You too are responsible*—addressed to the general public; *You are a leader*—addressed to members of the municipal committees; *Your name is action*—addressed to the group leaders in the communities; and *You are important*—addressed to the adult learners participating in the programmes.

In the national political arena, MOBRAL claims to have remained equidistant from the different political parties; and in order to build an image of effectiveness, it has used the strategy of promising conservatively and always delivering more than promised.

Internal mobilization

As the operational phase began in September 1970, it was necessary to invent and validate a national vision for MOBRAL. Meetings were convened, bringing together the Secretariat General of the Ministry of Education and Culture, the secretariats of education, regional superintendencies and other related ministries and secretariats, deans of universities, entrepreneurs, presidents of confederations, federations and unions to study and discuss MOBRAL's priorities and programmes in the immediate future. In a subsequent series of meetings and seminars, the purposes of MOBRAL were explained to state and territorial governors, mayors of municipalities and their council members.

As regards technical mobilization and technical system development, MOBRAL's work has been exemplary. Two mechanisms have been used with considerable effect to create a technical system that has common objectives, shared skills and resources, a functional division of labour and a suitable arrangement for information and feedback. These mechanisms are: (a) a system of manpower training and (b) an overall supervisory system.

The manpower training system
MOBRAL has trained almost all the personnel engaged in the implementation of its programmes: the pedagogical and technical agents in the state and territorial co-ordinations, and all the key personnel active at the municipal level. While the 'multiplier model' (professionals trained at one level train those at the next level and so on) has been used wherever possible, control over training content and training methodology has been retained through materials supplied by central MOBRAL. Thus the total MOBRAL system has come to share both the central MOBRAL's objectives and its basic technology.

The overall supervisory system
The overall supervisory system is directly under the Executive Secretary of MOBRAL at the centre and under an Assistant Co-ordinator at the state and territorial level. Each state and territory has supervisors, assisted in turn by, on average, nine area supervisors. Area supervisors each work in four to five municipalities, and each of these may have a municipal supervisor or an officer in charge of overall supervision. There are at present some 141 mobile state or territory supervisors, 869 mobile area supervisors, and a person in charge of supervision in each of the 4,000 municipalities—some 5,000 supervisors constituting the total supervisory system.

Supervisors are the eyes and ears of the Central MOBRAL, its agents of training and capacitation, the links in its logistical system for delivery of messages and materials. The overall supervisory system is the mechanism which creates both administrative and technical interfaces between and among the three levels of organization.

Collaborations with business

Yet another feature of MOBRAL is its collaborative arrangements with public and private business and non-profit organizations. Its collaboration, especially with publishers to produce, print and distribute teaching materials to Municipal MOBRAL, has been very successful. Four different publishing houses have printed and sold teaching materials to MOBRAL for cost-free distribution among individual learners. These business houses have priced their materials at a very low level. While leaving implementation to private publishers, MOBRAL is still able to keep control over the choice of content and the overall methodological conception through pre-publication review and by providing publishers with information to be reflected in subsequent editions.

Coverage, conception and incentives

MOBRAL's first step in the operational phase that began in 1970 was, comparatively speaking, a cautious one. Under the Concerted Action Programme (PAC), at that time being run by the Ministry of the Interior, an invitation was extended to the mayors of 500 municipalities to attend meetings in the respective capitals of the Federative Units. These PAC municipalities represented 11 per cent of the total number of municipalities in Brazil, but 75 per cent of the total Brazilian population. During the meetings, the mayors were supplied with information on MOBRAL's programmes and invited to establish municipal committees and to undertake surveys of illiterates in their areas so as to be able to administer MOBRAL literacy and continuing education programmes. By the time the agreements were signed, 611 municipalities were involved, covering more than half a million eligible students in MOBRAL's literacy groups.

The only material incentive the central authorities offered to the municipalities was the contract to provide funds for the local employment of literacy instructors, training for the personnel required, and teaching and learning materials for cost-free distribution among teachers and adult learners. But these incentives were also invitations to the municipalities to allocate their own resources, which sometimes added up to as much as 40–50 per cent of what was received from MOBRAL.

Table 7 gives MOBRAL's figures for the coverage of its literacy work over the years 1970-79. The last column represents the absolute number of illiterates still left in the population concerned.

MOBRAL: a comprehensive programme

MOBRAL is not merely an adult literacy programme or a functional literacy programme. It is much more comprehensive and can best be viewed as a battery of mutually reinforcing programmes of literacy and continuing education.

The functional literacy programme has already been described. In addition, there is an *Integrated Education Programme* that prepares learners for entry to the fifth grade of the formal school system. Some 720 hours of instruction are offered over periods of twelve or twenty-four months, depending on the learners' circumstances. Some 4 million students are said to have been reached between 1971 and 1978.

MOBRAL's *Self-Education Programme*, as its name suggests, provides opportunities to adult learners to pursue the Integrated Education Programme independently and individually. MOBRAL's cultural posts (described below) act as operational units for this programme. Individual participants are supplied with materials that have been specifically elaborated for the programme, four guidebooks making up the mathematical component. Additional reference material is made available at the cultural post.

Vocational Programmes of varied content and scope began operation as early as 1973, and since 1974 another programme, called 'Occupational Families', has been training students in a set of core skills applicable within a family of vocational and occupational skills. Most of these programmes are offered in co-operation with business and industry. When provided independently, placement services are offered and graduates are assisted in finding employment.

During 1971-73, MOBRAL offered *Community Development Courses* of two months' duration and sought to create *'mutiroes'*, self-help groups, to undertake development work within their own communities. In 1975, interest in community development reappeared under the *Diversified Community Action Programme* which seeks to generate local initiatives to meet local needs according to local approaches, with MOBRAL serving as a resource agent. Volunteer groups are encouraged and assisted in preparing diagnoses of problems in their communities, developing plans and taking the necessary action, with or without the help of public and private agencies. This programme is seen by MOBRAL as an operational synthesis of all its other programmes. During 1976-78, some 132 municipalities were reached and some 5,200 persons took part in community programmes.

A *Programme for Community Education for Health* was started in 1976. It is an important operation for a country where 60 per cent of all deaths of children under 5 are related to malnutrition and lack of health knowledge. The programme focuses on hygiene and nutrition and reached as many as 541,700 people during 1976-77. An important feature of the programme is that it aims not only to provide health information and services but to create an infrastructure of health services in the community itself.

Cultural MOBRAL has come to be an important programme component of 'Continuing Education MOBRAL'. Started in 1973, its operations cover radio, cinema, literature, theatre, arts, handicrafts and the plastic arts. In 1978 alone, some 750 new cultural posts were established bringing the total in the country to 3,150.

The *Sports for All* programme started in 1977 and claims to have involved 5.5 million participants in local and national events. The

TABLE 7. Results of the functional literacy programme

Year	Goal	Enrolment	Percentage of goal attained	Number of students made literate	Percentage of enrolment made literate	National illiteracy rate (%)	Number of illiterates
1970	–	507,567	–	172,089	33.9	33.6	18,146,977
1971	–	2,590,061	–	1,081,320	41.8	30.7	17,096,452
1972	4,214,540	4,234,871	100	2,042,683	48.2	26.6	15,262,227
1973	5,015,000	4,931,100	98	1,784,394	36.2	25.5	15,064,583
1974	5,098,000	4,738,131	93	1,923,922	40.6	21.9	13,318,120
1975	4,449,000	4,373,859	98	1,656,502	37.9	18.9	11,850,226
1976	4,634,387	3,923,365	85	1,415,687	36.0	16.4	10,643,730
1977	4,782,500	3,893,388	81	1,203,268	30.9	14.3	9,546,899
1978	4,439,650	3,932,726	89	1,262,405	32.1	12.3	8,371,244
1979[1]	4,351,350	3,000,000	70	900,000	30.0	11.1	7,700,000

1. Estimated.

Programme of Technology of Scarcity started in 1978 is an example of how MOBRAL responds to national educational needs as they arise. Under this programme, the technical culture of the Brazilian people is analysed and information is disseminated for use by others.

To sum up, MOBRAL's activities are truly comprehensive, but literacy—the teaching of reading and writing—remains the core of its work.

Sources of funding

In addition to government funding, MOBRAL receives 6.75 per cent of the gross income of the Sports Lottery, while companies are authorized to deduct up to 2 per cent of their taxable income as a voluntary contribution to MOBRAL.

In 1979, MOBRAL's total budget was US$66 million, of which 73.32 per cent was used for literacy work, 10.17 per cent for lifelong education programmes, and 16.51 per cent for administration and other activities. To provide a perspective, it may be noted that in 1979 MOBRAL's budget was 4.5 per cent of the total budget of the Ministry of Education and Culture, and that outlays on the first eight grades of basic education were twenty-five times MOBRAL's annual budget.

The pedagogical aspects of the Brazilian literacy movement

It is important to remember that while some of the methodological approaches and orientations of MOBRAL in the teaching of literacy have remained basically unaltered, others have changed in the process of trial and error over the last ten years.

The general approach

The general approach, as it has now emerged, is based on certain assumptions: adults can be and should be responsible for their own learning; individual development and community development should not be divorced from each other—the community should be the starting point in learning to read and the knowledge obtained by the individual should be applied back to the community; communal and cultural identities should be saved and protected and yet enriched by new technology; learning should not be confined to labour skills but should be humanistic and cultural; and, finally, there should be flexibility in delivery.

Objectives of the functional literacy programme

The objectives of the functional literacy programme are a combination of individual and community development. As regards the former, the objectives are to develop reading, writing and counting skills; to teach a vocabulary leading to mental enrichment; to inculcate reasoning power and positive attitudes towards work; and to teach the creative use of resources already available to the individual. As regards community development, the objectives are to acquaint students with their rights and duties; to enable them to make contributions to family and community health and the preservation of community assets and institutions; and to support general public welfare.

The teaching methodology

MOBRAL did not commit itself to any specific teaching method in its initial stages. All known methods were tried to determine which would best serve a particular population or region. To produce didactic materials appropriate to its own methodology, MOBRAL adopted a relatively novel approach. A number of publishing houses were invited to submit materials elaborated according to MOBRAL's established criteria. Materials submitted by publishers were tried out in the first courses given by MOBRAL before more extensive utilization. Thus, a whole programme of experimental work was begun and is still continuing.

The teaching of reading is currently based on (a) the generative poster (these posters are related to 'basic needs' and life experience of the individual and cover such topics as health, clothing, housing and work); (b) study of generative words derived from the poster (words such as school, vaccine, kitchen, brick, radio, soccer, machine, hospital, shoe, faith, love); (c) syllabic breakdown of the generative word; (d) study of related syllabic families; (e) formation and study of new words; (f) formation and study of new phrases and texts. It will be observed that the *technical* structure of this methodology is the same as that associated with Paulo Freire. The examples of life experiences chosen for the generative posters and generative words, however, set the two methods apart.

The methodology is now standardized, and standardization of the curriculum and teaching method is reinforced by the concept of the teaching kit. This includes *Guidelines for Orientation of the Literacy Teacher*, instructors' guides on the use of the basic kits sold by various publishing houses, generative posters, drill cards, and a reader for adult learners. Also included in the kit are a language exercise book, an arithmetic exercise book, follow-up books and a newspaper.

Modalities in the delivery of teaching vary widely. Typical literacy classes consist of twenty to thirty adults taught by one instructor; but other means include group or individual viewing of television and listening to radio programmes that teach literacy; literacy as an element in work and literacy-cum-cultural groups; and also a 'readers-create-readers' campaign. Courses usually last five months, meeting for two hours five days a week, giving a total of 200–240 hours of classroom instruction. Televised literacy programmes offer sixty transmissions of twenty minutes each, supplemented by 200–240 hours of self-instruction or assistance from a monitor. In addition, there are now special courses for particular vocational groups such as fishermen, rubber-latex gatherers and employees in the petroleum and lumber sectors.

More recently, literacy work has been conducted in two phases within the five-month period. The first phase is dedicated to teaching of reading and writing—skills of codification and decodification—and in a second phase functional materials are introduced.

Meeting local needs through diversification

MOBRAL has used one curriculum, one type of primer, one standardized kit of materials for teaching literacy all over Brazil, yet it has claimed to be flexible in meeting the diversified needs of communities all over the country. The contention is that the literacy instructor acts as the diversifier. In discussion of the themes in the generative poster, the teacher is encouraged to include local concerns and the local idiom and thus relate to the diverse and unique concerns of different communities. Scepticism creeps in, however, when we realize that the instructors who are supposed to diversify standardized curriculum through local adaptation and extension have often no more than four or five years of education and rather short initial training. Continuous on-the-job training and systematic supervision are said to cover for these deficiencies.

What is meant by literacy

To be declared literate, an adult should be able (a) to identify the content of the texts and sentences he reads; (b) to write sentences and phrases that make good sense; (c) to solve problems involving the four mathematical operations with one or two figures, with or without grouping; and (d) to solve problems involving measurements of length, calculation of perimeters, measurements of weight, volume, and time using whole numbers and fractions.

There is, however, no formal test of literacy. The teacher has complete autonomy to decide whether or not a student is literate. His evaluation is carried out during the process of literacy teaching itself.

Unit costs

MOBRAL's unit costs in making a student literate have been as follows: 1973: US$10.78; 1975: US$14.48; 1977: US$13.19; and 1978: US$22.62. (Unit costs on the basis of the number of students enrolled are about one-third of these figures.)

The rise in costs is explained in terms of more difficult (unmotivated) students and more distant (widely spread) communities which have now to be served in the north and north-east regions.

Motivations and incentives to learners

Official accounts of MOBRAL programmes assume motivated learners. People seem to understand the usefulness of literacy and to want it. In addition to the typical incentives provided by the programme, such as cost-free teaching materials, MOBRAL has, wherever possible, made use of other resources to stimulate learners: spectacles for those suffering from poor eyesight, school lunches, and wrist watches, alarm clocks, radios, bicycles, footwear and shirts for those who excel.

MOBRAL follow-up materials and integration across sectors

We have already noted the comprehensive nature of MOBRAL's overall programmes and seen how literacy has been integrated with home, work, health and culture. One of MOBRAL's follow-up programmes, enables adolescents and adults to enter the formal basic education system.

In terms of a traditional follow-up strategy, that is, in producing follow-up reading materials for new readers, MOBRAL has once again done impressive work. MOBRAL has used existing institutional structures such as the National Book Institute to promote and produce reading materials. Book contests and awards have been announced to generate general public enthusiasm and to discover creative talent. Popular novels have been adapted for new literates. The Bible has been issued in illustrated strip form and has, understandably, become one of the most popular works in a country where 80 to 85 per cent of the people are Catholic.

An oral literature project has valorized folk literature and launched new writers and poets on the literacy scene. Cultural MOBRAL has introduced new literates to non-print media and their educational and entertainment potential.

According to a study conducted by the University of Brasilia in 1977, MOBRAL can fairly claim that the rate of relapse into illiteracy among its graduates is low.

Distribution of reading materials

MOBRAL has an effective communication and logistical network, supported by computers and a telex system. While it has some warehouses to store materials and books, the transportation and distribution of reading materials is contracted out to private agencies. In 1977, MOBRAL and its agents distributed 1,755 metric tons of didactic materials constituting 3.5 million basic functional literacy training kits and integrated education sets, plus 2,100,000 copies of books for follow-up reading, in the two programmes being conducted in 3,755 municipalities.

Recruitment and training of literacy teachers

Teachers are chosen from the communities where classes are to be taught. They are semi-volunteers, receiving only a small gratuity for their work. Perhaps for this reason, 75 per cent of them are women. Most of the field-level supervisors are also women, usually selected from among successful teachers. As one would expect with a largely volunteer teaching force, the turnover rate is high (30.6 per cent) and qualifications relatively low (five years of schooling on average).

Because of the virtual absence of trained adult education personnel in Brazil in 1970 and shortages throughout the last decade, MOBRAL has had to develop its own training system at all levels from Central MOBRAL through the state and territorial co-ordinations to the municipal committees and literacy instructors in the communities.

In 1972, at the time of a large-scale expansion of the programme, MOBRAL trained 100,000 literacy instructors by radio under an agreement with the educational broadcasting service of the Ministry of Education and Culture. This so-called Minerva Project produced twelve broadcasts, ten of thirty minutes each and two of sixty minutes each, which were supplemented by appropriate training materials and teacher manuals. MOBRAL organized the teacher groups in the field. The project trained 90,500 teachers.

Content and duration of teacher training

Basic training of literacy instructors involves twenty-four hours of class time. The following topics are covered: literacy training of adults within the context of lifelong education; the characteristics of adolescent and adult students; the student-teacher relationship; the principle of acceleration and functionality underlying the methodology of the programme; the methodology of the functional literacy programme (the role of the generative posters, generative words, techniques of group activity, use of didactic materials); general subject matter required for development of the methodology, such as nutrition, work, communication, culture, hygiene, health, transportation; knowledge of other MOBRAL programmes; and evaluation of students and self-evaluation of teachers.

These twenty-four hours of instruction are supplemented by visits to classes by the supervisory staff and interviews with the teacher, orientation sessions with supervisors, the provision of didactic material written for teachers (such as the *Guidelines for Orientation of Literacy Instructor*), and a self-instructional programme for teachers. The opportunity to be trained, and thus to achieve personal growth, may be an important incentive for teachers who otherwise get no more than US$20 a month for their work with adults.

Area supervisors
Area supervisors receive forty hours of formal training and one month of in-service training under the guidance of an experienced supervisor. Monthly meetings, which last four days, are also used for training and orientation purposes. Area supervisors are supposed to supervise all MOBRAL programmes, and not merely the functional literacy programme.

Monitoring and evaluation of the campaign

MOBRAL has had a computerized data system since 1973, and this was expanded and further consolidated in 1978 into a fully-fledged management information system. The overall supervisory system already referred to monitors the total programme by anticipating, identifying and solving problems as they arise.

Besides having conducted a large number of internal evaluation studies, MOBRAL has encouraged outside evaluations and financed research projects for masters' degree theses whose results could be of interest to the organization. The great majority of these documents have been published and are readily available. External critical evaluations reveal some serious problems, such as: unsatisfactory training of instructors lasting only a few days; rigid structure of the literacy course with no regional adjustments; and failure, in many cases, in follow-up educational or cultural actions after the initial basic literacy course.

Effects of the movement

The Brazilian effort in the field of literacy during 1967-80, and its possibilities in the future, must be seen in the overall perspective of Brazil's political economy to be fully understood and properly evaluated.

Nicolas Ardito-Barletta, Vice-President of the World Bank Latin American and Caribbean Regional Office, wrote:

During the postwar years the economy of Brazil has grown more than twice as fast as the population. Although there has definitely been some 'trickle-down' of benefits to the poor in the areas studied in this report, the growth process has been very uneven: among sectors of the economy, among regions and urban-rural locations, and certainly among households. As a result, large differences in economic welfare among population groups persist. . . .

Rapid economic growth will be necessary to provide productive employment for the growing labor force and to meet the basic needs of the population. But growth in the modern sector alone is unlikely to absorb the bulk of the working-age population before the end of this century; it will take even longer for that sector to absorb the current and prospective supply of low-skilled workers. Therefore policies to increase productivity in the rest of the economy will be crucial in achieving more equitable socio-economic development.

Meeting the basic needs . . . of the entire Brazilian population by the end of the century is not, at its root, a major economic or financial problem. The problem lies rather with numerous administrative obstacles. Policies aimed at increasing provision of 'basic' services will therefore not only require increased financial backing on the part of the public sector but, what is perhaps more difficult, considerable efforts to overcome institutional problems.[1]

It is almost impossible to prepare an exact accounting of the socio-political and economic effect of MOBRAL. Because of its scale and importance among literacy movements in Latin America, MOBRAL has provoked a good deal of spirited discussion and debate. As earlier literacy efforts in Brazil were usually organized by non-governmental groups, and sometimes by groups in opposition to the government, it has been charged that MOBRAL was an attempt at depoliticization of popular education and those who participate in it. MOBRAL strenuously rejects this assertion and notes that its programmes have, in fact, generated increased pressures by participants for improved government services, especially in education and health. The fact that MOBRAL enjoys the support of all municipalities, regardless of the party affiliation of the mayor, is cited by the organization as proof that its programmes serve the nation and not any particular faction or interest. If MOBRAL's activities do not fully satisfy those who seek radical reform, they appear to have strengthened community awareness and collective action and to have created a demand for wider and more effective political participation. The

1. Preface to *Brazil: Human Resources Special Report*, Washington D.C., World Bank, 1979.

economic effects of MOBRAL have been important in promoting the upward mobility of some workers and have contributed to the national pool of skills.

MOBRAL has given a good deal of attention to measuring the quantitative dimensions of its work. As in other literacy campaigns, critics have not always been convinced of the validity of official statistics. Measured progress in literacy evidently depends upon the definitions used and the consistency with which they are applied. There are, no doubt, some conceptual and statistical problems in making reliable quantitative assessments of MOBRAL's work: there are, for example, significant regional disparities which may indicate either uneven success or differing standards of measurement, the enrolment figures may sometimes involve double counting and the use of self-reporting in enumerating literacy may inflate the figures. Yet, even when allowance is made for all such factors, MOBRAL's success remains undeniable.

Lessons from the Brazilian experience

The following lessons can be drawn from MOBRAL's experience with its mass literacy campaign:
1. A mass literacy campaign conducted at a national level has to have a national purpose.
2. For a national-level enterprise that might cover as much as 50 or 60 per cent of the nation's population and a tremendous proportion of the nation's institutional and material resources, the interest and support of the highest authorities is essential.
3. Literacy may be conceptualized in the context of an overall lifelong programme; however, the core objective of teaching reading and writing cannot be diluted or dissipated. As adults become literate, they should have opportunities for horizontal and vertical integration within the educational, economic, social and political systems.
4. Functionality in a literacy programme should not become an orthodoxy. In the first phase of a literacy programme it may be best to emphasize the teaching of reading and writing. Of course, the generative words chosen to teach reading may still reflect the readers' life experience but they may be only 'generally' functional and need not try to teach substantive economic or technical skills. Substantive functional content of a technical nature may be better taught in a second phase of teaching literacy.
5. The organizational aspects of a national literacy campaign should always be given paramount importance. A national movement must create a national vision and must sustain a national thrust. But a centralized bureaucracy cannot be at all places at all times to respond to local conditions and to take needed initiatives.

Therefore, the organization must include a centralized vision and direction but a decentralized implementation system.

6. It is not necessary for a literacy campaign organization to do everything on its own and under its own roof. Collaboration can be established with academic and public organizations and institutions while direction and control of overall purposes and objectives are retained.

7. In this age of technology, literacy campaigns should learn to put technology to work: to deliver teaching and training through radio, television, tape recordings; to develop management information systems; and to develop training, supervision and logistical systems.

8. Literacy campaigns need not be left to literacy workers alone. While this is not a suggestion to literacy workers to surrender control of literacy to the non-educator, it is recommended that the concept of multi-disciplinary teams of economists, sociologists, engineers, doctors, educators and literacy workers to implement mass adult literacy campaigns should be utilized.

BIBLIOGRAPHY

BOOTH, JOHN A. Political Participation in Latin America: Levels, Structure, Context, Concentration and Rationality. *Latin American Research Review*, Vol. 14, No. 3, 1979.

CAIRNS, JOHN. The Brazilian Literacy Movement—A First-hand Appraisal. *Convergence*, Vol. 8, No. 2, 1975, pp. 12-23.

CORREA, ARLINDO LOPES. *Educação de Massa e Acção Comunitária*. Rio de Janeiro, AGGS, MOBRAL, 1979.

DYE, DAVID R.; SAURA E SILVA, CARLOS EDUARDO DE. A Perspective on the Brazilian State. *Latin American Research Review*, Vol. 14, No. 3, 1979.

Literacy Campaigns in the Twentieth Century: Brazil. Report written for the Unesco/ICAE study of literacy campaigns of the twentieth century, 1980.

MINISTÉRIO DO EDUCAÇÃO E CULTURA, FUNDAÇÃO MOVIMENTO BRASILEIRO DE ALFABETIZAÇÃO. *The MOBRAL System*. Rio de Janeiro, 1973.

——. *Permanent Education and Adult Education in Brazil*. Rio de Janeiro, 1973.

UNESCO. *MOBRAL—The Brazilian Adult Literacy Experiment*. Paris, Unesco, 1975.

WORLD BANK. *Brazil—Human Resources Special Report*. Washington, D.C., World Bank, 1979.

CHAPTER 10

The Tanzanian mass literacy campaign, 1971-81

The nationwide mass literacy campaign of the United Republic of Tanzania was launched in September 1971. When Julius K. Nyerere emerged as leader of the newly independent nation, he already had a coherent vision for his country, a clear-cut developmental ideology, and the will to implement his vision with the participation of the people.

To fulfil the aspirations of the nation, its people had to be educated. The population had to learn the skills required for economic production and political participation. This meant not only elementary-school education for children but also education for adults. Some three years after Independence, when introducing the First Five-Year Development Plan (1964-69), President Nyerere emphasized:

First we must educate adults. Our children will not have an impact on our economic development for five, ten, or even twenty years. The attitudes of the adults . . . on the other hand, have an impact now. The people must understand the plans for development of this country; they must be able to participate in changes which are necessary. Only if they are willing and able to do this will this plan succeed.

The political and developmental agenda of the United Republic of Tanzania found formal expression in the Arusha Declaration of 1967 which stressed the achievement of socialism through self-reliance, and the role of adult education in the life of the nation became even more crucial. At about the same time, the United Republic of Tanzania agreed to participate in the United Nations Development Programme (UNDP)/Unesco Work-Oriented Adult Literacy Pilot Project (1968-72) in the Lake Regions of the country. But while literacy was important, it was not yet seen as central to the processes of socio-economic and political development. The educational needs of the people were placed in the general category of adult education; literacy was to be offered to the people when they were ready, and when they demanded it themselves.

The year 1971 saw a change in this approach. Literacy came to occupy the centre of the stage. In his New Year address in 1970, the President called literacy 'the key to further progress' and added that illiterates 'will never be able to play their full part in the development of our country'. The ruling party then adopted a resolution urging that all the 5,200,000 illiterates above the age of 10 be made literate before the end of 1975, and that a functional literacy approach be used in the campaign.

By the end of 1975, over 5 million people had enrolled in classes. The nationwide literacy tests conducted in August 1975 indicated that the illiteracy rate of 67 per cent in 1967 had dropped to 39 per cent. A second nationwide assessment in August 1977 showed that the illiteracy rate had dropped to 27 per cent, and a further assessment in August 1981 showed that the rate had been lowered to 21 per cent among the target age group.

The Tanzanian mass literacy campaign is impressive not only in numerical terms, but also in terms of significant programmatic and structural innovations. It provides an excellent example of how the special economic and occupational interests of learner groups can be accommodated within a mass campaign, thus integrating the mass and the selective approaches to literacy. It established an administrative system that achieved integration of the party, government and educational structures, both horizontally and vertically. While retaining a centralized direction, the campaign was able to decentralize instructional materials production and the training function through the establishment of regional writers' workshops and trainer teams. The campaign was able to establish a wide array of supporting instructional services—radio broadcasts, correspondence courses, rural newspapers, rural libraries, etc.—and later to institutionalize a very elaborate network of post-literacy programmes and organizations.

Historical background and setting

With an area of 945,000 square kilometres, the United Republic of Tanzania is the largest of the three East African countries. It is bordered by Zaire and Burundi in the west; by Kenya and Uganda in the north; by Zambia, Malawi and Mozambique in the south and by the Indian Ocean in the east. At the time of Independence in 1961, the population of Tanganyika was estimated to be about 9 million, 75 per cent of whom were illiterate. The 1967 census reported a population of 12.3 million and that of 1978 17.6 million, representing an annual growth rate of 3.3 per cent.

Some 90 per cent of the population still live in the rural areas, mostly engaged in subsistence agriculture. Cash crops include cotton, coffee, sisal, tobacco, cashew nuts, sugar, pyrethrum, oil seeds, maize and wheat. It is predominantly an agricultural country, agriculture constituting 38 per cent of GNP and 80 per cent of foreign exchange earnings. Industry contributes a mere 8–10 per cent of GNP. The annual per capita income of Tanzanians remains one of the lowest in the world at 1,360 Tanzanian shillings, or approximately US$170.

The country was colonized at the turn of the nineteenth century. In 1884, the Germans occupied the country and remained until 1919. From 1920 to 1961, the British ruled, first with a mandate from the League of Nations and then under a United Nations trusteeship. Tanganyika achieved its independence on 9 December 1961 and became a republic in 1962. In 1964, it entered a political union with Zanzibar and Pemba to form the United Republic of Tanzania.

The Tanzanian leadership inherited an economically poor country. The minimal communication infrastructures merely served the colonial government or the foreign-owned 'estate economy'. The school system was also inadequate and was designed solely to serve the manpower needs of the colonial administration.

The United Republic of Tanzania's real wealth was its people. There was a balance in its various ethnic groups and it possessed a language that could be developed as a national language in so far as Kiswahili was understood to a greater or lesser degree by as many as 95 per cent of the population. There were 126 ethnic groups in the nation but none was large enough to acquire a dominant position.

Driving forces behind the Tanzanian literacy campaign

The Tanzanian literacy campaign was not conceived in the aftermath of a revolution or any spectacular political event. It came about as the natural culmination of a decade of political developments and was woven into the very logic of the country's political ideology and developmental stance.

The developmental ideology of the United Republic of Tanzania found clear expression in the Arusha Declaration of 1967 adopted by the Tanganyika African National Union (TANU)—which in February 1977 merged with the Afro-Shirazi Party of Zanzibar to form the new party Chama Cha Mapinduzi (CCM)—as the blueprint for the nation's political and economic future. This Declaration, the most important political document produced since Independence, specified that the nation was to work for socialism and self-reliance, in other words eliminating dependency on foreigners; nationalizing key elements of the economy which were wholly in the hands of expatriates and foreign interests; defining development as 'rural development' by focusing on agriculture and giving priority to the provision of services to the rural masses; expanding labour-intensive manufacturing and industry; and decentralizing power so as to make participation by the people both possible and meaningful. Self-reliance was to be pursued at all levels: national, communal and individual. At the national level, it meant creating a non-dependent political economy; at community level, it meant creating self-governing village communities—the spirit of Ujamaa; and at the individual level, it meant education for both economic production and political participation.

The five-year development plans (1964-69 and 1969-74) were designed as instruments for bringing about socialism and self-reliance. The importance of education in the implementation of the plans and the actualization of the political programme embodied in the Arusha Declaration was self-evident. Development needed education; education was development.

Development strategy came to be educational strategy, centred on the education of adults. Inevitably, literacy came to be the core of the overall adult education and political programme. The statements that follow indicate the intellectual and political context of the 1971 campaign.

In a paper published on 16 October 1968, entitled 'Freedom and Development', President Nyerere commented that:

People cannot be developed; they can only develop themselves. . . . [Man] develops himself by what he does; he develops himself by making his own decisions, by increasing his understanding of what he is doing, and why; by increasing his own knowledge and ability, and by his own full participation— as an equal—in the life of the community he lives in.

The Second Five-Year Development Plan (1969-74), which followed on the Arusha Declaration, was directly aimed at the implementation of socialism and self-reliance and hence mass education which would enable people to become conscious and willing agents of transformation. In a New Year speech on 31 December 1969, the President said:

Although there has been a lot of talk about education for adults and quite a lot of people have been working in this field, we had not yet really organized ourselves for a major attack on ignorance. The Central Committee of TANU has decided that we must do this in 1970. The coming twelve months must be 'Adult Education Year' and we must give this work a very high priority.

The objectives he listed for Adult Education Year were the following:

In many cases the first objective of adult education must be to shake ourselves out of a resignation to the kind of life Tanzanian people have lived for many centuries past. We must become aware of the things that we, as members of our human race, can do for ourselves and for our country.

The second objective of adult education is to teach us how to improve our lives. We have to learn how to produce more on our farms and in our factories and offices. We have to learn about better foods, what a balanced diet is and how it can be obtained by our own efforts.

The third objective of adult education must be to have everyone understand our national policies of socialism and self-reliance.

The Second Five-Year Development Plan then being drafted emphasized adult education for rural development. Adult education was to cover elementary agricultural techniques and crafts, health, housecraft, simple economics and accounting, and politics and citizenship. Literacy was to be included 'in response to popular demand, as people become aware of its functional importance'. The Adult Education Year taught the lesson that literacy was 'the key to further progress' and that illiterates 'will never be able to play their full part in the development of (their) country'. Literacy thus became central to the development of the country.

On 31 December 1970, the President made a second appeal to the nation and directed that illiteracy be eradicated completely from six districts—Mafia, Ukerewe, Kilimanjaro, Pare, Dar es Salaam and Masasi—before the end of 1971. By September 1971, TANU had passed a resolution for the total eradication of illiteracy among all those above the age of 10, using the functional literacy approach.

Purposes and objectives of the campaign

As already noted, the Tanzanian mass literacy campaign was conceived in the context of the country's adult education policies, and indeed, within its overall development perspective. The objectives and purposes of the campaign did not have to be separately stated since they were inherent in the development approach itself. These objectives, to restate them briefly, were at the same time economic and technological, and in addition sought to bring about conscientization and communitarianism, a new political culture—in short, a new society.

Preparation for the mass campaign

There was no formally planned preparatory phase to the campaign, but the ground had been well prepared over a number of years. When the organizers announced the mass campaign in September 1971, the UNDP/Unesco Work Oriented Adult Literacy Pilot Project, 1968-72, was almost completed; a fairly well functioning system for mobilization, administration, extension and instruction was already in place; and the six-district mass literacy campaign had served as a 'pilot' to the nationwide campaign.

(a) UNDP/Unesco Work Oriented Adult Literacy Pilot Project (WOALPP)

The United Republic of Tanzania was one of eleven countries that collaborated with Unesco in implementing the concept of *functional literacy*—literacy directly linked to the economic functions of learners. The project started with pilot areas in the four Lake Regions—Mara, Mwanza, Shinyanga and West Lake—and first involved cotton farmers only, expanding later to cover larger areas and more diverse occupational groups. WOALPP (and the subsequent joint Tanzanian/UNDP/Unesco Functional Literacy Curriculum, Programmes and Materials Development Project) made some important contributions to literacy work in the United Republic of Tanzania and to the 1971 mass campaign.

1. It trained a whole cadre of specialists in literacy work—administrators, planners, trainers, evaluators, materials specialists, librarians, communicators—who later provided the much needed technical leadership in the mass campaign of 1971-80.
2. It made the concept of work-oriented functional literacy operational by producing and testing a variety of materials for specialized groups such as cotton farmers, banana growers, cattle raisers, fishermen, homemakers, etc. It was this work which later made it possible for the mass campaign to combine the mass and the selective approaches by using twelve different sets of primers, teacher guides and demonstration manuals to suit the diverse occupational interests of learners in different regions of the country.
3. It developed innovative methods, strategies, and structures to implement literacy programmes in the Tanzanian context, such as: writers' workshops to produce primers, follow-up reading materials and rural newspapers; training teams for the training of literacy teachers at the regional and district levels; organization for field-work and supervision; support programmes to assist in retention of literacy and to promote further learning; and tools and instruments for collection of data on the programme and for the evaluation of its impact on the lives of people.

(b) Roles and structures for the delivery of instruction

The mass literacy campaign of 1971 did not need to establish its own system of delivery. A comprehensive, nationwide system for adult education (and political education) was already in place. All that the organizers of the campaign had to do was to assign the existing system of adult education delivery a new educational task: to teach *literacy* to all learners over 10 years of age and to finish the task before the end of 1975.

During the first year of the Second Five-Year Plan, 1969, and especially during Adult Education Year, 1970, important steps had been taken to institutionalize the delivery of adult education in the United Republic of Tanzania. The first stage in this process was the careful and systematic integration of adult education with the existing structures of formal education. To begin with, all educational work, including adult literacy, became the responsibility of one ministry, the Ministry of National Education. A separate department of adult education was established within the Ministry with status equal to that of other departments dealing with various sectors of formal education. Adult education co-ordinators were appointed at all the various levels of administration from the region down through districts, divisions and wards to villages. More important, every elementary and secondary school became a centre of adult education classes and activities; the role of the teacher was redefined to include the teaching of adults in the community as well as children; and to enable teachers to do this, the curricula of colleges of national education were revised.

The structures of delivery of adult education (see Fig. 4) had been well integrated with the existing organization of party and government at various levels from the centre down to the party cell in the village. The interface with the party was particularly important since adult education was also to carry the burden of political education. Thus, horizontally, the system provided a frame for co-ordination and collaboration between the party, the executive and the education sector. Vertically, the system descended from the centre through regions, districts, divisions, wards and villages. Co-ordination committees were used as 'temporary systems' to enable the many diverse agencies and interests at various levels to act with one common purpose.

For mobility among field-workers in adult education, all ward co-ordinators were provided with bicycles; divisional co-ordinators were given motor cycles; and regional and district co-ordinators, who have to cover large areas, were provided with Land Rovers. Motor boats have been supplied to adult education officers in the Lake Regions.

Mobilization of the people. The party has been used as the main instrument of mobilization of learners and voluntary teachers. Both before and during the campaign, however, a variety of motivational and public relations approaches have been used. These have included the use of newspapers and radio broadcasts; songs and jazz bands; schools and the army; textiles printed with literacy themes and motifs;

	Political structure	Administrative structure	Adult education structure	Co-ordination committees structure
National	National party executive secretary	Prime Minister	Director of Adult Education in the Ministry of National Education	National Advisory Committee on Adult Education
Regional	Regional party executive secretary	Regional commissioner	Regional adult education co-ordinator (under the regional education officer)	Regional Adult Education Committee (Subcommittee of the Regional Development Committee)
District	District party executive secretary	Area commissioner	District adult education co-ordinator (under the district education officer)	District Adult Education Committee (Subcommittee of the District Development Committee)
Division	Divisional secretary	Divisional secretary	Divisional adult education co-ordinator	Divisional Adult Education Committee (Subcommittee of the Divisional Development Committee)
Ward	Ward executive secretary	Ward secretary	Ward adult education co-ordinator	Ward Adult Education Committee (Subcomittee of the Ward Development Committee)
Village	Village/urban/ workplace branch secretary	Village manager	Class/village adult education co-ordinator	Village Adult Education Committee (Sub-committee of the Village Development Committee)
	Ten cell leader(s)	Ten cell leader(s)		

FIG. 4. Structure for the delivery of the adult education programme.

special postage stamps; diaries and calendars; and competitions for literacy flags, sports, dances, demonstrations and exhibitions.

(c) The literacy campaign in six districts

The organizers of the nationwide mass literacy campaign were able to draw upon the experience of a campaign conducted in six diverse regions of the country in 1971, following the President's appeal to eradicate illiteracy within one year in these areas. This experience showed that the situation regarding the possible mobilization of voluntary teachers was highly favourable. In Pare district, well known for its co-operative social patterns, mobilization was of particular interest for the organizers. Finally, Dar es Salaam not only had a large number of literates (party cadres, union officials, civil servants) but also presented a literate environment and a whole network of institutions to provide continuing education. Table 8 shows the enrolment pattern for the 1971 campaign in these six districts.

TABLE 8. Enrolment in the 1971 campaign

District	Estimated number of illiterates	Numbers enrolled	Percentage enrolled
Mafia	8,545	8,549	100.0
Ukerewe	36,000	35,843	99.6
Kilimanjaro	46,510	45,466	97.0
Pare	24,121	24,121	100.0
Dar es Salaam	100,000	28,306	28.3
Masasi	51,973	45,364	89.0

A clear definition of what it meant to be literate had to wait until 1974 and the first nationwide literacy tests were administered in August 1975. It is not possible to determine how many of those enrolled in this campaign actually learned to read and write and at what level of competence. However, it cannot be denied that the Ministry of National Education gained valuable experience in organizing a literacy programme on a wider scale and under varied geographic and socio-economic conditions.

Conduct of the campaign

The Ministry of National Education in Dar es Salaam provided the central direction for the mass campaign. The Literacy Office in Mwanza which had implemented the two UNDP/Unesco functional literacy projects (1968-72 and 1972-76), provided the much needed technical assistance in training, instructional materials production, field organization and evaluation. The day-to-day implementation of the mass campaign, including the choice of classroom locations, recruitment and training of volunteer teachers, distribution of materials to learners, supervision of teaching, organization of practical demonstrations, and the establishment of co-ordination and advisory committees, was left to the regions, districts or divisions as appropriate.

Classes were conducted in all possible locations—schools, specially constructed centres, health centres, co-operatives, offices, factories, and in the open air. Typically, there were thirty learners in a class, and classes met three times a week for two hours a day.

When the campaign was launched in September 1971, the estimated number of illiterates aged 10 and above was 5,200,000. The enrolment figures available for the years 1970-81 are eloquent (see Table 9). In 1975, the first of the peak years, the composition of the teaching force was as follows: volunteers, 94,607; professional teachers, 14,917; students, 9,409; government workers, 6,777; party cadres, 3,477; workers of various religious affiliations, 946; and others, 3,752. This means a total teaching force of 133,885.

TABLE 9. Enrolments in literacy campaign, 1970-81

Year	Enrolments	Year	Enrolments
1970	261,369	1976	5,255,560
1971	908,351	1977	5,819,612
1972	1,508,204	1978	5,960,442
1973	2,989,910	1979	6,001,266
1974	3,303,103	1980	6,068,373
1975	5,184,982	1981	6,099,197

Three national tests were held in August 1975, August 1977 and August 1981, which differentiated between four different levels of literacy. (The levels of literacy and the testing procedures are described in the section on pedagogical aspects of the campaign.)

Participation in the August 1975 literacy test is shown in Table 10. The achievements, by level, of the 3.8 million men and women covered in the test were as follows: Levels III and IV, 1.4 million (37 per cent); Level II, 1.35 million (35 per cent); Level I and below, 1.05

TABLE 10. Numbers of illiterates and coverage of literacy test, August 1975

	Total illiterates	Registered	Underwent test
Male and female	5,860,473	5,184,982	3,806,468
Male	2,561,211	2,287,921	1,738,406
Female	3,299,216	2,897,061	2,068,062

million (28 per cent). This indicates a reduction in the illiteracy rate from 69 per cent (the figure in the 1967 census) to 30 per cent.

By September 1977, there were 140,829 more illiterate adults, bringing the estimated total of illiterates to 5,819,612. Those expected to take the test in August 1977 were estimated at 3,545,796. Actual participation, however, was as follows: 1,066,750 men, and 1,279,395 women, making a total of 2,346,154. The results of the test (see Table 11) show a reduction in the illiteracy rate from 30 per cent in August 1975 to 27 per cent in August 1977.

TABLE 11. Achievement, by level, in the August 1977 test

Level	Male	%	Female	%	Male and female
Below I	81,767	38	129,827	62	346,154
I	200,325	38	327,541	62	527,866
II	330,716	41	469,557	59	800,273
III	254,102	54	216,906	46	471,008
IV	199,849	60	135,564	40	335,413
TOTAL	1,066,759	45	1,279,395	55	2,346,154

By September 1981, there were a further 97,931 illiterates. Those expected to take the August 1981 tests were estimated at 3,524,442 (1,400,237 males and 2,124,205 females). As Table 12 shows, 3,107,506, some 88 per cent of those expected to take the test, actually did so. This represented a drop in the illiteracy rate from 27 per cent in August 1977 to 21 per cent in August 1981.

TABLE 12. Achievement, by level, in the August 1981 test

Level	Male	%	Female	%	Male and female
Below I	273,972	30	644,445	70	918,417
I	260,373	33	519,592	67	779,965
II	205,147	41	291,401	59	496,518
III	228,777	50	228,363	50	457,140
IV	262,563	58	192,873	42	455,436
TOTAL	1,230,832	40	1,876,674	60	3,107,506

In both the August 1975 and August 1977 tests, the number of those who actually took the tests was distinctly lower than expected. The reasons cited for not taking the tests were: sickness, heavy rains, farm work, distance from the test site, lack of materials at the test site, lack of understanding of the significance of the test, or shame at having to take tests. In the August 1981 test, participation was excellent, thanks to the interest shown by the President and the serious efforts of the party. Table 13 sums up the results of the literacy campaign.

TABLE 13. Illiteracy rates 1967-81

	Illiteracy rates (%)		
Year	Male	Female	Male and female
1967	54	80	67
1975	34	44	39
1977			27
1981			21

Costs and expenditure

It is noteworthy that throughout the campaign, government funds allocated to adult education represented no less than 10 per cent of the total allocations to the Ministry of National Education. The total cost of the programme to eradicate illiteracy has been estimated at 166.2 million Tanzanian shillings until the mid-1980s.

Pedagogical aspects of the campaign

Various pedagogical features of the Tanzanian campaign deserve special attention.

Multiple literacy primers

The United Republic of Tanzania was fortunate in having to use only one literacy language—Kiswahili. However, the campaign did not use a single primer for the whole nation. It was an unusual campaign in that it was able to offer functional literacy on a mass scale by using a mix of the mass approach to literacy and the selective approach. In other words, while it was a nationwide campaign, it offered different groups of learners a choice of curricula.

Thanks to the UNDP/Unesco projects which had first developed and tested many of the curriculum packages used in the campaign, twelve different primer sets were made available: cotton primer I and II, banana primer I and II, home economics primer I and II, fishing primer I and II, cattle primer I and II, tobacco primer I and II, maize primer I and II, rice primer I and II, cashew nuts primer I and II, coconut primer I and II, political education primer I and II, wheat primer I and II.

Each primer set was accompanied by a teacher's guide. Primers on home economics and on agricultural topics also had demonstration guides for making practical demonstrations. During 1972-75, some 25 million primers and 1.25 million teacher guides were produced and distributed.

The primers used an eclectic method of language teaching. They started with a simple sentence with a functional meaning, however elementary. The first sentence in the cotton primer, for instance, was: *Pamba ni mali* (Cotton is wealth). The home economics primer began with the phrase: *Mama na mtoto* (Mother and child) under a picture of a mother holding a child. The sentences or phrases were taught first; then the words; then the syllables, in as far as Kiswahili is a syllabic language. Syllables were then used to generate new words already in the vocabulary of the adult learners.

Writing and simple arithmetic were integrated into the teaching of reading from the earliest stages. Instructional materials were provided to learners free of charge. In some cases learners were fitted with spectacles.

Support programmes of instruction and extension

Another important feature of the Tanzanian campaign was the use of support programmes of instruction and extension, most of them already developed as part of the overall adult and political education programme or as part of the UNDP/Unesco project in the Lake Regions. These programmes and structures included: adult education centres to teach agriculture, crafts and home economics; educational radio programmes that started in the Lake Regions in January 1974 and, by the middle of the same year, were extended to the whole country; rural libraries; and rural newspapers.

Personnel training

Once again, the Tanzanian mass literacy campaign was able to use an already existing training system, with adequate capacity and excellent experience, for the training of the necessary personnel. The Institute of Adult Education (IAE) established in 1964 as an extension service of the University College, Dar es Salaam (now the University of Dar es Salaam) had been offering nine-month residential diploma courses in adult education (now of two years' duration). Over the years, the IAE had trained a large body of teachers and administrators, and some researchers in adult education who were well equipped to serve the literacy campaign. Its resident tutors, one in each region, gave the IAE a considerable coverage.

The University of Dar es Salaam offered a degree course in adult education, and training in the methodology of adult education was already part of the curriculum in all colleges of national education for the training of elementary school teachers.

The Tanzanian counterpart staff remaining from the UNDP/Unesco functional literacy projects, now employed by the National Literacy Centre, was a formidable resource which had already trained a large number of personnel. These included voluntary literacy teachers (6,658 trained in three-week courses); elementary school teachers (2,538 in one-week courses); civil servants (2,310 in one-week courses); students and instructors from national colleges of education (1,138); supervisors (556); writers (22); evaluators (54); rural librarians (18); and teacher trainers (129); as well as educational broadcasters, newspaper editors and others trained in courses that might be as short as one day or as long as several weeks. Most importantly, the National Literacy Centre in Mwanza trained regional and district teams for the purpose of decentralizing the training of literacy teachers. The permanent regional and district training teams represented an important strategic element in the mass campaign. Teams typically consisted of the regional adult education co-ordinator, the *ujamaa* and co-operative officer, an adult education tutor from the local college of national education, an agricultural officer, a secondary school teacher and national service leader, and the resident IAE tutor. The Tanzanian campaign did not have any serious problems in training teachers to go out in the villages and turn the whole country into one big classroom.

Four levels of literacy

While functional content was an important component of the total curriculum, the definition of literacy within the campaign context was based essentially on the ability to read, write and calculate. Four levels of literacy were singled out (I, II, III and IV), followed by three stages of post-literacy (V, VI, and VII). The idea of four levels of literacy was an excellent one in as far as it helped learners to think of literacy skills as a continuum. The four-level definition combined feedback on learners' achievement with a feeling of success. Those who qualified only for Level I could still experience success even though they knew that they had a long way to go to become functionally literate. (Those who passed Level IV were called literacy graduates, and to achieve functional literacy, Stages V, VI and VII had to be completed.)

Campaign documents define the four levels as follows:

Level I. Participants who have enrolled and attended at least two-thirds of the literacy sessions during any one year of the campaign.

Level II. Participants who are qualified for Level I but who have also successfully passed one or both tests for the following sub-levels: (a) able to recognize words and/or symbols and/or arithmetical signs and to carry out mental calculations; (b) able to read and write a short simple sentence and to add and subtract single-digit numbers.

Level III. Participants who are qualified for Level II but who have also successfully passed one or both tests for the following sub-levels: (a) able to read a short, simple sentence, able to add and subtract two-digit numbers; (b) able to read fluently a simple text, to write a short, simple message, to add and subtract three-digit numbers, multiply two-digit numbers and divide by single-digit numbers.

Level IV. Participants who are qualified for Level III but who are also able to read and write messages, to read newspapers so as to keep up with current events and obtain information, to read instructions, books on better living, better food, etc., to keep records and simple accounts of income and expenditure.

National examinations

The idea of levels of literacy was directly connected with the concept of national examinations. Three national examinations were conducted: in August 1975, in August 1977, and in August 1981. Tests were prepared by an ad hoc national committee and were administered by special examiners chosen from the party, the government, colleges of national education, universities, the army and the churches. Regional and district co-ordinators were trained to test the results of national seminars by the National Literacy Centre in Mwanza; they then returned to their districts and regions to train others.

While the national testing may be faulted by some for unnecessary formalization of a learning process that was meant to be non-formal and community-centred, certain advantages did accrue; among them standardization of the definition of literacy, legitimization of learners' achievements, and use of national testing as an opportunity for mobilization for the mass campaign.

Follow-up programmes, projects and structures

The mass literacy campaign was related to an impressive network of follow-up and post-literacy programmes, projects and structures. Note should be taken of the fact, however, that not all of these follow-up actions were conceived, designed and implemented within the framework of the mass literacy campaign. Most of the programmes, projects and structures preceded the launching of the campaign and had been established as part of the government's adult education and political education programme or had been brought into being on the initiative of the UNDP/Unesco pilot project. During the life of the mass campaign, many of these programmes served as 'support programmes' for the campaign and provided post-literacy activities for new literates. Brief descriptions of these follow-up programmes are given below.

Permanent workshops for follow-up books and materials

In order to ensure a continuous supply of suitable reading materials for new literates, permanent zonal and regional writers' workshops have been established. These workshops produce manuscripts for follow-up books and reading materials relevant to the interests of local communities and forward them to the department of adult education in Dar es Salaam for editing and publication.

Books for post-literacy Stage V

For those completing the four levels of literacy and wishing to continue, the Tanzanian campaign had conceptualized three additional stages for literacy education. Each stage (V, VI, and VII) involves two years of organized work in groups under trained instructors. Eleven books have been written and published for Stage V. (It is planned to have sets of eleven books each for Stages VI and VII as well). The books cover the following subjects: political education, mathematics, agriculture, Kiswahili, history, geography, political economy, crafts, health, home economics and English. Five of the eleven constitute the core on which the student must be tested before he or she is certified as having reached Stage V. The core subjects for farmers are political education, political economy, agriculture, mathematics and Kiswahili.

While Tanzanian organizers of the programme disclaim any intention of offering a parallel programme for adults equivalent to elementary education, the equivalence built into the idea of stages and curriculum is too evident to be missed.

Rural newspapers

Rural newspapers were first initiated by the Mwanza project within the Lake Regions in 1969. Currently, most of the regions and districts have already launched newspapers through their regional and district writers' workshops. In the meantime, the government has started three zonal newspapers: in the Lake zone, *Elimu Haina Mwisho* (Education Has No End); in the coastal zone, *Jiendeleze* (Develop Yourself); and in the northern zone, *Tujielimishe* (Let Us Educate Ourselves). *Elimu Haina Mwisho* has already attained a circulation of 100,000. The four remaining zones—the western zone, central zone, southern zone, and southern highland zone—will also soon have their own newspapers.

Rural libraries

First initiated in 1969, rural libraries already number some 2,781. Each has a collection of 500 titles and is looked after by a local volunteer with preliminary training as a rural librarian. It is hoped eventually to set up about 8,000 rural libraries, one in each village.

Educational campaigns through radio

The United Republic of Tanzania has become famous for its developmental/educational campaigns through radio, which are linked with discussion groups all over the country who receive supplementary reading materials for discussion under the guidance of a trained group leader. The first developmental/educational campaign on Tanzanian radio was called *To Plan is to Choose* (1969) and was designed to stress that a choice must be made in the planning process, and that priorities imply the inclusion of some programmes and the exclusion of others. *The Choice is Yours* (1970) offered education about voting; *Time for Rejoicing* (1971) celebrated the tenth anniversary of Independence; *Man is Health* (1973) taught health education; and *Food is Life* (1975) exhorted everyone to grow food wherever possible. A new campaign, *Trees are Wealth* (1980), is now in progress.

Correspondence education

An impressive correspondence school has been established since 1972 as part of the Institute of Adult Education in Dar es Salaam. A variety of courses—long and short, certificated and non-certificated—are offered in Kiswahili, political education, English, geography, history, bookkeeping, store-keeping, accountancy, business law and management.

Folk development colleges

Adapted from the folk high schools of Sweden, the African folk development colleges (FDCs) bring villagers who have been selected by their communities to attend residential courses so as to acquire information, knowledge and skills which they subsequently introduce into their communities. The curriculum includes general education, agriculture, handicrafts, leadership and culture. The first FDC was established in 1976 and 51 are already in operation. Ultimately, it is hoped to have 108 of them, one in each district.

Kivukoni colleges

Kivukoni colleges are colleges for political education and ideological training. The first Kivukoni college was started in the 1960s and ran courses for all levels of government and party officials, ranging from a few weeks to nine months. Five more zonal colleges have now been created to undertake political and ideological training of lower-level government officials and party cadres in the regions.

Evaluation of the mass campaign

No formal and systematic evaluation of the mass campaign has been undertaken but the experience of the Mwanza project indicates that an excellent monitoring system exists. The instruments for programme data collection developed and tested by the Mwanza project are being used to determine enrolments and enrolment patterns, participation in different functional specializations, patterns of attendance and teacher recruitment and performance.

Data flow from class centres to supervisors, to wards, to divisions, to districts, to regions and then to the centre. Special questionnaires are occasionally administered to develop feedback on various aspects of the programmes. Monthly and quarterly reports supply useful qualitative data which are supplemented by visits, annual conferences and correspondence.

Effects of the mass campaign

In numerical terms, the effects of the mass campaign have already been indicated. Illiteracy in the United Republic of Tanzania dropped to 27 per cent in 1977 and to 21 per cent by August 1981. The more significant effects, even though not well documented, should be measured in individual and social terms. Individuals, it has been asserted, have changed their ways of thinking, feeling and envisioning. They have lost their sense of marginality, alienation and fear. They have become self-confident and assertive. In broader social terms, the most important effect of the mass campaign (and of adult education in general) may have been the politicization of the masses, a real change in the political culture of the United Republic of Tanzania.

The Tanzanian mass campaign is also noteworthy as the adult literacy campaign that led to the declaration of universal primary education (UPE). In 1974, the party declared that UPE should be completed before the end of 1976. By 1979, 93 per cent of all eligible children were actually in school.

Lessons of the Tanzanian campaign

1. The very first lesson from the campaign is that even the poorest of countries must eradicate illiteracy in order to achieve development and that they are capable of doing so. The United Republic of Tanzania was seeking socialism and self-reliance and it needed literacy. It did not wait for the economy to take off and for a literate environment to emerge; it used literacy as an instrument to bring this about.

2. The United Republic of Tanzania could declare and implement a mass campaign because it had the political will to do so to produce the needed structures and allocated the needed resources.
3. The Tanzanian mass campaign once again points to the important role of effective leadership in such large-scale transformational actions.
4. The role of the mobilizational agent—in this case TANU—is once again brought home. While the government had established an extensive structure for adult education, it still made use of the party cadres' literacy committees and volunteers to make the campaign a people's campaign.

BIBLIOGRAPHY

The Arusha Declaration and TANU's Policy on Socialism and Self-reliance. Dar es Salaam, Publicity Section, Tanganyika African National Union (TANU), 1967.

KASSAM, Y. O. *Illiterates No More: The Voices of New Literates from Tanzania*. Dar es Salaam, Tanzania Publishing House, 1979.

KUHANGA, N. A. Organization and Administration of Adult Education in Tanzania. *Literacy Discussion*, Vol. 6, No. 1, 1975.

MALYA, SIMONI. Tanzania's Literacy Experience. *Literacy Discussion*, Vol. 6, No. 1, 1975.

MPOGOLO, Z. J. *Tanzania Case Study*. Report written for the Unesco/ICAE study of literacy campaigns of the twentieth century, 1980.

NYERERE, J. K. Education for Self-reliance. In: *Freedom and Socialism*. Dar es Salaam, Oxford University Press, 1968.

——. *Ujamaa—Essays on Socialism*. Dar es Salaam, Oxford University Press, 1968.

——. *New Year Speeches*, 31 December 1969; 31 December 1970.

——. *Freedom and Development*. London, Oxford University Press, 1974.

Resolutions of the Fifteenth TANU Biennial Conference. Dar es Salaam, National Printing Co., 1973.

TANU Constitution, Promise No. 6.

UNITED REPUBLIC OF TANZANIA. *The People's Plan for Progress*. Dar es Salaam, Ministry of Economic Affairs and Development Planning, 1969. (A popular version of the Second Five-Year Plan for economic and social development, 1969-74.)

——. *Third Five Year Plan for Economic and Social Development, 1976-81 (Part I: General Perspectives)*, Dar es Salaam, Ministry of Economic Affairs and Development Planning, 1976.

VISCUSI, M. *Literacy for Working; Functional Literacy in Rural Tanzania*. Paris, Unesco, 1971. (Educational Studies and Documents, 5.)

CHAPTER 11

Literacy in the context of a rural development campaign: the Somali experience of 1973-75

The Revolutionary Government of the Somalia Democratic Republic took power on 21 October 1969. Literacy was one of its main preoccupations.

The Somali language has a long and rich oral heritage. Spoken all over Somalia, it had remained an unwritten language. For centuries, Arabic had been used in the cultural and religious contexts; and during the colonial period, the business of the state has been conducted in English in British Somaliland and Italian in Italian Somaliland. Somali remained the language of everyday communication.

To make the revolution meaningful in the lives of the people, to create a new political culture, to integrate the people into one nation, and perhaps to develop one national economy, there had to be a dialogue between the government and the masses. This dialogue had to take place in the language of the people, which was Somali; this meant that Somali had to become a written language and that the people had to become literate in it.

The choice of a script for Somali had been under discussion for many years. The prevalence of Islamic culture and religion suggested that the Arabic script should be used, but non-religious and functional considerations favoured the Latin script. On 21 October 1972, the Latin script was chosen and, exactly one year later, Somali was made the official language of the country.

Immediate steps were taken to teach reading and writing in Somali to the Somali people. Since most of those who were literate in English, Italian or Arabic (some 5 per cent of the total population of over 3 million) lived in the urban areas, the teaching of reading and writing in Somali was initiated in those areas. The literacy campaign involved two phases: the urban literacy campaign and the rural literacy campaign which became a rural development campaign in which literacy played a central role.

The urban campaign was launched in March 1973 and began with literacy teaching for government workers, teachers and school children. This was a comparatively easy task since these groups knew the spoken language and almost all of them knew the Latin script. This first group of literates in Somali then taught other urban residents. By the time it ended, the urban campaign had reached some 400,000 people.

The rural campaign was launched in August 1974 and ended in February 1975. This was a more difficult phase. First of all, objectives were redefined to include community development, though literacy remained central to the total set of objectives. The campaign was named 'Campaign for the Advancement of the Rural People' and included among its objectives: (a) eradication of illiteracy among rural people; (b) public health improvement; (c) animal health improvement; and (d) a census of both people and livestock.

Another factor that contributed to the difficulty and complexity of the rural phase was the nature of the populations that had to be served. Most of the people involved were nomadic or semi-nomadic. These groups were perpetually on the move looking for water and grazing grounds for their animals. Few among them, if any, could be mobilized as literacy teachers. Infrastructures of transport and communication were lacking. The environment was harsh, and particularly so during the campaign: a serious drought caused literacy operations to be suspended somewhat prematurely only seven months after they had begun. By the time the rural campaign ended, some 795,000 adults had been declared literate on the basis of tests.

The historical context and the socio-economic setting of the campaign

Modern Somalia has a population of over 3 million spread over an area of 650,000 square kilometres.

The country is culturally, ethnically and religiously homogeneous. Eighty-five per cent of the people are Hamitic, and almost 100 per cent are Sunni Muslims, Islam having been introduced by the Arabs as they settled along the coast early in the seventh century.

Somalia is mostly semi-arid and only 13 per cent of the land is cultivated. Fifty to 60 per cent of the population is nomadic or semi-nomadic (some estimates put the figure as high as 75 or 80 per cent), split up in different tribes. The nomads keep moving from one place to another in search of water and pastures, and do not always stay within the jurisdictional territory of the Republic.

The living culture of Somalia is deeply rooted in the Muslim faith, and nomadic values are clearly defined in terms of the roles of men and women. Days are taken up with the care of livestock on which the nomadic communities almost entirely depend. Evenings are spent in entertainment, including the recitation of poetry. Poetry recitation has become an important art form and plays a key role in the communication of knowledge and skills from generation to generation.

The colonization of Somalia began during the mid-1800s. French Somaliland, today the independent nation of Djibouti, was established in 1860; British Somaliland, now northern Somalia, was established in 1884; and in 1889 Italy took control of what is now southern Somalia to establish Italian Somaliland.

Independence came about in 1960 when the Somali Republic was established by unifying British and Italian Somaliland. The colonial experience left Somalia with two European languages—English and Italian—the rudiments of Western institutions of government and formal education, a dualistic economy, and general underdevelopment. The years 1960-69 were marked by political and social chaos with some eighty political parties vying for power and fanning the fires of tribalism and nepotism. This led to the army coup of 1969 that established a government committed to scientific socialism. During 1969-76, military leaders ruled the country through a Supreme Revolutionary Council (SRC). In 1976, the Central Committee of the Somali Socialist Revolutionary Party replaced the SRC under the same leadership.

The nature and extent of the developmental task

The country which the Revolutionary Government sought to reconstruct represented one of the most difficult challenges in development anywhere in the world. The SRC inherited a country of vast distances, of sparse population, with a minimum of communicational and institutional infrastructures. The total length of roads in 1970 was estimated at 13,541 kilometres, only 582 kilometres of them tarmac. The majority of villages had no roads at all. There were 50,000 radio sets in the country—one for every fifty-six people—and most of these were concentrated in urban areas such as Mogadishu, a city of about 445,000. Estimates of radio sets for 1974 were 67,000. There were altogether 4,740 telephones in the country—one for every 600 people.

The SRC also inherited a country that was and remains among the poorest in Africa. The GNP in 1970 was estimated at US$70 per capita. (More recent figures indicate a per capita GNP of US$110.)

The population estimates in 1970 were around 3 million with a *natural* population increase of 21.9 per 1,000 during the years 1965-70. Life expectancy during the late 1960s was estimated at 38.5 years. The nomadic population owned 4.8 million goats, 4.6 million sheep, 2.2 million camels, and 2.1 million cattle (1970 figures). Such a population was obviously hard to serve and yet their needs were the greatest and most urgent.

Fifty-six per cent of the population was below 24 years old and mostly uneducated. The education system was outmoded and irrelevant and was concentrated almost exclusively in the urban areas. Some idea of the dimension of the educational enterprise may be gained from the figures for school enrolment in 1969-70: there were 31,589 students enrolled in primary schools; 17,394 in intermediate schools; 6,040 at secondary schools; and 548 in higher education. Many Somalis had had their only formal education in Koranic schools run by Koranic teachers (*Her*) who often travelled with the nomads. The extra-scholastic modes of education available were minimal. The total circulation of newspapers, for example, was 4,900 in 1970—1.8 newspapers for every 1,000 readers.

The government resources were, on the other hand, very scarce. The total state revenue in 1970 was 327,927,595 Somali shillings.[1] Of this sum, 5.8 per cent went to education in that year and 6.7 per cent to health. Understandably, self-help—*iskaa wax u qabso*—became central to the developmental strategy.

The only advantages the government enjoyed were its own ideological commitment, a homogeneous culture and a single language. It was within this historical context that the government sought to make independence real in the lives of people, to bring them development in the form of basic services and an opportunity to participate in building the nation.

Driving forces and objectives

The main driving force behind the Somali literacy campaign was the politics of language which were inextricably mixed with the politics of development. If development was to become a reality, a dialogue had to be conducted between the government and the people in Somali. In a very real sense, the literacy campaign of Somalia was inevitable if the language policy was to be implemented with reasonable speed.

The objectives of the urban campaign which preceded the rural one were more oriented to language and culture, though practical information was also offered. Those of the rural campaign were more in the nature of community development, though literacy remained a central objective. It has been said that through a dialectical process the rural campaign also became an urban campaign in as far as the teachers learned as much as they taught.

---

1. 7.50 Somali shillings = US$1.00 (approx.)

The following excerpt from a lecture by Adan, the then Director-General of the Ministry of Education, details the objectives of the campaign:

The campaign, the first of its kind, is part of our endeavour to fight against society's three main enemies: hunger, disease and ignorance. Its aim is two-fold, namely: to bring about the alphabetization of the rural masses as one of the prerequisites for development, and also to render the masses cognizant of our needs and orient them towards the right path to national progress. Equal weight is attributed to these two aspects of the campaign. In fact as the rural people become literate, the tasks of the staff in the medical, agricultural and veterinary services will be made easier and their instructional activities, which can also be carried out by means of written material, will be more far-reaching. At the same time, through the teaching of our revolutionary principles, i.e., the teaching of socialism, and through self-help (*iskaa wax u qabso*), the rural masses will be brought to the same level of political consciousness as the population in urban centres.

Some added benefits expected of this campaign are: the strengthening of national unity by demolishing the barriers between the urban and the rural masses; the revival of our traditional culture through the intimate contacts between the students/teachers and the nomads; a new awareness of the problems confronting the rural masses and of the need for their solution; a greater degree of involvement in these problems on the part of the various organs of the Central Government.

The comprehensiveness of the objectives should be obvious. They include not only literacy but also political consciousness; ideological orientation and the liquidation of rural-urban barriers; socio-economic development to end hunger, disease and ignorance; revival of the traditional culture; and, on the part of central government, greater sensitivity to the people's needs and better returns on its extension services.

Planning and conduct of the campaign

Some interesting features are to be found in the planning and preparation for the Somalia literacy campaign. To begin with, the campaign was so conceived that the first urban phase itself prepared the second rural phase. To compensate for the lack of systematic research surveys, a national seminar was used to bring together all the available information for use in the planning process. This seminar, which was attended by some 700 people from all levels, also started a communication network. Finally, the administration was mobilized through the establishment of various policy-making and technical committees and a whole network of committees was established from the centre down to village level to enable participation by the people.

Planning and organization of the urban campaign

With the adoption of a script, Somali became the language of administration. On 8 March 1973, the political decision was made to launch a national mass literacy campaign to cover both urban and rural areas and to eradicate illiteracy in two years. This was a truly radical decision, because it necessarily depended upon the mobilization of the people for self-help and because schools would have to be closed for a whole year to supply the 20,000 teachers needed for the rural phase of the campaign. 'If you know, teach; if you do not know, learn' demanded commitment of a very serious type.

The urban phase of the campaign was supervised by a Central Committee, composed of three vice-presidents of the country and three secretaries of state, which was the supreme policy-making body. There was also a separate Co-ordination and Implementation Committee consisting of nine members who came from all the ministries and public agencies concerned, such as the ministries of education, the interior, and information and national guidance; the state printing agency, the broadcasting service, finance, transport, national curricula and the press.

Three subcommittees were established under the Co-ordination and Implementation Committee: the Preparation Subcommittee to plan, execute and evaluate all publicity programmes to promote the urban campaign; the Inspection Subcommittee to guide the establishment and working of parallel committees at lower levels, to supervise the establishment of learning centres and allocation of teaching personnel to those centres, to help in the formulation of enrolment procedures and to evaluate the various operational aspects of the campaign; and the Production and Publication Subcommittee to prepare and distribute materials for teachers and learners in collaboration with the National Adult Education Centre (NAEC). A separate Secretariat served this committee structure by co-ordinating all the activities of the campaign, maintaining communications and records, and keeping minutes and statistics.

Long before the campaign was conceptualized and launched, the government had evolved a new political-administrative structure covering the whole country which sought to decentralize the administration and to promote mass participation. Somalia had been divided into administrative zones, each zone having an orientation centre which served as the government body at local level, as a structure for representation of the local people, as a mobilization centre for the zone, and as a centre for training in community leadership. The campaign, of course, used the political-administrative structure already in place and especially the orientation centres.

Within the context of the urban literacy campaign, these orientation centres were assigned the tasks of: bringing together state employees, military personnel, literate businessmen, students and teachers living within the zone and to recruit them as voluntary literacy teachers, inspectors, and orientation personnel for the campaign; motivating the illiterate population to join the literacy campaign as learners; locating learning centres so that no one would have to travel a long distance to attend literacy classes; providing learning facilities and materials needed at learning centres; instilling among teachers and learners a healthy sense of competition with their counterparts in other zones and regions; nominating people to represent the community at various levels of the committee structure; ensuring optimal use of resources in men and materials, space and time; and establishing flexible timetables to suit the convenience of learners.

Conduct of the urban phase of the literacy campaign

The campaign was implemented purely with indigenous expertise and indigenous resources. The government did allocate some resources to the campaign and provided teaching and learning materials, but much came from the people themselves in cash and kind, in terms of classroom space and in terms of voluntary work in teaching, organizing and inspecting.

The preparatory phase developed slowly into action. Soon organizers and committees were moving from place to place distributing materials and observing classes being set up or in operation. Instructional programmes were continuous from morning till evening. The early morning sessions were reserved for housewives, who often left the household chores to a relative or helper. Classes in the afternoon and evening were intended for workers. Typically, three sessions would be conducted: 3.00–4.30 p.m.; 5.00–6.30 p.m.; and 7.00–8.30 p.m. Thus the timetable was flexible enough to suit anyone wishing to participate.

Even though facilities in makeshift classrooms were often less than satisfactory, participation was high and the level of interest and enthusiasm excellent. People would assemble for classes with their own *qabaros* (traditional seats used in Somalia) and writing implements. Mothers came to class with babies on their backs and toddlers playing around them. Often a learning group would be composed of pregnant mothers, children and grandparents struggling to master the skills of reading and writing.

In the words of a Somali Government document on the campaign:

After the final evening class, committee meetings were convened for reviewing the day's work, seeking solutions to problems that had cropped up, writing letters to the teachers which would provide them with feedback on their performance and sending any other communication. At the local level, the committee evaluated progress in every section under their jurisdiction and announced which section had excellent records at weekly meetings held for the residents of the particular zone; rewards were given for good performance. People were inspired to achieve their goals with will and determination, withstanding personal difficulties and hardships. That people rose to the occasion is evident—they had to work against all kinds of odds, attending classes in addition to their normal work, learning to concentrate on their lessons despite distractions, such as passing cars and playing children.

To maintain the tempo of the campaign and to demonstrate the continued commitment of the central leadership, classes were often visited by the top officials. By the time the campaign ended, 400,000 people had been made literate, according to Ministry of Education estimates. The campaign laid the foundations for a written culture in Somalia and thereby started a cultural revolution. At the same time, it had important dynamic effects on the economic and social life of the people.

Planning and organization of the rural campaign

The rural campaign launched on 1 August 1974 should be seen as a continuation of the urban literacy campaign and as a climax to all the preceding socio-political campaigns launched by the government. It was an important communication between the government and the people.

Before the campaign was actually launched, a technical committee was established to develop a design for the campaign and to determine its *modus operandi*. This committee consisted of representatives from various ministries and other government institutions concerned with rural administration. The first problem faced by the committee was to choose between a pragmatic and a revolutionary approach to the rural campaign. The realities of Somalia with its great distances, nomadic population, lack of communicational and institutional infrastructures, scarcity of teachers and teaching materials suggested a need for pragmatism. That would have meant a five-year campaign to parallel the government's Five-Year Plan, covering two regions each year. The needs of the revolution demanded a one-year campaign, with total mobilization of people and resources to do whatever was needed. It was the second alternative that was chosen.

The crux of the problem and the heart of the challenge was to mobilize the 20,000 teachers needed for the conduct of the rural campaign. Civil servants, members of the armed forces, and volunteers were considered but not actually used. They had essential tasks which could not be carried out if they were to spend weeks and months teaching illiterate nomads and semi-nomads in rural areas. Students and teachers of intermediate and secondary schools were an obvious alternative resource. In order to make use of them on a full-time basis, rather than intermittently during the summer vacations, the radical decision was taken to close schools for a year, a decision which was approved by the SRC. All students below the age of 14 were excluded from this mobilization, as also students in the eighth, eleventh and twelfth grades in order to guarantee their graduation and continuity within the education system. Vocational and technical schools also remained open.

Another most important decision taken by the technical committee and approved by the leadership was to conceptualize the rural campaign as a campaign for rural development, with literacy as its central focus. As indicated earlier, the objectives of the campaign were oriented towards community development and included eradication of illiteracy among the rural masses; public health improvement; animal health improvement; and a census both of people and of livestock.

The technical committee needed information to make operational plans for the campaign but unfortunately, virtually none was available. Census data were lacking, and little was known about population densities or about the seasonal movements of the nomads. The technical committee began by sending letters and questionnaires to the regions and districts, but the information received was so sketchy as to be wholly inadequate for the formulation of plans for the campaign.

Accordingly, a three-week symposium was organized in Mogadishu to discuss the planning, organization and implementation of the campaign with representatives of the regional and district authorities. This was an excellent strategy for systematizing the information already within the system. The 700 participants in the symposium included all chairmen of the regional and district councils; all regional and district education officers; all headmasters in the districts; all regional and district representatives of the political office of the SRC; all heads of regional and district police stations; all heads of the regional and district National Security Service; and all regional transport officers.

The symposium carried out detailed discussions and made concrete proposals concerning the conduct of the campaign, including:

identifying possible obstacles and resources; determining common solutions at the national, regional, district and community levels; establishing manpower requirements for every district, e.g. of literacy teachers, health and livestock extension workers, census-takers, political-orientators and supporting staff; outlining plans regarding transport and media of communication; preparing a list of basic equipment needed for instruction, health care and treatment, a literacy census and political mobilization at the community level; delineating organizational structures needed for the campaign; and determining procurement of resources.

Besides information gathering, the symposium had other important objectives. Since a whole cross-section of the leadership participated in the decision-making, they were later able to identify with the campaign and its objectives. By bringing them together in Mogadishu, the government made the campaign everybody's business; all governmental agencies, at all levels, were responsible for ensuring mass participation and institutional action. Participants were asked to convene similar symposia and seminars at the regional, district and village levels on their return home.

The organizational framework developed for the rural development campaign is shown in Figure 5. This committee structure was integrated, of course, level by level, with the political-administrative system already established by the Revolutionary Government after the October Revolution of 1969.

The Central Committee was the policy-making organ of the campaign and was chaired by the Secretary of State for Education. Other members of this committee were the secretaries of state for interior, health, livestock, transport and planning, and the general manager of the state printing agency.

The Central Office brought together all the institutions and agencies concerned through the full-time participation of representatives of each of those institutions and agencies. Each of these representatives was responsible for communication with his or her parent institution or agency to ensure co-ordination and operational decision and action where necessary. The Director-General of the Ministry of Education became the head of this office, and his duty was to administer the campaign at the central level and collect all related information and documentation.

The Regional Committee played the same role at regional level as the Ministry of Education at the centre. Membership of Committees was more or less the same as that of regional councils. This meant that representatives of ministries and other state institutions in the regions all served on these committees.

The District Committee was the direct agent of the Ministry of Education at the centre and played in the district the role which the Ministry of Education played at national level. The district education officer was the chairman of this committee.

The District Inspection Office was composed of the district education officer, various school inspectors sent by the Ministry of Education and certain headmasters in the district. The district was the real operational unit of the campaign, and the district committees and inspection offices were the institutions nearest to the people and were thus involved in the day-to-day conduct of the campaign.

To facilitate work and to guarantee effective communication with front-line workers, each district was further divided into smaller units, taking into consideration population density and transportation and

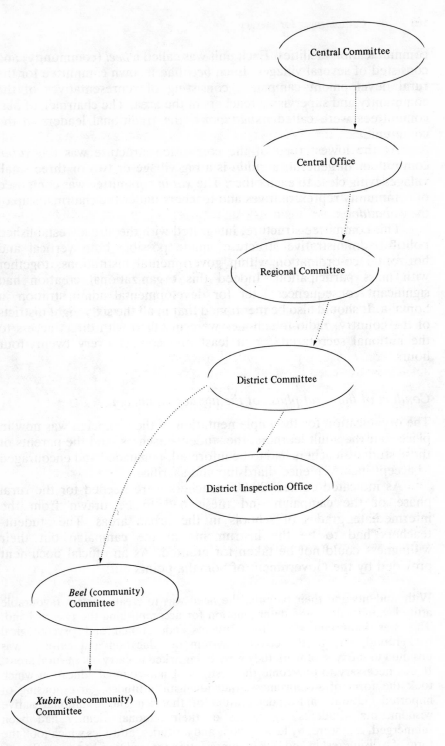

FIG. 5. Organization for the rural development campaign. in Somalia, 1974-75.

communication facilities. Each unit was called a *beel* (community) and consisted of several villages. Each *beel* had its own committee for the rural development campaign, consisting of representatives of the community and supervising teachers in the area. The chairmen of *beel* committees were called *nabaddoons*, the traditional leaders in the communities.

At the lowest rung of the committee structure was the *xubin* committee. In general, a *xubin* is a big village or two or three small villages lying close to each other. The *xubin* committee was composed of community representatives and teachers under the chairmanship of the *nabaddoon*.

This committee structure, integrated with the already established political-administrative structure, made possible both vertical and horizontal co-ordination within governmental institutions, together with mass participation. Indeed this organizational creation had significant consequences later for developmental administration in Somalia. It should also be mentioned that in all the sixty-eight districts of the country, radio-telephones were installed with direct access to the national secretariat for at least one contact every twenty-four hours.

Conduct of the rural phase of the literacy campaign

The organization for the implementation of the campaign was now in place, but the adult learners, the student-teachers, and the parents of those student-teachers had to be informed, persuaded and encouraged to accept inconvenience, hardship and sacrifice.

As indicated earlier, 20,000 teachers were needed for the rural phase of the campaign and these had to be drawn from the intermediate grades of schools in the urban areas. The student-teachers had to be the instruments of the campaign but their willingness could not be taken for granted. As an official document provided by the Government of Somalia points out:

With students and their parents, the need was to create certain favourable attitudes and values and determination for accomplishing the task at hand. This was important since the students' educational and psychological background, due to the colonial system of education and culture, was unsuited to the type of work they were being asked to carry out in rural areas. It was necessary to overcome the vestiges of neo-colonial education which took the form of snobbishness, individualistic attitudes, an espousing of imported cultural values, denigration of the rich and traditional native wisdom, etc. Students' awareness of their national identity had been submerged, as it were, by false notions and attitudes, attitudes which took the form of a disinterest in and lack of appreciation for tradition-honoured Somali values in contrast to a preference for modern Western values and ways of living and a tendency to look down upon rural life and rural people without realizing that these were the very people upon whom the nation depends for its economic resources and whose work enables urban dwellers to lead a more sheltered life. In certain respects, the students' parents shared these attitudes.

To encourage students to undertake the task, both positive and negative inducements were used. According to the *Sharciga Ololaha* (The Law of the Campaign), students who refused to participate or who withdrew before the end of the campaign were faced with dismissal from school for three years and were to be prohibited from working for the same period. On the other hand, those who performed well were to have priority for entry into higher educational institutions and were to be given preferential treatment for government jobs. Ultimately, 15,681 student-teachers volunteered for the campaign. Only 400 students refused to serve while another thirty-eight abandoned their adult classes after agreeing to work.

But sanctions were not the only thing that induced student-teachers to undertake this work. Publicity campaigns were conducted in the urban areas; orientation centres organized symposia, lectures, and plays; radio, cinema, newspapers and street displays were all employed to drive home the importance of the rural campaign and the need to contribute to its success.

On 1 August 1974, the campaign was officially opened and as the student-teachers prepared to take up their posts, the SRC chairman addressed them and extended his personal good wishes. As the cars carrying the students passed through the streets of Mogadishu, they were applauded by the population.

Meanwhile, the mobilization of potential learners had continued in the rural areas. Special symposia were conducted in the rural areas for *beel* and *xubin* leaders in order to prepare them for mass mobilization and to impress upon them the value of self-help programmes.

Student-teachers had nowhere to live except with the families of nomads. At first, they were not over-welcome; but after they had shown what they wanted to teach and what they wanted learn, they became part of the families in which they lived. Each received 3 shillings a day from the government for personal expenses. For this they taught literacy classes, and assisted the 416 livestock extension workers and 497 health educators who were also involved in the campaign. Female student-teachers frequently doubled as nurses and the male student-teachers doubled as animal health assistants. The drought that Somalia suffered during that time forced a premature termination of the campaign, but before it ended, considerable results had been achieved. Of the 1,257,779 learners registered at the start of the campaign, 912,797 sat the final test (a drop-out rate of 27 per cent); and 795,099 passed (a failure rate of 14 per cent). In addition, 1,612,241 persons received health treatment; 1,418,798 persons were immunized; 11,048,176 animals received treatment; and 2,313,670 animals were vaccinated.

The unplanned actions and the results of the campaign were even more impressive. A large number of feeder roads were built to connect isolated villages with district centres. This often led to new marketing possibilities and to new trade. A village which earlier discarded any milk it could not use was now able to sell it to those in need. Water resources were identified, or developed where none existed. The introduction of the orientation centres in rural areas was a most significant result. *Ubaxa Kacaanka* (the Somali Youth Organization) became accessible to rural youth. Many taboos about food were removed; new games were introduced (football, for example); and traditional culture was enriched with the introduction of rural drama as a mode of conscientization. Most importantly, the campaign resulted in the training of community leaders. The *nabaddoons* and *sabaddoons* affirmed that they now understood the function of the government, had learnt how to co-operate with it, and, above all, realized what it meant to mobilize people for particpation in their own work.

The need to act and to succeed even under the most difficult conditions challenged all concerned to give their best. Many innovations resulted: camels were brought in for transportation when jeeps were not to be had or simply could not go where they were required to, and local plants were put to new uses.

The campaign achieved these results with the minimum of governmental allocations. The whole budget approved by the Ministry of Finance for the campaign was 21,620,000 Somali shillings (US$3.4 million). Of this only 5,500,000 shillings (US$870,000) had been allocated to the Ministry of Education.

Pedagogical aspects of the rural campaign

The student-teachers had come to work with a kit which included a blanket; a textbook; a register; a pencil and a pen; a small water-container; a rubber; a razor; and a blackboard which could be folded in the form of a box for keeping all the other things.

The only textbook available was *Buugga Meer Miyiga*, a primer originally written for nomads. Produced by the NAEC, it followed the analytical method and used a semi-functional approach. Its content dealt with cattle-breeding, overgrazing and general hygiene. Since this was the only book the teachers had to rely upon, one additional chapter, called 'Teachers' Guidelines', was added to the primer.

There were serious shortages of instructional materials in terms of both quantity and quality. *Buugga Meer Miyiga*, although intended only for nomads, had to be used throughout the rural areas.

Unfortunately, not all students in the literacy classes had a copy of their own. To help matters a little, NAEC published in 1974 two issues of a newspaper called *Codka Macallinka iyo Miyiga Maanta* (The Voice of the Teachers and the Students in Rural Areas Today). This gave teachers guidance in methods of teaching adults and also contained several articles which dealt with cattle-breeding, overgrazing, and general hygiene. Seven thousand copies of each of the two issues were published but only two-thirds of each could be distributed to learning groups because of lack of communication. This newspaper later became a newspaper for self-learning groups for use in the post-literacy stages.

Teaching places

The principle followed was to use all possible sites for teaching. In settled agricultural areas, lessons took place either under the trees or in huts built on a self-help basis. Open-air classes were, however, preferred since it was uncomfortable to bring 30 to 40 learners together in small huts in very hot weather.

In the case of nomads, classes were first held near wells and pools where the nomads brought their cattle to water; the nomads were required to attend classes as a condition for using the water. This approach proved unsatisfactory. The nomads did not have to water their cattle every day and, in any case, could not really be denied the use of water under common law. Finally it was decided that teachers should move with the nomads in the same way as the traditional *Her* not so long ago. Thus the mobile school unit came into existence and later provided the model for the 'nomad education centres'.

Teaching methods

It should be noted that teachers were for the most part untrained. They were left free to develop their own teaching methods since they had nothing to go by except for the one chapter of guidelines in the primer. Naturally, these student-teachers turned to the method they had themselves been subjected to—the alphabetical method involving extensive drill to ensure recognition of characters. While the method presented problems—many students memorized rather than learning to recognize characters—it did have the advantage of being culturally familiar since it was the method used in Koranic schools.

Consolidation and follow-up of the campaign

The problems of follow-up were considered even while the rural development campaign was proceeding. A national seminar (very much like the one held at the beginning of the campaign) was held with representatives from all the regions and districts that took part. The seminar devised a three-year plan and recommended that the activities initiated by the campaign be continued but that the responsibility for such continuation be given to the Ministry of the Interior, which was the national institution nearest to the rural populations.

An effort was made to institutionalize follow-up activities by establishing the Interministerial Committee for the Permanency of Literacy. Literacy was now conceptualized as *functional* so that the link between literacy and development was more clear and direct. There was thus an important shift from conscientization to economic productivity.

The strategy for delivery was once again to depend on self-help. The best literacy students in the communities were to be given further teaching in literacy and were to be trained in subjects concerning the development of rural communities so as to be able to take over the tasks so far being carried out by students from the cities.

Finally, there was to be more professionalism in the conduct of literacy work. The NAEC was to be strengthened to undertake the more important role of producing curricula and curriculum materials and was to undertake the training of personnel.

Literacy work did continue, at least during the years immediately following the campaign. In 1976, 568,546 persons were enrolled in literacy classes and in 1977 another 487,180.

Evaluation and results

No formal evaluation of the campaign is available. The testing procedures and criteria used to determine whether literacy had been achieved are not quite clear and statistical data are both scarce and ambiguous. Qualitative results claimed for the campaign are, however, impressive. The most significant gain was in the emergence of a new consciousness among the people, and of a political consciousness among the rural masses. There was, it is claimed, a deep transformation in the rural personality which created a dynamic revitalization in all the various aspects of rural life. Some food taboos were discarded, roads were built, and new markets came into being. Most important, the rural people came to understand what development was and how they had to bring it about themselves, at the same time achieving individual realizations. The presence of the government was felt in many places for the first time, new institutions such as orientation centres and youth clubs came into being, and community leaders acquired new skills of animation, organization and leadership. The old divisions between rural and urban were less pronounced at the end of the campaign, and both laymen and social scientists began to make an effort to understand nomadic and rural life.

Lessons of the Somali literacy campaign

1. While one set of economic and social pre-conditions may be preferable to another, it is difficult to imagine any conditions which would preclude the launching of a mass adult literacy campaign, provided only that the necessary commitment for the eradication of illiteracy exists. Given that commitment, organizational action can be taken, and public and private resources can be marshalled.

2. The mass adult literacy campaigns by their very nature acquire broad political objectives which may, at the same time, involve the need for a national language to facilitate communication, to help in mobilization of the masses for nation-building and development, and to abolish class feelings between rural and urban people, and also the need to establish secular institutions and services to serve the masses.

3. Even a serious lack of resources is not an insoluble problem in launching a literacy campaign if an effective mobilization of the masses can be undertaken.

4. Lack of planning information may make things difficult but does not make them impossible. Indeed, planning strategies can be so designed that the gathering and utilization of information can be built into the planning process itself.

5. If political commitment is the first essential condition, then organization is the second condition for the successful launching of a mass literacy campaign. Such organization must achieve vertical integration between various levels of administration and leadership. At the same time, it must achieve horizontal integration between the ministries and agencies of the government and between official and non-official leadership in the nation.

6. Methodologies are marginal to mass literacy campaigns. If political commitment exists and if effective organization can be projected, even the most orthodox methodologies can be used to do the job.

BIBLIOGRAPHY

ADAN, HUSSEIN MOHAMED. *Notes on Somali Studies in Somalia*. Baltimore, Md., 1976.
——. *The Revolutionary Development of the Somali Language*. Lagos, 1978.
ADRZEJEWSKI, B. W. The Rise of Written Somali Literature. *African Research and Documentation*, Nos. 8 and 9, 1975.
ELMI, ABDI HEYBI. *The Nomadic Education Project*. Mogadishu, Ministry of Education, 1977.
INTERNATIONAL LABOUR OFFICE (ILO)/IASPA. *Economic Transformation in a Socialist Context*. Addis Ababa, 1977.
KINNANE, DERK. How Somalia Put its Native Language Down on Paper. *UNESCO*

Features; A Fortnightly Bulletin for News Media, No. 695/696, 1976, pp. 11-13.

The Literacy Campaign. Mogadishu, Ministry of Information, 1975.

MOHAMED, OMAR OSMAN. *From Written Somali to a Rural Development Campaign*. Mogadishu, Somali Institute of Development Administration and Management, 1975.

——. *Administrative Efficiency and Administrative Language in Somalia*. Mogadishu, Somali Institute of Development Administration and Management, 1976. (Occasional paper.)

PESLATOZZA, LUIGI. *The Somalian Revolution*. Translated from Italian by Peter Glendining. Société d'Édition Afrique, Asie, Amérique Latine, 1974.

Report of the Franz Fanon Center Conference on Human Development in Action. Mogadishu, 1979.

SOMALI INSTITUTE OF DEVELOPMENT ADMINISTRATION AND MANAGEMENT (SIDAM). *Somali Development Administration*. Vol. I, No. 2, April-June, 1976. (Special issue devoted to the Rural Development Campaign).

A Study on the Somalia Literacy Campaign. Study submitted to Unesco on behalf of the National Adult Education Centre, the Government of Somalia, n.d.

UNESCO. *Mass Education in Somalia*. Paris, Unesco, 1978. (Sectoral Report.)

UNICEF. *Country Kit on Somalia*. Nairobi, 1979.

UNICEF/UNESCO. *Report of Basic Education Seminar, Mogadishu, 1 to 9 April 1978*. 1978.

CHAPTER 12

Planning, implementing and evaluating literacy campaigns: a memorandum to decision-makers

One practical purpose of the present study is to contribute to the development of an international strategy for the eradication of illiteracy worldwide. So far, the study has offered descriptive-analytical reconstructions of some mass literacy campaigns, articulating in each case the relationships between ideology, policy, planning, instructional methodology, and the results obtained within each campaign.

It is now time to draw some lessons of direct importance to policy-makers, planners, administrators and programme specialists who may be concerned with mass literacy campaigns or similar large-scale programmes of adult literacy. For this purpose, use will obviously be made of the experiential base represented by the foregoing case-studies, but the analysis will by no means be limited to them. The following discussion will also reflect the experience derived from some of the mass literacy campaigns recently completed in Nicaragua and elsewhere, and some still in operation, as in India, Ethiopia and Kenya. It will also embody some of the most useful practical knowledge about literacy work accumulated over the years by practitioners in the field; and some of the relevant theoretical knowledge systematized and organized under the disciplines of communication, management, pedagogy and evaluation.

Purpose and scope

The term 'decision-makers' as used in this memorandum does not refer to literacy planners and specialists alone, but also to educational planners and media specialists, to development planners with interests covering many different sectors, as well as administrators, programme specialists and technicians who must understand each other's roles and act in concert to plan and implement a successful literacy campaign.

The essential aim of this memorandum is to present an *ideal* model of how best to plan and implement a mass literacy campaign. The assumption is made that a theory and a technology of literacy campaigns has already emerged; and that the technology of literacy campaigns can be used by planners and administrators to increase the probability of success and to improve the instructional, social and economic returns on their campaigns.

One qualification is, however, called for. In presenting a general theory and technology of literacy campaigns, we do not claim that there is only one correct way of planning and implementing a mass literacy campaign. In other words, what is offered is not a set of instructions which must be followed, and followed in one particular order. In actual practice, political will and popular mobilization have often more than compensated for shortcomings in planning and management. The commonsense of those involved and their ability to learn from their own experience have sometimes resulted in success where linguists, psychologists and pedagogues have failed. It is not intended to teach a new orthodoxy, but merely to delineate some ideas that have worked before in various places, and which seem to be full of promise. It is hoped that planners, administrators and teachers in future literacy campaigns will invent fresh solutions as they face certain familiar problems and certain new ones uniquely their own, thereby adding to the experience already available.

A general model for the planning and implementation of literacy campaigns

On the basis of the analysis of literacy campaigns in this study (and an examination of other educational and developmental campaigns recently conducted in various parts of the world), it is possible to propose a theory of the mass literacy campaign.

To be so called, a campaign must be an organized large-scale series of activities, focused with some intensity on a set of objectives to be achieved within some predetermined period of time. A campaign suggests urgency and combativeness; it is in the nature of an expedition; it is something of a crusade. Thus a 'literacy campaign' is markedly different from a 'literacy programme' which, though also planned systematically to meet certain objectives, may lack both urgency and fervour. A literacy programme may seek to provide a useful service, yet not claim to wage war on an intolerable social condition. Many of the campaigns described in this book were campaigns within campaigns, and some were expanded incrementally over a long period of time; yet all had an intensity of purpose expressed in a series of mobilizations and all were highly combative in trying to achieve their goals. The fact that they range over half a century, from the Soviet campaign in 1919 to the Somali campaign in 1973, adds to the richness of the comparative analysis and makes the model proposed here widely applicable.

A potentially successful mass literacy campaign has to be, at the same time, an educational and a political event. A useful theory of the mass literacy campaign must, therefore, include both ideological and technological dimensions.

The prevailing ideology of a society will, first of all, determine whether universal adult literacy is indeed considered central to the achievement of overall national developmental goals. Ideology will also determine the articulation and maintenance of the 'political will' to achieve universal literacy in a society—a necessary condition for a successful mass literacy campaign. At another level, the prevailing ideology will reflect a particular political culture which, in turn, will determine the organizational, mobilizational and technological choices that can be made in the planning and implementation of a mass literacy campaign within a particular society.

Political will is a pre-condition, but technology is the crucial factor in the planning and implementation of a successful mass literacy campaign. A general model for such planning and implementation is presented below. The basic processes involved are:

Articulation of the nation's political will;

Temporary institutionalization of the first policy initiative; and later

Development of a comprehensive policy-making and legitimizing body;

Study and diagnosis of pre-conditions;

General mobilization of the public; and

Establishment of structures of mass participation;

Development of inter-ministerial and inter-agency structures (a) administrative, and (b) technical;

Pre-operational preparation;

Implementation of developmental and instructional actions;

Evaluation of context, processes and results; and

Design and establishment of post-literacy programmes.

These processes have been designed against a time dimension (t) from t_1 to t_8 providing the outline of the PERT chart (Fig. 6).

1. Birth of a mass literacy campaign

Mass literacy campaigns have typically been born of ideological commitment, on the one hand, and utilitarian considerations of nation-building and socio-economic development on the other. For literacy campaigns to come about in the developing countries that need them, there must be a mating of ideas among politicians, development

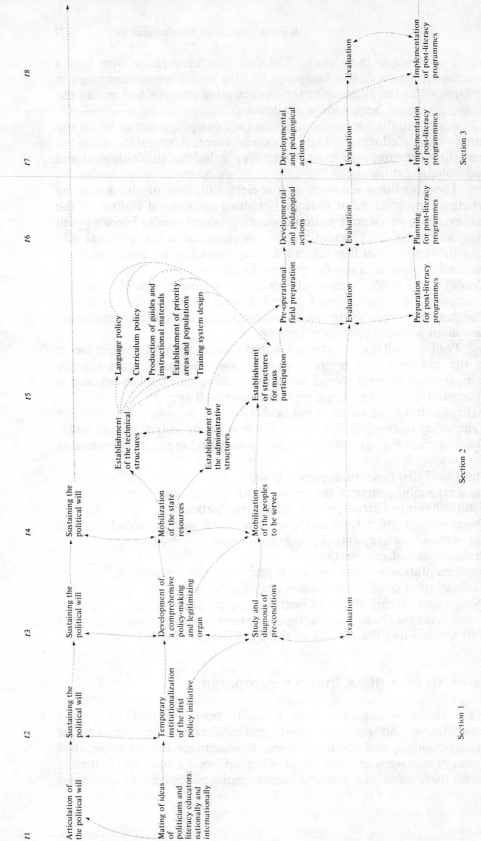

FIG. 6. A general model for the planning and implementation of literacy campaigns.

planners and literacy educators. This can be promoted by bringing political figures, development planners and literacy workers together at symposia under the auspices of multilateral organizations such as Unesco. The newly independent countries, all struggling to reconstruct their societies in the post-colonial period, are, in ideological terms, highly sensitive. Socio-economic development, again, is on the national agenda of almost all of the developing nations. Unesco's role can be especially fruitful in terms of providing opportunities for discussion and disseminating successful national experiences and the newly emerging technology of mass literacy campaigns. The role of the intelligentsia in each country is, of course, significant in preparing the ground for the campaign.

Political will—what it means and why it is needed

The political will of a society is expressed by making clear and conscious choices and by carrying them out with unfaltering determination. It may not be easy to develop an operational definition of political will, or to measure it in relation to a particular policy choice at a given time in history, yet it is a useful concept. There is hardly any doubt about its existence or about its central role in successful implementation of policy. Its presence is revealed in the statements and action of the leadership, and its strength may be gauged by weighing the political, institutional and material resources allocated to the implementation of a policy.

Political will is a necessary, though not a sufficient, condition for a successful mass literacy campaign. Without its clear expression by a society's leaders, a successful campaign is most unlikely. A mass literacy campaign must be conceived as the political equivalent of the Long March if it is to have a chance at all. Without the existence of a dominant political will, there will always be competitive claims from other development sectors on the scarce resources of the nation. Even literacy workers will be ready with lists of reasons why a mass literacy campaign is impossible or at least altogether premature.

The question that must be asked is: How does the political will of a nation for launching and implementing a literacy campaign emerge? No simple answer is possible. The expression of political will in regard to a particular policy choice is the product of a multitude of political forces coming together at a given time. What political forces are in play and how those various forces interact will differ from country to country. The agency responsible for initiating the campaign may also differ from country to country—the state authorities in one case, the governing party in another, and a consortium of voluntary agencies in yet another.

Two interrelated observations are, however, in order. First, the expression of the political will of a nation is almost always rooted in the ideological fervour prevalent at the time. Second, political will crystallizes more easily within 'mobilizing societies'—societies where the leadership possesses great power to set directions and allocate resources and, through a mixture of persuasion and sanctions, can gain the support of the masses. Socialist and revolutionary societies have been able to create and sustain the political will necessary to launch and implement successful mass literacy campaigns. However, it must be stated emphatically that the articulation of the political will is not the special preserve of socialists or revolutionary states. All societies are capable of ideological commitment and can draw upon the cultural, moral, and spiritual resources of their peoples. Again, all societies, including those in which the power of the state is limited by tradition or constitutional provision, can challenge their peoples to action and mobilize them around nationally defined issues.

It should be clear from the foregoing that political will cannot simply be grafted on to the psyche of a nation. It should be possible, however, for institutions such as Unesco to contribute to the emergence and articulation of the political will in a society. This would require convincing political and development leaders in different societies of the possibilities and the promise of literacy campaigns; organizing the exchange of international experience; and providing technical assistance in the actual planning and conduct of mass literacy campaigns.

At a more practical level, literacy workers must be concerned with the problem of sustaining the political will of the nation once it has been articulated. This requires the expression of national concern for the eradication of illiteracy through the country's creation of popular institutions. Both the USSR and China offer examples of how a commitment to mass literacy was sustained over the decades by setting up different anti-illiteracy institutions and by making literacy teaching part of the agenda of most mass organizations of workers, peasants, women and youth. Brazil offers another example of sustaining commitment to literacy through the country's institutional arrangements formalized as MOBRAL. A second strategy for sustaining political will is to continue to associate the political leadership with ongoing literacy programmes through ceremonies and celebrations, and to provide public opportunities for them to renew their commitment to the eradication of illiteracy.

2. Institutionalization of policy initiatives

It is important to institutionalize the first policy initiatives for the eradication of illiteracy with a sense of urgency and in an appropriate form. The level of the national response to the problem of illiteracy must not only be sound and forceful but must be seen as such by the general public.

Formation of a national council

A body such as a 'Supreme National Council for the Eradication of Illiteracy' would seem necessary as part of this institutional response. It should be a supreme body in that it brings together the leadership from all sectors of society, in and outside of the government. For the legitimization of the campaign, the most popular and powerful leaders of the people must be associated with the Supreme Council. Such a council should not be an advisory body merely making recommendations to the government. It should be able to lay down policy goals and targets for the government and for semi-government mass organizations with the expectation that their resolutions will be fully implemented whatever the difficulties involved.

It should be a national council in that it should not be merely a special committee or a technical board pursuing the narrow interests of a special group but a body representing all aspects and sectors of national life—government, army, media, communication, education, agriculture, industry, banking, labour, religion, and culture. By representing all aspects and sectors of the nation, it should be able to make literacy the nation's business.

On the other hand, the focus on the eradication of illiteracy should be kept clear and unmistakable. While some literacy campaigns have used larger categories such as 'national adult education programmes' or 'spare-time schools', it seems more promising to concentrate on literacy as such. This, of course, does not mean simply teaching the Three Rs; literacy can be defined in more comprehensive curricular terms when programmes are actually taken to the communities. The use of a larger category such as adult education and its subsequent operational definition as a mere literacy programme may seem to the people to represent the breaking of a promise, a regression and a failure.

Codification of the goals of the campaign

The Supreme National Council for the Eradication of Illiteracy, as here proposed, can and should play an important part in the conceptualization of a mass literacy campaign and in codifying for the nation its purposes, goals and expectations. It is important to note that such a council will need to develop and use two different codifications of goals and purposes: one for the people at large, the other for officials in the secretariats of ministries and government departments.

Codification for the people at large: choosing the language of justification. Literacy planners seem impelled to justify their literacy plans and campaigns in utilitarian, often economic, terms. A review of the literacy campaigns so far described would suggest that this need not be so. On the contrary, it appears that policy-makers and planners might do better to justify their literacy plans to the masses in general categories of a cultural revolution; socialization for a new man to handle participative decision-making and to use the new tools of production; abolition of class-based social structures; etc. The justification of literacy to the masses in narrow economic terms can in fact be counter productive. When literacy is justified in this way, adults may begin to expect economic returns in the form of well-paid jobs or cash income as soon as they have finished learning. There is, of course, seldom any such direct connection between literacy and income. The relationship is not always immediate or always direct. Literacy, and the knowledge subsequently acquired through the practice of literacy, may bring returns in terms of physical health, quality of family life, improved production in the field, and increased self-esteem, but such advantages cannot be expressed in financial terms. It is thus a matter of both strategy and good sense to justify literacy in broader terms that relate not to economic returns but to individual identities and cultural identities.

Codification for the secretariats: putting literacy in a larger planning perspective. A different set of codifications should be developed for the secretariats of planning commissions and government ministries. These technical codifications should link literacy simultaneously with development planning, the planning of development support communication systems and educational planning. This requires the establishment of clear connections between literacy and agriculture, literacy and industrial policy, literacy and new technological and scientific contexts, literacy and communication through the non-print media, and finally, adult literacy and the formal education of children. A Supreme National Council for the Eradication of Illiteracy should not only develop these perspectives but ensure that those working in the various secretariats of commissions, ministries and departments accept them.

Clear and unequivocal goals for the literacy campaign

While the language used to justify a literacy campaign to the masses may sometimes be an exercise in generalization (and studied ambiguity), the operational goals must be clear, unequivocal and unmistakable. There should be no scope for misunderstanding and unstated compromise. Indeed, it may be important for literacy campaigns to have goals that are comprehensive and all-inclusive, for example: to make literate every individual above the age of 6, omitting only the blind and the seriously ill. Such an operational goal leaves no scope for local compromise which may often mean limited coverage because of the alleged need to establish functional priorities. Where some economic zones must be given priority or particular occupational or age groupings must be selectively and intensively served, it should be seen as a pragmatic compromise on the way to the final goal.

What it means to be literate should also be made absolutely clear by the Supreme Council. To ensure that every adult learner 'passes' and yet to give each man and woman a correct view of his or her literacy skills is an aim reflected in the Tanzanian concept of different levels of literacy.

Campaigns are not campaigns if they last forever. The definition of a time-frame is one of the most important requirements for a successful literacy campaign. It may cover a few months or ten years. A second campaign may be needed to complete the work left undone by its predecessor or to build upon the work already accomplished. The first campaign, for example, may be a literacy campaign and the second a post-literacy campaign.

3. Optimal pre-conditions for mass literacy campaigns

When is a society ripe for a mass adult literacy campaign? What set of pre-conditions is required in order to launch it successfully? What circumstances might hinder it?

A technician would prefer it if there were a weighted check-list to provide a social diagnosis of a society with a clear 'Go/No go' decision on the bottom line, to determine whether or not the nation should proceed with plans for a mass literacy campaign. A review of the adult literacy campaigns described in this study (and of some other campaigns recently implemented) suggests that the existence of the political will among the leaders and the accompanying social energy of the people in a post-independence or revolutionary era or in a period of confidence in the future is the only absolute pre-condition. All other conditions in regard to material resources, infrastructures and technology can be seen as enabling conditions, which may make things easier but the lack of which seldom renders a mass literacy campaign impossible.

This is confirmed by the experience of the campaigns of Burma, Ethiopia, Nicaragua and Somalia among others, all of which declared and implemented mass adult literacy campaigns with extremely limited material resources. Indeed none of the countries whose campaigns have been examined here had great material resources at the time they initiated literacy campaigns. They also lacked infrastructures and professional and institutional capacities. Somalia had to use ministry officials to teach urban illiterates, who then went to the rural areas to teach illiterates in the countryside. Schoolchildren were pressed into service in Cuba, Somalia and more recently in Nicaragua. Old school books and children's primers were used in many literacy campaigns since new ones, more appropriate to the interests and needs of adults, could not be had. Old newspapers were used to write on, since proper paper was not available. Systems of decision-making, administration and delivery of services were created as part of the campaigns, as in Burma, the United Republic of Tanzania, Somalia and even India. The problems posed by a multiplicity of ethnic groups and languages have not prevented campaigns being successfully launched. Similarly, campaigns have been conducted in countries shattered by war where peace has been precarious and the economy very far from the 'take-off' point. Campaigns have been launched where illiteracy was almost universal as well as in countries where the rate was only relatively low. The only common factor in all these cases was the will for decisive action.

This should not, however, be interpreted as a criticism of efforts to study prevailing conditions. The point is simply that it is hard to imagine conditions so severe that a mass literacy campaign is out of the question. The study of conditions is necessary not as the basis for a decision as to whether or not a campaign should be launched, but in order to furnish information for its effective implementation once it is launched. Such a study should include at least: (a) a census of the population to establish the number of people to be served by age, sex, ethnicity, language, education, occupation and, possibly, income; and (b) a comparative study of regions indicating population densities, modes of production, existence or otherwise of infrastructures, and economic possibilities.

These studies do not need to be conducted in a formalized professional mode but may be conducted—as part of the planning process—with the participation of officials, community leaders and the people themselves.

4. Mobilization of the masses and mobilization of the state

Mobilization of the masses and of the state must take place simultaneously to ensure the success of a mass literacy campaign.

(a) Mobilization of the masses

To mobilize can mean to make ready for 'war'. It is not surprising that many of the literacy campaigns described in this study have used the war theme to mobilize the masses for literacy work: they have trained 'soldiers of learning', put them in uniform, organized them in brigades and encouraged them to attack the enemy, who is ignorance and poverty.

Mass mobilization may be seen as a popular expression of the leadership's political will. No mass literacy campaign has succeeded or even will succeed without mass mobilization. Only the masses, through genuine participation, can make a literacy campaign a mass campaign. They are the learners and at the same time must be the teachers. More importantly, the people must be willing to invest voluntary effort, rent-free facilities and contributions of both money and materials.

Mass mobilization strategies have to be a combination of the symbolic and the structural. The symbolic strategies involve both the message and the media. The words of the slogans must touch the hearts and souls of the people—serving as epitaphs for the past they are glad to put behind them, and as signposts for the future to which they aspire. The media used should be popular media that people encounter every day of their lives, ranging from billboards, leaflets, posters and puppets to theatre, radio, film and television. The masses should be able to devise and disseminate messages. In other words, wherever possible, the media should be used participatively. The structural strategies may involve the management of incentives at one level and the use of social and economic sanctions at another; both incentives and sanctions will differ from one society to another. However, it must be clearly understood that mass mobilization is not simply a matter of a well-run publicity campaign.

(b) Mobilization of the state

It is important, too, to realize that mobilization is not merely an externally oriented process. It must also involve mobilizing personnel and resources within the government and the governing party. This internal mobilization, in turn, must involve re-education of officials at various levels. It should be clear that their commitment and enthusiasm cannot be taken for granted. Moreover, the mobilization of state resources must cover both administrative/material and intellectual/technical resources.

As Figure 7 indicates, mobilization is a comprehensive process that must cover the public as distinct from the private dimension on the one hand, and the general (administrative and material) as distinct from the technical dimension on the other. The focus on the technical aspect should be particularly noted. A successful mass literacy campaign requires both commitment and competence. An effective use of the professional and technical resources available within and

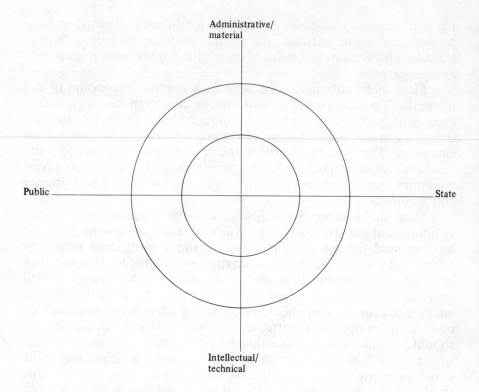

FIG. 7. Mobilization as a comprehensive process.

outside the government is an important part of the mobilization effort. Mobilization is in essence a marriage of imagination and practical strategy, of emotion and intellect. It is a belief in the possibility of success in actualizing a new social order; it is a discovery of unsuspected resources; it is putting old things to new uses; it is a declaration of 'business *not* as usual'; it is acting against all the odds; it is changing adversity to advantage. No mass literacy campaign can succeed without effective mobilization.

5. Establishment of administrative structures for conducting a mass literacy campaign

The mobilization of the resources of the state, as we have indicated, must work along two dimensions: administrative and technical. This means that the state has to establish two parallel and integrated structures, one administrative and the other technical.

In the language of the Burmese literacy campaign, illiteracy cannot be eliminated among the masses without 'organizational power'. Organization is important for the implementation of ideology, it is indeed the operational aspect of a nation's will. Without effective organization that will can all too easily be dissipated.

Formal organization is, of course, neither culture-free nor ahistorical. History determines organizational structures and organizational innovations which subsequently and inevitably undergo cultural adaptation. However there are certain organizational principles which override local manifestations, and can be put to use in developing effective administrative systems:

1. The leadership should have the will and the ability to change, modify, eliminate and create legal and administrative structures.
2. A harmonious balance should be established between centralized direction and decentralized initiative and implementation.
3. The literacy organization created should not be linked to one ministry or department (such as the ministry of education or department of economic planning, etc.) but should be so placed within the governmental structure that it can demand identification with, and support from, all the various organs of the state.
4. A mass literacy organization should be created (especially in countries where political parties do not play a mobilization role) to provide opportunities to the people for mass participation.
5. The overall administrative organization of the government should be linked on the one hand with the organization of the ruling party (or parties) and on the other hand with the mass organization for literacy both horizontally and vertically.

Institution building to achieve the right level of response

On their own initiative and on the advice of top-level planners, the nation's leaders should be ready to make whatever changes in legal and administrative structures are necessary for the implementation of the campaign. This may mean taking a utilitarian view of organization and experimenting with different institutional forms. It will also mean experimenting with the design of new instructional functions at all levels of training. This is not to say that literacy organization should be constantly changing but there should be a readiness to experiment and to make changes as experience in the delivery of instruction and services accumulates.

Even more importantly, literacy organizers should be able to ensure the right level of response to the organizational needs of the campaign. The worst enemies of a literacy campaign may be the organizers themselves. They may not 'think big enough' and may make organizational responses which are completely inadequate to the real needs of the campaign. A literacy campaign, it must be understood, is not one more file or dossier in the central ministry. It is not a matter of transferring half a dozen people to a new unit or section within the existing bureaucracy. It may well require manpower greater than the total strength of the ministry concerned. It is thus absolutely necessary that the organizers of literacy campaigns should have the right organizational aspirations if they are to do the job assigned to them.

Centralization versus decentralization

A national campaign must have a national direction from the centre, but no national campaign can be successfully implemented under a national command. The centre should inspire, demand and enable, without extinguishing local initiatives and local adaptations. Decisions on implementation, both administrative and curricular, should be left to local workers. This arrangement, sometimes characterized as democratic centralism, would seem to be an important principle in the management of mass adult literacy campaigns.

Location of literacy organizations within the overall governmental structure

The government authority for the organization of a mass literacy campaign must not be limited by assigning the campaign to any one governmental ministry or department—a ministry of education or a ministry of social welfare, for example. The campaign administration should be in the office of the president or prime minister or in another overall administrative unit such as the planning commission. In addition, temporary systems such as inter-ministerial and inter-departmental commissions must be created for a national co-ordination of effort by bringing together all the various government ministries and agencies, as well as popular volunteers.

Linkage of administrative organization with political and popular organization

The literacy campaign organization must be linked with the political organization of the party (or parties) as also with the organization of the people. Governments should avoid employing literacy teachers and supervisors as civil servants to carry out the campaign. A literacy movement cannot be handled by career-oriented, hierarchy-conscious officials. Literacy work can best be handled by political parties and voluntary organizations because party cadres and voluntary workers are easy to employ, deploy and separate without concern for rules as to travel allowances, salary increases, and severance payments. Above all, a successful literacy campaign requires ideological energy which bureaucracies can only rarely supply but which party cadres and voluntary associations usually can.

Finally, the organization of the operational system must be interfaced with the popular organization of client groups. Illiterate adults and local leaders should be organized from village and community levels up to the highest levels, and interfaces must be built between the popular leadership and the corporate leadership of the literacy campaign.

Vertical and horizontal integration

The three streams of government, party and popular literacy organization (sometimes the party and popular organization may be combined into the same stream) must be both vertically and horizontally integrated. (See Fig. 8). A system of committees is needed to bring together representatives of the government, the party and the people, and secondly to co-ordinate different levels of decision-making.

6. Technical structures for conducting a mass literacy campaign

A successful literacy campaign is not merely a matter of administrative organization; it also involves technical organization and decision-making. The following elements must be elaborated and embedded in the technical organization for successful implementation of a mass adult literacy campaign:

Decision on a clear-cut language policy.

Setting up unambiguous goals as regards coverage of populations and priorities in regard to participant groups.

Well-defined curricular goals with clear demarcations between national and local community needs.

Development and production of materials for the teaching of reading and writing, and of related materials for the teaching of functional skills.

Training of staff and orientation of those collaborating with the programme.

Establishment of coalitions with institutions of formal and non-formal education, development support communication systems, and research and development agencies in the field of education.

Planning of follow-up and continuing education programmes.

Evaluation and information management systems.

The technical organization of the campaign may be seen as separate and distinct from the administrative organization for the purposes of analysis and planning. However, the two organizational branches will have to intersect at many levels and at many different

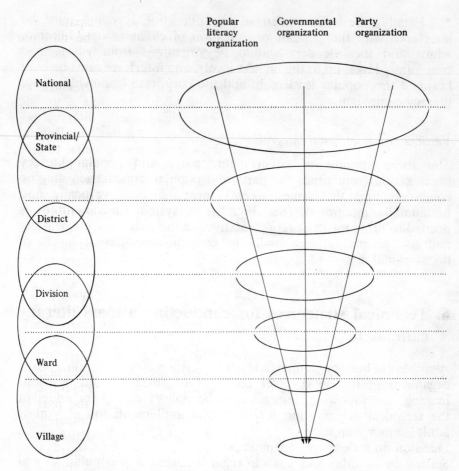

FIG 8. Vertical and horizontal integration of administration for the launching and conduct of a mass adult literacy campaign.

points and in some cases will merge into a single process of delivery of services.

The need for a clear-cut language policy

A clear-cut language policy will have significant implications for the technical system established for a mass literacy campaign.

Language is clearly the most significant expression of a culture; rejection of a language is often viewed by the culture or sub-culture concerned as a rejection of itself, an attack on its identity and its existence. But language is not merely a matter of cultural identity; it is also a matter of economics and politics. In the modern world of the nation-state based on science and technology and bureaucracy, it is essential to know the language of politics in order to share political power, and the language of the economy in order to participate in the economic system. Literacy in a language other than the national language may doom those involved to a limited, parochial and marginal existence.

It is impossible to provide a general prescription for language policy in all Third World countries since each presents a unique cultural and political situation. A single language of literacy has contributed to the success of mass literacy campaigns in Burma, China, Cuba, the United Republic of Tanzania and Somalia, to give only a few examples. But there is nothing sacred about the idea of a single language of literacy. A nation may be genuinely multilingual, as in the case of India where some fourteen languages are spoken, each by millions of people, and where each language has a literature and traditions going back hundreds, and sometimes thousands, of years. On the other hand, the retention of many different languages of literacy may signify failure to manage the politics of language rather than the adoption of a policy of cultural pluralism.

The only suggestion that can be made in regard to language policy is that the question of the language of literacy be faced squarely and honestly. In a number of Latin American countries, for many years, the leadership based its language policies on the assumption that everybody in the country understood and spoke Spanish when in fact this was by no means the case. The majority of the people neither spoke nor understood Spanish but used instead one of the two Indian languages, Aymara or Quechua. Such assumptions on the part of policy-makers can, of course, be fatal to a mass literacy campaign. In the United Republic of Tanzania, it was possible to adopt Kiswahili as the national language and as the language of literacy instead of artificially strengthening the 150 or more tribal languages spoken in that country on the eve of independence. Such decisions should be made where feasible. Where there are many local languages, one of which is chosen as the language of literacy (or even where a foreign metropolitan language is chosen as the language of literacy), clear strategies must be laid down about teaching literacy in the mother tongue and about a later shift to the national language.

Unambiguous coverage goals

A national adult literacy campaign is by definition a mass campaign. However, the definition of the masses may vary from country to country. In some countries, the term may be applied solely to the labour force in a so-called productive age group: 15-35 or 18-45, for example. Elsewhere, the masses may exclude children below 13 years old since they are seen as belonging to the formal school systems; but in some countries children as young as 5 or 6 years old may also be included to compensate for the lack of formal schooling.

Absolute goals for literacy campaigns (e.g. to leave no one illiterate except the sick and the blind) are most helpful. Such goals leave no psychological escape hatches for planners and implementers, and yet priorities and phases can be accommodated within these goals.

Definition of curricular goals; a dialectic between national visions and local community needs

Various curricular issues will be involved in the execution of a mass literacy campaign. First and foremost, there is the issue of nationally determined needs and community determined needs. Both are, of course, important. The nation-state cannot be wished away; it would be absurd to dismiss the national visions of the leadership as arrogant and unjust impositions. On the other hand, individuals and communities must not be mere pawns. The people must participate in planning their own destinies; they must have a voice in changing their world. This can be made possible only through a dialectic between the national and the local, between the visions of the central leadership and the felt needs of the local communities. Through a process of needs assessment and needs negotiation, national visions must be reinvented in local settings.

Secondly there is the issue of the 'soul' of the curriculum, should the curriculum chosen be aimed at conscientization; should it be problem-solving; or should it be a bread-and-butter curriculum based on economic and life skills? A related curricular issue is one of integration with economic and social functions. Finally, there are the questions of levels of literacy and the equivalence of literacy with elementary school education.

If a literacy campaign requires more than the teaching of the Three Rs (as mostly it will), literacy workers will have to collaborate with various ministries, departments, media and extension workers to develop a division of labour for carrying out the total curricular load.

Production of training and teaching material

Mention has already been made of the twin roles of ideology and organization in the success of mass literacy campaigns. By implication, the essential role of mobilization-motivation in the process of teaching literacy should also be quite clear. Where strong motivation to learn exists, the methodology material used becomes of marginal importance. In other words, highly motivated individuals can learn to read even from indifferently prepared reading material. But this does not mean that no effort should be made to produce the best material possible. Linguists, reading teachers, literacy and adult educators, and graphic artists should join together in teams to produce basic reading material as has been done in the Tanzanian campaign.

The problem of material must be defined in dual terms: material for learners and material for teachers. Especially when untrained or hastily trained monitors are used to conduct learner groups, the development of appropriate materials for teachers in the form of guidebooks and discussion plans takes on paramount importance.

Uses of literacy primers have varied from one mass literacy campaign to another. Many national literacy campaigns have used a single primer for the whole country, as in Burma, Brazil, Cuba and Somalia. The USSR used more than one national primer. The United Republic of Tanzania is perhaps the sole example of a country using many different primers, all in one language, but each differentiated in regard to the occupational groups concerned—cotton growers, fishermen, banana growers, stock breeders, coffee growers, house-wives, etc. India has used primers differentiated both in terms of occupations and in the language of literacy.

It is important to note that a typical first primer cannot teach retainable literacy. It must be followed by suitably graded readers. Where different primers are used for different occupations, but employ the same language, a single set of graded readers may still be used; for example, occupation-differentiated primers P_1, P_2 and P_3 may each be followed by the same graded readers, first G_1 and then G_2.

If one primer is used for the whole country, the themes included will have to have a national orientation and the book might be centrally produced. Where regional and occupational differentiations are to be reflected, primers may best be produced by teams close to the situation of specific learner groups. While there has been some discussion with regard to 'learner-designed' primers, no mass literacy campaign seems to have made use of this technique.

Training of teachers and supervisors and orientation of organizers and administrators

The need for appropriate training of teachers and supervisors and orientation of officials should not be overlooked. Formal training should be provided for literacy teachers and supervisors. At the same time, administrators and organizers of mass literacy campaigns must be provided with continuous orientation in more or less non-formal settings of committees and discussion panels.

The content of training for literacy teachers has varied from one campaign to another. Some campaigns provided hardly any training at all; in other cases, where mobilization was an important consideration, training of teachers was seen as a new socialization and had a strong ideological content. The training provided political education for teachers while enabling them to become familiar with the teaching and learning materials. In other campaigns, training has been defined more formally as 'professional capacitation for a role' and has included adult psychology and the teaching of reading, writing, class organization and similar subjects. In countries where a more formal definition of training was used, it has been possible to make use of electronic media such as radio and television in the training of large numbers of literacy teachers on tight time schedules.

Teachers have been drawn from a variety of sources. The campaigns of Cuba, Somalia and Nicaragua were able to close schools for several months to deploy students as teachers of illiterates and thus eradicate illiteracy in one massive effort. Typical volunteers have included primary school teachers, school-leavers, literate farmers and workers, retired civil servants and army officers, young people on national service, and clergy of various religions.

The best training approach seems to include a ten-day workshop (providing some teaching experience in real or simulated conditions) supplemented by one-day-per-month refresher courses. It is also important that the whole process of administration and supervision should become a continuous training process for campaign officials.

Institutional coalitions and professional collaboration

The campaign administration must establish coalitions and collaboration with three types of institutions: institutions of higher education and centres of research; institutions of non-formal education such as family planning groups, co-operative alliances, etc.; and media institutions such as television, radio, press and official publicity agencies.

The institutions of higher education and research must conduct the basic and applied research needed by the campaign organizers. Some, though not all, of the training responsibilities must also be assumed by these institutions. As indicated earlier, the campaign cannot and should not carry the whole curricular burden for the mass education of the people. Other non-formal education and extension services must play their part. Finally, the media of development support communication should play their part to supplement and support the objectives of the campaign. The Tanzanian development campaigns by radio provide an excellent model.

Post-literacy and continuing education programmes

The effects of a mass literacy campaign may disappear like a river in the desert unless a systematic post-literacy and continuing education programme is established and a 'literate environment' created to sustain the effects of such a programme. These programmes should be institutionalized so as to facilitate their long-term survival. Multi-purpose centres, such as learning resource centres, may be used to provide new literates with opportunities and settings in which to continue their education and enhance their social and economic mobility.

Evaluation and information for management

An evaluation unit should be established as soon as the processes of conceptualization and planning begin. But evaluation should not be carried out solely by the evaluation unit. It must be everybody's business. To this end, the evaluation responsibilities of everyone engaged in the campaign must be clarified and made concrete in terms of what information will be collected, when, in what form, and how it will be collated. Such information is an essential part of a well conceptualized management information system.

BIBLIOGRAPHY

BAUER, RAYMOND A.; GERGEN, KENNETH J. *The Study of Policy Formation*. New York, The Free Press, 1968.

BERLE, ADOLF A. *Power*. New York, Harcourt, Brace and World, 1967.

BHOLA, H. S. Notes Toward a Theory: Cultural Action as Elite Initiatives in Affiliation/Exclusion. *Viewpoints*, Vol. 48, No. 3, May 1972.

——. The Design of [Educational] Policy: Directing and Harnessing Social Power for Social Outcomes. *Viewpoints*, Vol. 51, No. 3, May 1975.

——. *Curriculum Development for Functional Literacy and Non-formal Education Programs*. Bonn, The German Foundation for International Development, 1979.

——. *Evaluating Functional Literacy*. Amersham, Bucks., Hulton, 1979.

——. *Program and Curriculum Development in the Post-literacy Stages*. Bonn, The German Foundation for International Development, 1980.

CHODAK, S. *Societal Development: Five Approaches with Conclusions from Comparative Analysis*. New York, Oxford University Press, 1973.

EATON, J. W. *Institution Building and Development: From Concepts to Application*. Beverly Hills, Calif., Sage Publications, 1972.

FAURE, E., et al. *Learning to Be*. Paris/London, Unesco/Harrap, 1972.

FISHMAN, J. A., et al. (eds.). *Language Problems in Developing Nations*. New York, Wiley, 1968.

HORNSTEIN, HARVEY A., et al. (eds.). *Social Intervention: A Behavioral Science Approach*. New York, Free Press, 1971.

LINDBLOM, C. E.; COHEN, D. *Usable Knowledge: Social Science and Social Problem Solving*. New Haven, Conn., Yale University Press, 1979.

SIGMUND, PAUL E. (ed.). *The Ideologies of the Developing Nations*. New York, Praeger Publishers, 1972.

UNESCO. *Meeting of Experts on the Use of the Mother Tongue for Literacy, Ibadan, 13-23 December 1964: Final Report and Recommendations*. 1965. (Unesco/MELIT/6. Limited distribution.)

CHAPTER 13

Conclusions

Looking back on the history of literacy promotion in the twentieth century, two different approaches to the eradication of adult illiteracy seem to have been employed: the 'campaign approach' and the 'programme approach'.[1]

Literacy campaigns have been national or regional in scope, involving a series of intense, well-organized activities aimed at the eradication of illiteracy within a particular time-frame. They have been urgent and combative, undertaken in the spirit of expeditions or crusades. Those campaigns that, at first sight, might seem to have dragged on for long periods were in fact campaigns within campaigns, involving a series of mobilizations, reviewing gains, rectifying errors, setting new goals, re-committing institutional support, throwing in new resources, and challenging the masses to achieve the new goals set before them.

The justifications used by the organizers of mass literacy campaigns have been at the same time ideological and economic. They have sought to create new political cultures as well as economies based on new scientific and technological knowledge. They have challenged illiterate men and women to become literate, to come into the political scene, to mould political, social and economic institutions to their needs, and to master science and technology so as to contribute to both agricultural and industrial productivity.

Most of the successful mass literacy campaigns have taken place within revolutionary conditions or during the early post-independence periods when the nations conducting those campaigns were in the

---

1. In Chapter 3, Section 3, three policy options for literacy promotion within societies were conceptualized. However, what was characterized as the 'diffusion approach' has seldom been used as a deliberate policy option. The 'selective-intensive approach' came to be called the 'programme approach' by the delegates to the International Seminar, Campaigning for Literacy, held at Udaipur, India, 4-11 January 1982. We have opted here for the term 'programme approach'.

process of reconstructing their societies and were not afraid to make new departures, to conceive new visions, or invent new institutions. Nations that can boast of successful mass literacy campaigns simultaneously implemented important structural changes. Thus, the mass literacy campaigns were embedded in what we have elsewhere called the structural-developmental model of social change.[1] National development was defined primarily as a problem of change in existing political, social, economic and educational structures. Literacy was then used as preparation for participation in the new social order.

The programme approach to literacy (as distinguished from the campaign approach) has been selective in nature. Even when programmes were established all over a country or region, there was an intensive focus on particular communities, occupational groups or economic and industrial sectors. Literacy programmes may also be well-organized and sharply focused on specific objectives, but they have lacked the urgency and the fervour of literacy campaigns and the mass line. Literacy programmes have typically arisen from the calculations of development planners rather than from the intense commitment of politicians and ideologists.

Justifications used by the organizers of literacy programmes in recent years have been economic and technological. It has been rightly argued that economic deprivations are the most acutely felt deprivations among the poor in the Third World. It is suggested that if literacy is linked with economic rewards, adult illiterates will be motivated to learn and nations will have literate workers capable of transforming agriculture and industry by using new science and technology. It is also argued that literacy will inevitably lead to the literate's social and political promotion. Literacy is expected to play a generative role in the life of the newly literate, who will then be able to exert pressure on social and political structures and demand that they be changed and serve the adult literate's needs.

While some literacy programmes have concomitantly sought changes in social and economic structures or have offered 'package programmes' to illiterate farmers, their basic focus has been on the motivations of individual adults. These programmes can thus be seen as rooted in the motivational-developmental model of social change.

Literacy programmes rooted in the motivational-developmental model have been less than spectacular successes. This was because programme organizers were not always able to manage even the economic incentives on behalf of the new literates. Within the wage sector of the economy, it was sometimes possible to achieve higher wages for workers certified as literate, but in the rural sector of

---

1. H. S. Bhola, 'Justifications for Literacy: A Speculative Essay', paper presented to the Twenty-fifth Annual Conference of the Comparative and International Education Society held at Tallahassee, Fla., 18-21 March 1981.

subsistence agriculture, gains from literacy were often delayed, diffuse and intangible. Programme organizers were not able to reform the overall political structures which determine economic relationships and thereby the allocation of economic rewards.

In comparison, mass literacy campaigns seem to have done much better. These campaigns have made large numbers of adult men and women literate, and in the process, have created new social organizations and infrastructures; they have changed existing political, social and economic arrangements, and achieved new distributions of social, economic and educational goods among the people. They have helped the newly literate to shed their marginality and to acquire full membership of their own societies.[1]

With the exception of Brazil, all the literacy campaigns discussed in this report were conducted by states that profess to practise some form of socialism. While the political culture of the socialist state may have been favourable to the conduct of successful mass literacy campaigns, socialism is neither a necessary nor a sufficient condition for the implementation of campaigns. The set of conditions conducive to launching mass literacy campaigns can be obtained within a whole range of socio-economic settings and under a variety of political structures.

Irrespective of the different labels applied to the political arrangements in various countries, the following conditions are a prerequisite of the conduct of successful mass literacy campaigns:

1. *A political ideology that is humanistic, egalitarian and democratic.* The political ideal being sought must be one of political and social equality. The individual must be central to all national concerns. All the citizens of a nation must find their due place within the new social order envisioned.

2. *A conception of the role of literacy that is not merely economic.* The conception of literacy in development should include not only the economic but also the social, political and cultural aspects. Literacy should be seen at one level as an instrument of scientific production and management; at another, it should be seen as an instrument for creating a new social order and a new political culture.

3. *The articulation of the political will to eradicate illiteracy.* It is necessary that the various political figures within a society should come together to develop a national consensus for the eradication of illiteracy and that they should forge this national consensus into the nation's political will. The processes involved in the articulation and renewal of this political will must differ from one nation to another, but the need for such articulation is incontestable.

1. H. S. Bhola, 'Notes Towards a Theory: Cultural Action as Elite Initiatives in Affiliation/ Exclusion', *Viewpoints*, Vol. 48, No. 3, May 1972, pp. 1-37. See also H. S. Bhola, *Social Change and Education*, Morristown, N.J., General Learning Press, 1976.

4. *The ability to mobilize the resources of both the state and the people.*
   The resources of both the state and the people must be mobilized.
   Mass campaigns cannot succeed without the participation of the
   masses. To provide a rallying point for mass mobilization, society
   must draw upon its specific ideological, spiritual and moral
   resources, which may vary from Marxism to Democratic Socialism,
   from Gandhiism to Sarvodaya. Again, different instrumental
   strategies and institutional arrangements may be invented for the
   mobilization of the masses.
5. *A commitment to structural reform on behalf of the people.* Finally,
   the leadership must show a serious commitment to structural
   reform on behalf of the people and not depend solely on the
   motivation of the people to become literate and then make
   demands on the system to serve their special needs. The rules of the
   political game must also be changed and made more equitable.

To sum up, successful mass literacy campaigns are not the exclusive
province of one particular ideology, nor of one-party political cultures.
The achievements of successful mass literacy campaigns are possible
within any society that desires them. All that is needed is the will to
commitment and action.

APPENDIX

Udaipur Declaration on International Strategy for Literacy Promotion

An international seminar, organized jointly by The German Foundation for International development (DSE), The International Council for Adult Education (ICAE) and Seva Mandir (India), with close collaboration of Unesco, UNICEF and IIEP, was held in Udaipur, India from 4-11 January 1982 to discuss the Unesco /ICAE Report, *Campaigning for Literacy*. The Seminar was attended by delegations from seventeen countries: Bangladesh, Botswana, Burma, Cuba, Ethiopia, India, Iraq, Kenya, Nicaragua, Nigeria, Sierra Leone, the Socialist Republic of Viet Nam, Somalia, Sudan, Thailand, the United Republic of Tanzania, and Zambia.

In showing their deep commitment to the cause of universal literacy and in proposing an international strategy for the eradication of illiteracy worldwide by the year 2000, the international seminar adopted the following Declaration on 11 January 1982.

The Udaipur Literacy Declaration

Recognizing that literacy is a decisive factor in the liberation of individuals from ignorance and exploitation and in the development of society,

Conscious of the need to arouse awareness, nationally and internationally, that the struggle against illiteracy can be won, to demonstrate solidarity with those working on behalf of the thousand million adult illiterates in the world, and to vigorously mobilize the resources and will to eradicate illiteracy before the end of this century,

We representatives of national literacy programmes from Africa, Asia and Latin America, representatives of international organizations, and adult educators from all parts of the world, assembled in Udaipur, India, from 4 to 11 January 1982, to draw and apply the lessons deriving from campaigns for literacy in many countries,

Hereby adopt this Declaration as a testament of our commitment to the quest for a world in which human dignity, peace, freedom from exploitation and oppression are shared by all.

The Declaration

1. One out of every four adults in the world cannot read or write, victims of the discrimination, oppression and indignity that illiteracy breeds. And yet, the clear lesson from efforts in many countries is that nationally motivated mass campaigns can banish illiteracy, regardless of the adversity of conditions a country faces.
2. The magnitude of the problem in many countries calls for massive efforts. Only specific campaigns with clearly-defined targets can create the sense of urgency, mobilize popular support and marshal all possible resources to sustain mass action, continuity and follow-up.
3. It is not enough merely to teach skills linked to general economic development if the poorer classes remain as exploited and disadvantaged as before. A literacy campaign must be seen as a necessary part of a national strategy for overcoming poverty and injustice. A realistic campaign focuses on levels of skills and knowledge achieved, rather than on more numerical enrolment, and takes into account cultural, geographic and linguistic issues.
4. A literacy campaign is a potent and vivid symbol of a nation's struggle for development and commitment to a just society. It creates a critical awareness among people about their own situation and about their possibilities to change and improve their lives.
5. An effective literacy campaign is part of a comprehensive and continuing effort to raise the level of basic education of women and men. These efforts include universal primary education, post-literacy activities and opportunities for adult education—all of which are necessary components of a true and lasting learning society.
6. The participation of disadvantaged groups that historically have remained subjugated and marginal, especially women, demands the priority of special attention. The identification of groups that may require different approaches, such as out-of-school youth, is essential.
7. Legislative measures and resolutions should reflect a national sense of urgency, define the order of priorities attached to the elimination of illiteracy, and set out the responsibilities and rights of citizens taking part in the campaign and carrying out its priorities.
8. National popular resolve sustains the political, legislative and administrative measures needed to support the campaign and raises it above partisan politics and changes in political viewpoints and personalities.
9. While societies in the midst of profound and structural changes find a favourable climate for successful campaigns, all societies, irrespective of political systems, can activate forces for change and create a supportive political environment.
10. Literacy campaigns succeed and realize their liberating and development potential when there are avenues for popular participation in all phases. Participation can be gained through ensuring that all levels and sectors of government take a leadership role in the campaign and that the full range of voluntary and people-based organizations are partners in mobilizing citizens and resources.
11. Decentralized sharing of responsibility and decision-making in the administrative structure creates both participation and responsibility.

Decentralization also implies that central authorities have well-planned roles in policy-making and supportive actions. Clear delineation of responsibilities at different levels means that planning and implementation decisions can be taken close to where the campaign operates.

12. It is desirable to establish equivalence of literacy and post-literacy activities with formal education and to make appropriate linkages with other education work and with such cultural expressions as folk media and the arts.

13. The resources of modern communication and information technology are to be brought to bear on both the creation of a national sense of purpose and on the implementation of the campaign.

14. Research and experimentation are to be directed at improving the pedagogy of the acquisition of literacy skills and at reducing to a minimum the time and effort needed to acquire these skills. Participants should be involved at every stage of monitoring and assessment.

15. Efforts have to be made to mobilize private, voluntary and community resources, both in cash and in services rendered. But effective national campaigns also require a significant allocation of state resources commensurate with the priority attached to the elimination of illiteracy.

16. The eradication of illiteracy is the responsibility of every citizen—leaders and people. Literacy work symbolizes in a powerful way the unity and solidarity of individuals and groups within a country and offers people from all walks of life the opportunity to help others learn and to widen their horizons.

17. In a divided world, where understanding and co-operation often appear as elusive and intangible, the moral imperative of the eradication of illiteracy can unite countries in the sharing of knowledge and in a common and achievable goal.

18. Renewed dedication and effort at the national, regional and international level is required to overcome the intolerable situation in which hundreds of millions of people find themselves. The planetary dimensions and the unjust social and human implications of illiteracy challenge the conscience of the world.

In consequence of the above, and bearing in mind that the United Nations Third Development Decade has specified the elimination of illiteracy as an essential strategy in the struggle against poverty and inequity,

We call upon the United Nations and its agencies and organizations, and particularly Unesco, to take the necessary action to declare a World Literacy Year as a concrete step in our common goal of achieving a literate world by the year 2000.

ED.83/D.145/A